The Business

C1 ADVANCED Student's Book

John Allison, Rachel Appleby and Edward de Chazal

MACMILLAN

The **Business** 2.0

C1 ADVANCED

To the student

The objective of *The* **Business** 2.0 is to help you learn two things: how to do business in English and the language you need to do it. The new language and structures are presented in the Student's Book whilst the eWorkbook provides language practice and extension.

Here is a summary of what you will find in each.

Student's Book

The modules

The Student's Book contains 48 modules in eight units. Each unit deals with a key sector of activity in the business world. There are six different types of module:

1 About business

These modules contain information and language for the topic area of each unit. The focus is on understanding the topic and the general sense of the texts – don't worry too much about details such as new vocabulary.

2 Vocabulary

These modules build on the important words and phrases associated with the topic and provide thorough practice.

3 Grammar

These modules help you practise the grammar in a communicative and meaningful way, in business situations relating to the unit topic. Before you start, read the 'Did you know?' box to remind yourself of the key grammar points. Use the Grammar and practice section at the back of the book for consolidation.

4 Management skills

These modules develop important skills and techniques for managing your work and the people you work with, together with the relevant language you will need. Some will be familiar, others may be new; use the speaking activities as the opportunity to experiment with and hone your people skills as well as your language.

5 Writing

These modules provide practice for the most important types of document you will need to write at work. You analyse a model text, focus on key language and use both as a basis for doing a writing output activity.

6 Case study

The case studies provide an opportunity to apply all the language, skills and ideas you have worked on in the unit. They present authentic problem-solving situations similar to those you will meet in business.

Internet research

Every module includes an Internet research task to encourage you to explore the topic in more detail. The tasks can be done before or after working on the module. Remember that to search for an exact phrase, you may get more accurate results if you put quotation marks around it.

Other features

In addition to the eight main units, the Student's Book contains the following:

Business fundamentals

This opening section introduces you to basic business principles and vocabulary. It provides a solid foundation for you to build on in the course and will help you get the most out of all components of *The* **Business** 2.0.

Reviews

These units can be used in three ways: to consolidate your work on the units, to catch up quickly if you have missed a lesson, and to revise before tests or exams.

Additional material

This section contains all the extra materials you need to do pairwork or group work activities.

Grammar and practice

This section gives a useful summary of grammar rules with clear examples, and also provides further practice of the essential grammar points in this level of the course.

Recordings

Full scripts of all the audio recordings arc provided, allowing you to study the audio dialogues in detail. However, try not to rely on reading them to understand the listenings – very often you don't need to understand every word, just the main ideas.

Glossary

In most modules, there is a short glossary of words you may not know. The definitions for these are in the Glossary at the back of the book. Words in red are high-frequency items, which you should try to learn and use. The others, in black, are words you just need to understand.

eWorkbook

The **Business** 2.0 eWorkbook provides everything you would find in a printed Workbook, as well as extra multimedia resources. It is mainly intended for self-study or home study and contains material to support and enhance the activities in the Student's Book.

Language practice

This section contains activities to consolidate the language presented in the Student's Book. You can practise grammar, vocabulary, listening, pronunciation, reading and writing.

Watch

This section contains a video clip and worksheet to accompany each unit in the Student's Book. The video clips are episodes of a mini-drama that illustrate the communication and people skills in each unit. The exercises allow you to practise the functional language in the video.

Tests

You can test yourself at any point in the course using the eWorkbook, by setting either the time or the number of questions. Your test scores are recorded for your reference.

Print and work

This section offers a pen-and-paper version of the activities in the Language practice section. You can also download the audio tracks required for these activities.

Grammar help

You can refer to this section for helpful grammar rules and examples.

Word lists

This section contains the keywords and definitions from the Vocabulary modules in the Student's Book.

Dictionary

Use the Dictionary Tool to link to the *Macmillan Dictionary* online http://www.macmillandictionary.com.

Writing tips

This section provides explanations and exercises on aspects of writing, such as spelling, punctuation and paragraphing.

Listen

This section contains all the audio recordings from the Student's Book and eWorkbook, together with the audioscripts. You can download all the material in this section to a mobile device for listening on the move.

We sincerely hope you will enjoy working with *The* **Business** 2.0. Good luck!

John Allison   Rachel Appleby   Edward de Chazal

Contents

Management skills	Writing	Case study
1.4 Self-awareness and communication Personal qualities The Johari window© Roleplay: play the Truth game	**1.5 A professional biography** Analysis: structuring a biography Language focus: participle clauses	**1.6 Case study: The glass ceiling** Discussion, reading and listening relating to challenges in career development for women
2.4 Time management Prioritizing Effective delegation Roleplay: practise delegating and give feedback	**2.5 Newsletter articles** Analysis: structuring a newsletter article Language focus: perspectives	**2.6 Case study: Pixkel Inc.** Reading, listening, discussion and presentation related to improving the corporate image of an electronics company in California
3.4 Managing change Force field analysis Cleft sentences Roleplay: presentation of a change management plan	**3.5 Emails** Analysis: greetings and salutations Language focus: expressions with *as* Levels of formality	**3.6 Case study: WEF Audio** Reading, discussion, listening and simulation related to the production strategy of an audio technology company in Austria
4.4 Assertiveness Assertive, aggressive or passive Assertiveness techniques Roleplay: conflict situations in the workplace	**4.5 Letters** Analysis: tone Language focus: sounding diplomatic, assertive or forceful	**4.6 Case study: Olvea Brasil** Discussion, reading, listening and presentation related to conflictual relationships in a Brazilian engineering firm
5.4 Active listening Active listening techniques Asking questions Roleplay: discussion with active listening	**5.5 Business proposals** Analysis: structuring a proposal Language focus: reason, purpose and concessive clauses	**5.6 Case study: Presnya Taxi** Discussion, listening, reading and simulation related to a new marketing strategy for a Moscow-based taxi service
6.4 Communicating in a crisis Crisis communication strategies Analogies and alliteration Roleplay: interview in a crisis situation	**6.5 Reports: making recommendations** Analysis: structuring a report Language focus: key expressions for corporate reports	**6.6 Case study: Périgord Gourmet** Discussion, reading, listening and simulation related to a crisis at gourmet food company in France
7.4 Decision-making Decision-making tools Grid analysis Roleplay: a decision-making meeting	**7.5 Financial reporting** Analysis: structuring a financial report Language focus: metaphors, useful finance-related expressions	**7.6 Case study: Lesage Automobile** Discussion, reading, listening and simulation related to a small car manufacturer's future investment strategy
8.4 Leading the team Team roles Team functions Roleplay: meetings with team roles	**8.5 Style** Analysis: appropriate style Language focus: pairing, adverb and adjective collocations	**8.6 Case study: The cartel** Discussion, reading, listening and negotiation related to the expansion plans of two technology companies

Business fundamentals

▶ economic sectors

▶ ERP

Industry groups, company types and structure

Vocabulary

1 Match the industry groups with the appropriate economic sector.

Industry group	Economic sector
auditing, consulting	basic materials
chemicals, mining	capital goods
food, beverages	commercial services
machinery, equipment	consumer discretionary
restaurants, hotels	consumer staples

Industry group	Economic sector
telecoms, software	energy
electricity, water	financials
banking, real estate	technology
oil, gas	transportation
airlines, logistics	utilities

2 Put these company types in the most likely order of size, from smallest (1) to largest (4).

☐ private company/corporation ☐ public company/corporation ☐ partnership
☐ sole trader/sole proprietorship

3 Use words from the box to complete the text about ERP.

forecasting   functions   overview   platform   ~~processes~~   repository   software   umbrella

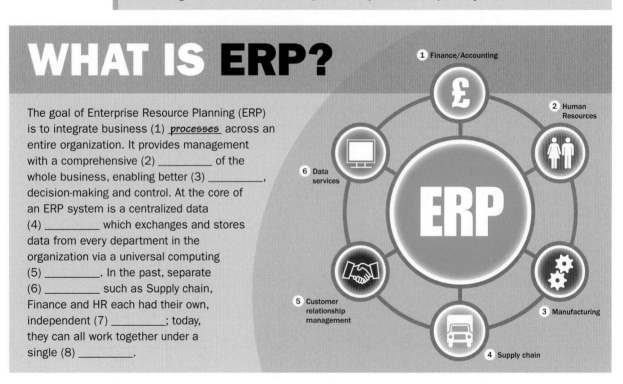

WHAT IS ERP?

The goal of Enterprise Resource Planning (ERP) is to integrate business (1) _processes_ across an entire organization. It provides management with a comprehensive (2) _____ of the whole business, enabling better (3) _____, decision-making and control. At the core of an ERP system is a centralized data (4) _____ which exchanges and stores data from every department in the organization via a universal computing (5) _____. In the past, separate (6) _____ such as Supply chain, Finance and HR each had their own, independent (7) _____; today, they can all work together under a single (8) _____.

1 Finance/Accounting
2 Human Resources
3 Manufacturing
4 Supply chain
5 Customer relationship management
6 Data services

4 With a partner, decide which department 1–6 in the chart the following ERP functions are usually associated with. The first two have been done for you.

1	access control 6	6	customer service	11	payables	16	recruiting
2	budgeting 1	7	sales & marketing	12	payroll	17	engineering
3	call centre support	8	inventory	13	purchasing	18	shipping
4	cash management	9	manufacturing process	14	quality control	19	user interfaces
5	supplier schedules	10	order entry	15	fixed assets	20	training

Discussion

5 In small groups, give examples of friends or family; which industries, types of company and departments do they work in, and what are their activities? How desirable are their jobs in your opinion?

the business cycle

the investment cycle

Business and investment cycles

Discussion

1 Why is it unusual in sport or in music for one team or one band to be consistently successful over a long period? What parallels can be drawn with economic and business life?

Listening

2 1:01 Listen to a presentation of the business cycle and label items 1–6 on the chart with the words in the box.

peak   recession   slump   trough   recovery   boom

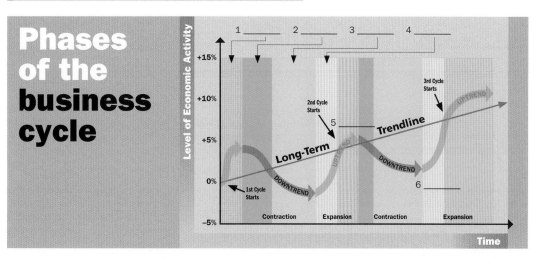

3 1:01 Listen again and answer the questions.

1 What average growth rate is given as an example in the presentation?
2 What phase of the business cycle is the economy in at the moment, and how long has it been so?
3 What possible causes for variations in the cycle are mentioned in the presentation?
4 What is the current growth rate in your country? Is it below average or above average?
5 Give examples of factors that have contributed to recent changes in the business cycle.

4 1:02 Listen to a presentation of the investment cycle. What four phases of the cycle does the presenter mention? Listen and label them on the chart below.

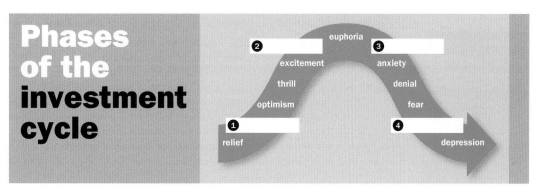

5 1:02 Listen again and answer the questions.

1 What kinds of securities do investors prefer in each of the four phases?
2 What is the term used to describe a situation where investors expect prices to fall?
3 What is the term used to describe a situation where investors expect prices to rise?
4 What is the term used to describe investors who buy when the share price is lower than the company is really worth?

Glossary   PAGE 152

cyclical
slump
trough

6 Which phase of the investment cycle do you think the market is in at the moment? Which companies are considered a good investment?

Business fundamentals

- ▶ profit and loss account
- ▶ balance sheet
- ▶ cash flow statement

Financial statements

Reading

1 The P&L (profit and loss account, or income statement), the balance sheet (BS) and the cash flow statement (CFS) are a company's three most important financial statements. Match descriptions 1–3 with the documents A)–C).

1 a picture of what a company owns and what it owes at a single moment in time ☐
2 money received or spent on business activity, investments or financing ☐
3 revenue minus expenses equals profit ☐

Ⓐ P&L

Revenue
- Cost of sales
  Gross profit
- SG&A
  Operating profit
+ Non-operating profit
  EBITDA
- Interest
- Tax
- Depreciation
- Amortization
  Net profit after tax
- Dividends
  Retained profit

Ⓑ Balance sheet

Assets
Current assets
Cash
Accounts receivable
Inventories
Long-term assets
Fixed assets
Intangible assets
Financial assets
Liabilities
Current liabilities
Bank debt
Accounts payable
Liabilities for tax
Short-term provisions
Long-term liabilities
Bank loans
Bonds payable
Shareholders' equity

Ⓒ Cash flow statement

Cash at beginning of year
Operations
+ Cash receipts from customers
- Cash paid for inventory, general expenses, wages, interest, tax
Investing
+ Cash receipts from sale of property, equipment and securities
- Cash paid for property, equipment and securities
Financing
+ Cash receipts from issuing stock, borrowing
- Cash paid for repurchase of stock, repayment of loans, dividends
Net increase/decrease in cash
Cash at end of year

2 Look at the P&L (document A). With a partner, find the words that match the definitions 1–10 below.

1 money paid to the government *taxes*
2 the cost of materials and labour for production
3 payments received from customers
4 money paid to shareholders
5 value lost on vehicles as they get older
6 the cost of advertising the product
7 value lost on patents as they get older
8 payments received for the sale of land
9 the cost of loans from the bank
10 money reinvested in the business

3 Mark the following statements about the balance sheet (document B) *T* (true) or *F* (false).

1 A BS can only be completed at the end of the financial year. ☐
2 Current assets include money owed by customers but not yet paid. ☐
3 Inventories include stock which has been sold but not yet delivered. ☐
4 Fixed assets do not include vehicles because they are mobile. ☐
5 Patents, copyrights and shares in other companies are financial assets. ☐
6 Current liabilities are items that have to be paid within the next year. ☐
7 Accounts payable are invoices that customers have not yet paid. ☐
8 Short-term provisions include money the company expects to lose in court. ☐
9 Bonds payable are amounts of capital the company will receive in the future. ☐
10 Shareholders' equity is the value that would be left if all the assets were sold and all liabilities paid. ☐

4 Choose the best option to complete these statements about the cash flow statement (document C).

1 For a typical company, most cash comes from a) operations b) investing c) financing.
2 The figure for cash receipts from customers comes from the a) P&L b) BS c) bank.
3 Investing includes money spent or made on a) equipment b) shares c) equipment and shares.
4 Tax payable is a) deducted b) added c) ignored.
5 A company can improve cash flow by a) issuing b) purchasing c) borrowing shares.

Glossary   PAGE 152

EBITDA
SG&A

CVs

job interviews

Recruitment

Writing

1 Using the framework below, write a CV. Include three items of information that are not true.

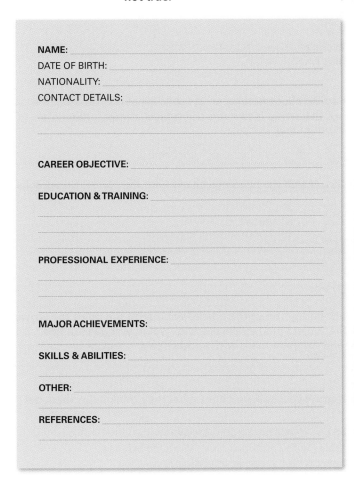

NAME: _____

DATE OF BIRTH: _____

NATIONALITY: _____

CONTACT DETAILS: _____

CAREER OBJECTIVE: _____

EDUCATION & TRAINING: _____

PROFESSIONAL EXPERIENCE: _____

MAJOR ACHIEVEMENTS: _____

SKILLS & ABILITIES: _____

OTHER: _____

REFERENCES: _____

Speaking

2 With a partner, exchange CVs and interview each other. Try to identify the three items in your partner's CV that are not true.

Listening

3 🔊 1:03 Listen to a consultant presenting the recruitment process to a group of HR Directors. Match the seven steps in the process with the summaries a)–g).

1	Set-up	a)	The consultant adjusts all the variables to ensure the best candidate takes the job.
2	Sourcing	b)	The consultant and the line manager meet to draw up a profile of the ideal candidate.
3	Screening	c)	The consultant makes appointments for candidates to meet the line manager.
4	Interviews		
5	Feedback	d)	A consultant uses phone conversations to eliminate or interest candidates.
6	Offer	e)	The consultant uses old and new channels to contact and attract the right profiles.
7	Onboard	f)	The consultant continues to advise the new employee until they start work.
		g)	The consultant gathers data to improve the process and help the line manager.

Glossary   PAGE 152

flawlessly

screen

Discussion

4 As candidates, what can you do at each stage in the recruitment process to maximize your chances of success?

Top tips for getting on in the workplace

Life at work is a potential minefield: if your boss isn't out to get you at any opportunity, it will be your colleagues. But don't worry, as there are many things you can do to make your life at work a little easier (and even to get yourself ahead). Aside from such illegal strategies as blackmail and kidnap, a number of less drastic and more legal ones exist. So, next time you are having a hard time at work, try using a few of the tips opposite.

Internet research

Search for the keywords *success at work* to find other tips. Choose the best five to compare with a partner.

Glossary   PAGE 152

dress-down Friday
mind share
office politics

1.1 About business Developing your career

Discussion

1 Work with a partner. What advice would you give to a new employee on how to make a good impression and 'get on' in their career? Think about the issues below and agree on five top pieces of advice.

> dress   meetings   colleagues   your boss   business lunches
> conferences   dealing with emails/phone calls

2 Read an introduction to an article about getting on at work. What do you think the attitude or stance of the writer of the article is towards the subject matter? Underline words in the text which support your view.

Scan reading

3 Read the whole article quickly. Match the headings below with the correct paragraphs.

a) Dress up not down
b) Get yourself noticed
c) Remember that less is more
d) Steer well clear of all meetings
e) Manage without bosses

f) Be nice to PAs
g) Ignore all emails
h) Learn to recycle reports
i) Treat appraisals as auditions for pantomime

Reading and discussion

4 Work with a partner. For each paragraph of the article, summarize the point the writer of the article is making about the subject matter. What advice would you give on this topic? Write down your ideas, and compare them with another pair.

Listening for gist

5 🔊 1:04–1:06 Listen to three employees talking about what they think helps them get on at work.

1 Make notes of the advice they give under the headings below.
   • Promotion   • Relationships with your boss   • Work-life balance
2 How do their comments compare with the tips in the article?

Top tips for getting on in the workplace

1

Getting ahead in business means getting noticed, but working hard makes you almost invisible. Therefore it's a lot better to work hard at getting yourself noticed. What senior management likes more than anything else is junior managers who show signs of initiative and volunteer to do things. Most of the reason for this is that the more junior managers volunteer to do, the less senior managers will have to do themselves. Of course, volunteering for things and doing things are two different matters. Once you have got the credit for volunteering for a project, it's best to get as far away as possible from the project before the work kicks in. The best way to do that is to volunteer for another project.

2

Working in the post room is not generally a career choice for most people. Yet with the epidemic of email most people spend half their working lives slaving away in their own personal computer post room. Most emails are biodegradable, however. If you let them sink to the bottom of the pile and go unanswered they will eventually become irrelevant. To some people, doing this might seem like just about the most daring and suicidal thing you could possibly do in an office but, if something really matters, the person who sent it will eventually call you to ask you about it.

3

The difference between a boss and a high street bank is that a bank sometimes gives you credit for things. Bosses give you things to do and then blame you for doing them. What they never understand is that if they didn't give you things to do in the first place, you wouldn't make so many spectacular foul-ups. Naturally there are good bosses and bad bosses. Some take the trouble to get interested in what you are doing, encourage your personal development and generally provide you with a stimulating and challenging environment in which to work. There are also good bosses who lock themselves in their rooms, have five-hour lunches and leave you completely alone.

4

Since the collapse of communism, dress-down Fridays have done more than anything else to impair the smooth running of capitalism. Business suits are for doing business in. If you are wearing a welder's helmet people expect rivets; if you are wearing a suit people expect business. But if you are wearing shorts and sandals, people expect you to be on your way to San Francisco with flowers in your hair. On the other hand, never look too businesslike. This marks you out as someone who works in organized crime or as an undertaker, if not both.

5

An appraisal is where you have an exchange of opinion with your boss. It's called an exchange of opinion because you go in with your opinion and leave with their opinion. When you have had a bad year, the best approach is a balance between cringing apology and grovelling sycophancy, something like: 'My respect for you is so intense that it sometimes distracted me, thereby causing the continual string of major cock-ups that have been the main feature of my performance this year.' Interestingly, giving appraisals is actually as hard as getting them. The secret is to mix criticism with recognition. For example: 'You've made a number of mistakes Martin, but we recognize you made them because you are a total idiot.'

6

Reports are the office equivalent of cones in the road. They are not actually work themselves, but they are a big, clear sign that real work might be done at some stage. In the meantime, they slow everything down and cause anger and annoyance all round. The quickest and easiest way to write a report is to change the names in the last report. When you do this, be aware that there will always be one name that escapes your changes and that will be in the sentence, 'We are committed to personal service to ...' The other thing people always forget to change in reports are the headers and footers which you only notice are completely wrong in the lift on the way to your presentation.

7

If you put all the country's chief executives in one room, all they would produce would be a range of jammy share options for themselves and some meaningless corporate waffle for the City. Give them one good PA and they might get some useful work done. That's why it's very difficult for PAs to become managers. It's not that PAs couldn't do management jobs, it's because management couldn't do management jobs without PAs. Remember that for every senior executive on the golf course, there is a PA running the business back in the office.

8

You would think that lazy people would form an inert mass at the bottom of an organization. On the contrary they are found at all levels in business, right up to chairperson. The reason for this is simple: when something goes wrong in business it's generally because someone somewhere has tried to do something. Obviously, if you don't do anything, you can't be blamed when it goes wrong. People who sit all day like a lemon, busily straightening paperclips, are therefore the only people with a 100% record of success, and with that sort of record, promotion is inevitable.

9

Half of every working day is spent in meetings, half of which are not worth having, and of those that are, half the time is wasted. Which means that nearly one third of office life is spent in small rooms with people you don't like, doing things that don't matter. The only reason people have so many meetings is that they are the one time you can get away from your work, your phone and your customers. People say that the secret of a good meeting is preparation. But if people really prepared for meetings, the first thing they would realize is that most are unnecessary. In fact, a tightly run meeting is one of the most frightening things in office life. These are meetings for which you have to prepare, in which you have to work and after which you have to take action. Fortunately, these meetings are as rare as a sense of gay abandon in the finance department.

Getting ahead in business means getting noticed

- ▶ skills and qualities
- ▶ SMART objectives

Behavioural competencies

1 You work for Global Sounds, a tour management organization, arranging tours and concerts for musicians from around the world. What challenges and obstacles does this present you with? What skills are key in your job?

2 Behavioural competencies are observable skills and qualities required for effective performance in a job. Look at Global Sounds' list of behavioural competencies and put them into the correct column.

> analytical thinking   client focus   decision-making   effective communication   flexibility
> holding people accountable   innovation   intercultural competence   leadership
> managing change   networking   results orientation   self-awareness   self-development
> time management

Teamworking	Managing and developing yourself	Customer service	Problem-solving

3 Use the correct form of the words in the box to complete the definitions of five behavioural competencies below.

> analyse   apply   communicate   expect   prioritize

1   being able to bring disciplined _____ to data and situations, to see cause and effect and to use this to make effective decisions
2   the ability to use the appropriate channel, means and style of _____ with tact in a variety of situations
3   the willingness and ability to give _____ to customers, delivering high-quality services which meet their needs
4   the ability to adapt with ease to a variety of situations; it is also about not being disconcerted by the _____
5   the ability to find opportunities to develop your skills and attributes through self-study, training, practical _____, and/or support from others

Now match each definition with a competency from Exercise 2.

Listening

4 🔊 1:07 Tony is a Project Manager at Global Sounds and is having a performance appraisal with his manager. Which of the behavioural competencies from Exercise 2 do they discuss?

5 🔊 1:07 Now listen again. What examples does Tony give to support his points?

Glossary   PAGE 152

astute
SMART
time-bound

Setting goals

6 Read the text below. Choose one word from each box to make a suitable collocation to fill in the spaces.

clear   measurable   performance   realistic   valuable   written

appraisal   guidelines   insight   objectives   record   targets

This section aims to provide you with (1) _____ in setting objectives.

- First, be sure to make sure you set (2) _____. This means being precise in terms of time and quantity, and will ultimately help you to achieve your goals. It's also advisable to set short- and long-term objectives: concentrating only on the final outcome gives minimal chance for reviewing the stages you reach on the way.
- Secondly, make sure you set (3) _____. You must know you'll be able to achieve them. Being overambitious won't help, and won't help your confidence in achieving them. Make sure you have all the support you'll need, in terms of both people and resources.

- Remember also that a (4) _____ of your goals means you'll have a document to refer to regularly. Don't just keep your plans in your head!
- Don't forget that having a clear plan of your objectives gives you (5) _____ into your priorities and aspirations – for yourself, or others.
- With this in mind, your (6) _____ should be a meeting you can look forward to, and use as an opportunity to set more exciting and challenging goals for a bright future!

Vocabulary

7 Read this extract taken from the end of the conversation between Jill and Tony. Complete it with the given word in the correct form.

Well, I think overall you've had a pretty (1) _____ (succeed) year, with a number of major (2) _____ (achieve). In particular, your (3) _____ (perceive) of how your own team of staff are doing is very astute. I'm pleased about that, as good (4) _____ (evaluate) skills are important in managing a department. However, when things go wrong, try not to get (5) _____ (defend). I understand it's difficult, but as you've seen, your colleagues have been so (6) _____ (respond) that I don't think you need worry. It's much better to be upfront, and work together to put things right.

Out on the road you experienced a few problems in relation to the behaviour of the musicians on the Bosnian tour. We discussed the importance of communicating (7) _____ (effective) and making it clear that any costs incurred from damage to hotel rooms or facilities will not be met by Global Sounds. This should avoid a rerun of the infamous swimming pool incident! Standards of behaviour vary across the world and you may want to think about focusing on intercultural communication in the coming months, especially given the tour of the Far East you're going to be working on with the American youth orchestra.

We've also talked about setting targets, and I think what's key for you, rather than be (8) _____ (commit), is to be more precise about what you want to achieve and by when, and to set more interim targets.

8 Look at some of the objectives from Tony's job plan. For each objective, <u>underline</u> the SMART aspects, indicating which criterion it relates to.

(Reminder: SMART = Specific, Measurable, Achievable, Realistic, Time-bound)

Internet research

Search for the keywords *behavioural competencies* and find out what other companies use these, and why. Report your findings back to your group.

- To finalize 80% of promotional plans for artist publicity eight weeks before any planned tour date begins.
- To involve junior staff in at least 50% of arrangements.
- To ensure publicity exposure covers at least three different channels (print, radio, the Web, mail, etc.).
- To update budgets by the end of each quarter.

9 Make a list of three short-, three medium- and three long-term objectives. Make sure they are SMART. Read and compare your lists in small groups and give feedback to each other on how realistic or idealistic these goals could be. Be prepared to outline, defend or change your decisions!

1 | Personal development

1.3 Grammar   Tense, aspect and voice

Did you know?

English has just two tenses – *present* and *past*, plus two aspects – *perfect* and *continuous*. Aspect is how we see things: the perfect aspect describes complete actions, *They have built a new research centre* (present perfect) and the continuous aspect describes actions in progress, *They have been building a new research centre for the last three years* (present perfect continuous). There are eight possible tense/aspect combinations, six of which we can put into the passive voice. About 90% of verbs used in English are in simple forms, i.e. neither perfect or continuous.

▶ Grammar and practice
pages 122–123

Review of aspect

1 With a partner, brainstorm as many different verb forms as you can. Organize the forms in a logical way, for example, past forms, future forms, active and passive, etc.

2 Check your list of possible verb forms from against the *Did you know?* box in the margin.

3 Read the conversation between two colleagues and <u>underline</u> the most suitable verb forms. With a partner, discuss the reasons for your choices. What different meanings are expressed by the other choices?

Ed: So, what (1) *have you been up to / are you up to* since I last (2) *saw / have seen* you?

Jon: Oh, (3) *hasn't anyone been telling you / hasn't anyone told you*? I (4) *decided / have decided* to go for promotion. You know, for the new Area Manager job.

Ed: Great! What exactly (5) *would you be doing / would you have been doing* in the new job?

Jon: Well, you need to be quite flexible as there's a lot of travel involved – in fact, the responsibilities (6) *cover / have covered* six different countries.

Ed: That'll suit you down to the ground – you (7) *have always got / always got* out and about a lot I seem to remember. By the way, you know Jacob (8) *is going / has been going* for it as well?

Jon: No, but I'm not threatened – he (9) *blew / has blown* his reputation for competence over that lost documents episode.

Ed: OK, but what (10) *have you done / have you been doing* to make sure you actually get the job?

Jon: Well, by the end of the week I (11) *will have worked out / will be working out* my interview strategy and there's no question they can ask me I can't answer.

Ed: (12) *Aren't you being / Aren't you* a bit overconfident, or should that be arrogant?

Jon: We'll see. Drinks are on me if I get it.

Ed: Deal.

🔊 1:08 **Listen and check your answers.**

Glossary   PAGE 152

blow your reputation
Peter Principle

Speaking

4 Interview your partner about their career, education and training path over the last few years. What have they been doing and what have they achieved? What will they be doing in the near future?

Using the passive

5 Complete the pairs of sentences below with a) an active and b) a passive verb form. Decide how the choice of the active or passive voice affects the meaning and emphasis of the sentence.

1 **target** (present continuous)
   a) We _____ the training initiative at those employees who need it the most.
   b) The training initiative is _____ at those employees who need it the most.
2 **make** (past perfect)
   a) The Chairman of the board admitted that 'mistakes _____'.
   b) The Chairman of the board admitted that they '_____ mistakes'.
3 **cover** (present simple)
   a) The course _____ all the areas of confidence building, fostering team spirit and self-awareness.
   b) All the areas of confidence building, fostering team spirit and self-awareness _____ by the course.
4 **bring under control** (present perfect)
   a) The government _____ massive arrival of illegal immigrants, particularly the influx of refugees fleeing civil war in neighbouring countries at the end of the decade.
   b) The massive arrival of illegal immigrants, particularly the influx of refugees fleeing civil war in neighbouring countries at the end of the decade, _____.
5 **transform** (past perfect)
   a) From a backward agricultural society, by 1970, the people _____ the country into a powerful industrial state.
   b) From a backward agricultural society, by 1970, the country _____ into a powerful industrial state.
6 **rate** (present perfect)
   a) People _____ this product highly since it was released.
   b) This product _____ highly since it was released.

6 Work with a partner. Is the active or the passive voice the most appropriate for each of the pairs of sentences? Use the list of reasons below to help you.

- We want to avoid mentioning who did the action so the passive is appropriate.
- The passive is appropriate because it is unimportant, or unnecessary, to say who did the action.
- The subject of the sentence is extremely long, so the active sounds better because it puts the long material at the end.
- There is no reason to use the passive, so the active is better.

Tense, aspect and voice

7 Work in small groups. Play noughts and crosses. Draw a grid and number the spaces as shown. The first team chooses either noughts or crosses and then picks a number and a topic from the box. If they can make a correct sentence about the topic using the corresponding tense and aspect (either active or passive) they win the square and fill it with either a nought or a cross. The winning team are the first to get a horizontal, vertical or diagonal line of noughts or crosses.

> how I've been developing my career   how communication has changed
> the most influential business people of our time   the qualities of the best leaders
> how to make a good impression

Square 1 present tense, simple		
Square 2 present tense, perfect		
Square 3 present tense, continuous		
Square 4 present tense, perfect continuous		
Square 5 past tense, simple		
Square 6 past tense, perfect		
Square 7 past tense, continuous		
Square 8 past tense, perfect continuous active or passive		
Square 9 any tense or aspect, passive voice		

1	2	3
4	5	6
7	8	9

e.g. 2 communication
The way colleagues in the same office communicate with each other has been changed by technology. They send each other emails instead of talking.

1 Personal development

1.4 Management skills — Self-awareness and communication

Discussion

1 How do you know what other people think of you and your behaviour? In small groups, make a list of all the possible ways you can find out. Which kinds of feedback do you feel are most reliable, most sensitive, and most difficult to obtain?

2 Divide into pairs. Working individually, first choose five or six adjectives from the list below which you feel describe you and how others might perceive your behaviour at work. Then, still individually, choose five or six adjectives which describe your partner.

able	dependable	intelligent	patient	sensible
accepting	dignified	introverted	powerful	sentimental
adaptable	energetic	kind	proud	shy
bold	extroverted	knowledgeable	quiet	silly
brave	friendly	logical	reflective	spontaneous
calm	giving	loving	relaxed	sympathetic
caring	happy	mature	religious	tense
cheerful	helpful	modest	responsive	trustworthy
clever	idealistic	nervous	searching	warm
complex	independent	observant	self-assertive	wise
confident	ingenious	organized	self-conscious	witty

3 With your partner, compare your lists. Write the adjectives into the quadrants below as follows.

1. In the top left quadrant, write any adjectives that both you and your partner chose to describe you.
2. In the bottom left quadrant, write any adjectives that you chose to describe yourself but that your partner did not choose.
3. In the top right quadrant, write any adjectives that your partner chose to describe you but that you did not choose.

Johari window

	Known to (1) _____	Not known to (2) _____
Known to (3) _____	(5) _____	(7) _____
Not known to (4) _____	(6) _____	(8) _____

Listening

4 🔊 1:09 Listen to a presentation of the Johari window and complete the labels 1–8 on the chart above.

Discussion

5 With your partner, discuss how well your Joharis describe you.

> I think of myself as someone who ...   I hadn't thought of myself like that.
> I (do) tend to ..., so, yes, perhaps I am a bit ...   I consider myself ...
> I'm rather a(n) ... kind of person.   Do you think so? I'm really hopeless at ...

Glossary   PAGE 152

Arena
Blind spot
Façade
Johari window
megabucks
Unknown

6 The Johari window also offers insights into personality and communication skills by comparing the relative size of each quadrant. Discuss how managers with the Joharis below might be perceived.

Which type of manager would you prefer to work with?

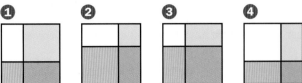

Listening for gist

7 🔊 1:10–1:14 The Truth game is designed to encourage sharing and feedback in order to enlarge the Arena and reduce the other areas. Listen to two people playing the game; which questions are they talking about?

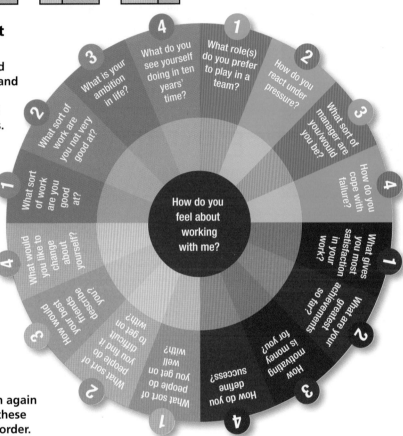

8 🔊 1:10–1:14 Listen again and put the words in these phrases in the correct order.

1 a at go have I Shall this? _____
2 confess have I that to ... _____
3 like one take this to Would you? _____
4 about it I've much never really that thought. _____
5 haven't I idea slightest the! _____
6 have honest I'd If I'm myself, say to totally with ... _____
7 don't if I'll mind on one, pass this you. _____
8 leave Let's one, shall that we? _____
9 a clue got honestly haven't I! _____
10 I I'd If me, pushed really say suppose you ... _____

9 Find two expressions in Exercise 8 which are used for:

a) taking turns
b) talking about one's weaknesses
c) saying you have no strong opinion
d) saying you don't know
e) not answering a question.

Truth game

10 Work with a partner and play the Truth game. Start with different colour questions from the group next to you. Go round the board clockwise until you have discussed all the questions, then answer the question in the middle. Ask supplementary questions to help your partner develop their answers.

11 Repeat the process in Exercises 2 and 3 to draw a second Johari. Have your windows changed after playing the Truth game?

1 | Personal development

▶ structuring a biography

▶ participle clauses

▶ writing a professional bio

1.5 Writing   A professional biography

Discussion

1 Which of the items a)–h) below would you include in a professional bio for the following publications?

1 a bid document   2 a conference programme   3 your company website

a) a photo
b) marital status and family
c) address and phone number
d) hobbies
e) professional achievements
f) professional objectives
g) academic qualifications
h) positions held and dates

Model

2 Read Erica Winter's bio and number the paragraph headings in the order they appear.

☐ background   ☐ other   ☐ current position   ☐ recent achievements

---

ERICA WINTER

A recognized expert with more than 15 years of successful experience in HR, Erica has a proven ability to identify and develop management talent. She heads up Black, Bone & Winter's executive search team, filling strategic positions for industrial clients and government departments.

Having earned her Master's in Management from the London School of Economics, Erica first went to work in the car industry, quickly earning a reputation for boosting productivity while maintaining quality. She then moved into HR, steadily making the transition from shop floor management to global responsibility for managing 4,500 people.

Erica is most fulfilled when helping people to maximize their potential, and having championed numerous personal development initiatives in the car industry, in 2010 she co-founded BBW, an executive search firm that specializes in placement of executives. To date, she has successfully completed hundreds of successful searches.

Leveraging her professional network (she is an active member of the Chartered Institute of Personnel and Development), Erica also chairs 'Work on wheels', an association that lobbies the car industry to employ more disabled people. She has made numerous TV appearances and is the author of a best-selling book, *How to be headhunted*. Erica lives in London with her husband, two children and three cats.

Analysis

3 Which of the following recommendations did Erica *not* follow in the model bio above?

1 Ideally your bio should be between 150 and 300 words long, and never more than one page.

2 Use the third person (*he, she*) to sound more professional.

3 Include a head and shoulders photo of yourself in business clothes.

4 Give a brief description of your business and your customers.

5 Describe your key professional achievements.

6 Include any professional qualifications and awards you have received.

7 Mention organizations, associations or clubs you belong to.

8 Add to your credibility by mentioning media appearances and publications.

9 Include your contact details in your final paragraph.

10 Add a human touch that people will remember you for, such as mentioning your family life, hobbies, etc.

Internet research

Search for the keywords *sample professional bio* for more models and tips. Be critical; not all the advice you will find is helpful!

Language focus

4 Adverbial participle clauses provide more information about the verb or the main idea in a sentence. They can use present or past participles, and come before or after the main idea:

She heads up Black, Bone & Winter's executive search team, filling strategic positions for industrial clients and government departments.
Having earned her Master's in Management from the London School of Economics, Erica first went to work in the car industry …

Find and <u>underline</u> six more examples in the model bio.

5 Rewrite these extracts from biographies using participle clauses.

1 Jack works at Bell Labs, where he manages a mobile communications research team.
2 Because he didn't know what else to do, Bobby started playing in a piano bar.
3 Suzanne served her apprenticeship with the legendary Paul Bocuse, then opened her own restaurant.
4 Marie didn't wish to spend all her life in the family business, so she undertook a round-the-world tour.
5 Jochen took up teaching because he failed to qualify as a lawyer.
6 Fran got the idea for the new product while she was a research scientist in the chemicals industry.
7 Because he met a lot of doctors in his previous job, Frederick realized there was a gap in the market.
8 Once Henry's new business had been launched, it grew fast.

Output

6 Using the notes below write a bio for Ned Fordyce, a leading economics analyst. Make sure you use some participle clauses in your writing and add at least three ideas of your own.

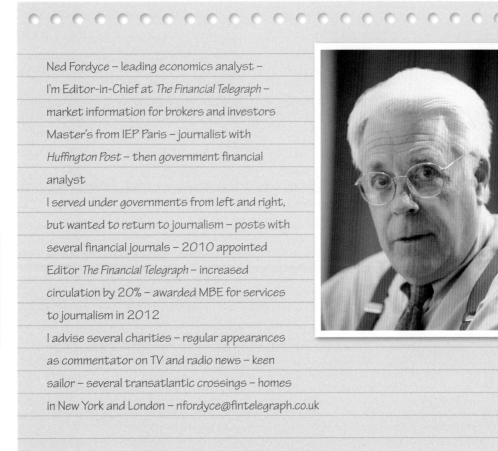

Ned Fordyce – leading economics analyst –
I'm Editor-in-Chief at *The Financial Telegraph* –
market information for brokers and investors
Master's from IEP Paris – journalist with
Huffington Post – then government financial
analyst
I served under governments from left and right,
but wanted to return to journalism – posts with
several financial journals – 2010 appointed
Editor *The Financial Telegraph* – increased
circulation by 20% – awarded MBE for services
to journalism in 2012
I advise several charities – regular appearances
as commentator on TV and radio news – keen
sailor – several transatlantic crossings – homes
in New York and London – nfordyce@fintelegraph.co.uk

Glossary   PAGE 152

bid
broker
circulation
leverage
lobby

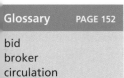

7 Write your own bio. You can either write your current profile or imagine yourself ten years in the future.

1.5 Writing

1 | Personal development

▶ strengths and weaknesses

▶ professional image

▶ strategic career development

1.6 Case study The glass ceiling

Discussion

1 In small groups, discuss your reactions to these statements from a survey on equal opportunities.

Women, ethnic minorities and gay people have got nothing to complain about. It's the disabled who are really hard done by. **NITA FIGUEROA, SOCIAL WORKER**

There's no denying that in some industries, it's a man's world – it's a fact of life, always has been, always will be. **CARLOS ALEGRIA, TRADE UNIONIST**

The glass ceiling is as much a reality today as it ever was in the past, and most men want to see it stay that way! **CATALINA VALLEJO, FEMINIST**

Business is a jungle; only the fittest survive and make it to the top. But as a shareholder, why would you want it any other way? **RAUL SOTO, COMPANY DIRECTOR**

Glossary   PAGE 153

comfort zone
devil's advocate
glass ceiling
headhunt

Reading

2 Work with a partner. Gemma Álvarez Garcia works for SEVS, the Spanish subsidiary of a US-based high tech glass manufacturer. Read the extract from her personnel file, and answer the questions.

INTERNET

| NAME | Gemma Álvarez Garcia | JOB | Product Manager | Annual appraisal interview, 18 December |

Gemma continues to be a valuable and dependable member of her team. Her efficiency is widely appreciated: she is outgoing, has strong communication skills and is keen to take initiative. She has performed well in her current position, with the exception of the tendency to overreach her authority and to favour unconventional methods, which was discussed last year.

Gemma makes no secret of her ambitious career objectives: she is intensely disappointed that her application for the position of Marketing Manager was unsuccessful. This very publicly expressed frustration underlines a certain lack of maturity. She remains determined to move into management, despite the difficulties of reconciling the care of her four-year-old daughter with an inevitably heavy travel schedule. She does not appear to realize that SEVS has never employed a woman as a Marketing Manager; however, she agrees that she lacks a formal marketing and management background, and we discussed the possibility of her following an MBA course to enhance her personal development prospects.

1 What are Gemma's strengths and weaknesses in her current job?
2 What reasons are given for not promoting her to Marketing Manager?
3 How objective is she about her suitability for the position?
4 Transfer these key points to Gemma's Johari window© opposite.

Johari window

	Gemma knows	Gemma doesn't know
others know		
others don't know		

Listening

3 🔊 **1:15** Work with a partner. Listen to a conversation between Gemma's manager Steve and Ruben, the HR Manager at SEVS, and note the key points they make about Gemma. Decide what information to add to the Johari window.

Reading

4 Read Gemma's email to her mother. Decide what information to add to the Johari window.

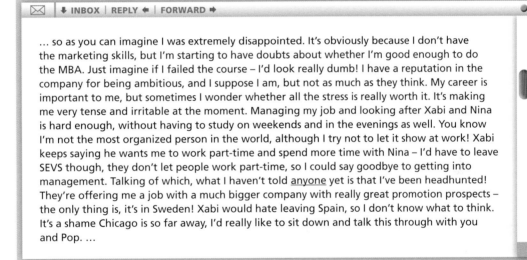

✉ | ⬇ INBOX | REPLY ⬅ | FORWARD ➡

… so as you can imagine I was extremely disappointed. It's obviously because I don't have the marketing skills, but I'm starting to have doubts about whether I'm good enough to do the MBA. Just imagine if I failed the course – I'd look really dumb! I have a reputation in the company for being ambitious, and I suppose I am, but not as much as they think. My career is important to me, but sometimes I wonder whether all the stress is really worth it. It's making me very tense and irritable at the moment. Managing my job and looking after Xabi and Nina is hard enough, without having to study on weekends and in the evenings as well. You know I'm not the most organized person in the world, although I try not to let it show at work! Xabi keeps saying he wants me to work part-time and spend more time with Nina – I'd have to leave SEVS though, they don't let people work part-time, so I could say goodbye to getting into management. Talking of which, what I haven't told <u>anyone</u> yet is that I've been headhunted! They're offering me a job with a much bigger company with really great promotion prospects – the only thing is, it's in Sweden! Xabi would hate leaving Spain, so I don't know what to think. It's a shame Chicago is so far away, I'd really like to sit down and talk this through with you and Pop. …

Discussion

5 With a partner, make a list of Gemma's options, then discuss the pros and cons of each strategy.

Listening

6 🔊 **1:16** Listen to a conversation between Gemma and her husband Xabi and answer the questions.

1 What points in Gemma's Johari window does this conversation confirm?
2 What can be added to the Johari window?
3 What can be added to the list of Gemma's options?

Discussion

7 In small groups, hold a meeting to decide what advice you would give Gemma. Report back to the class on your conclusions.

Student A turn to page 114.
Student B turn to page 116.
Student C turn to page 115.
Student D turn to page 118.
Student E turn to page 119.

1.6 Case study

2 | Corporate image

▶ reputations

▶ corporate makeovers

2.1 About business Corporate image

Discussion

1 Work with a partner. What do you know about McDonald's™, the global fast food chain? How would you describe its corporate image? Complete as much of the information below as you can.

Company founded in (place/date)	Company founded by
Logo	Mascot
Products/menu	Appearance of restaurants
Core market	Image of the company

Reading for gist

2 Read the text about the McDonald's corporate makeover.

1 Add any missing information you can to your table in Exercise 1 above.
2 Why was the company in trouble at the end of the 1990s? Summarize the reasons in one sentence.
3 In what ways has McDonald's recently changed the following?
   - the way the restaurants look
   - the menu
   - the corporate values

Reading for detail

Glossary PAGE 153

back-to-basics
fruits of its labours
green on the inside
green on the outside
greenwash
in your face
McLibel

3 Use the context to work out the meanings of the following expressions from the text.

1 *golden arches* (line 14)
2 *dead-end McJob* (line 35)
3 *BSE scare* (line 35)
4 *PR pratfalls* (line 45)
5 *'less is more' treatment* (line 82)
6 *corporate scam* (lines 87–88)
7 *in your face* (line 114)
8 *'Starbucksy' image* (line 138)

4 Who or what are:

1 *Arne Jacobsen* (line 5)
2 *Hemel* (line 12)
3 *Prince* (line 46)
4 *Watford FC* (line 90)
5 *Steve Easterbrook* (line 92)
6 *Jamie Oliver* (line 139)

Internet research

Search for the keywords *building corporate image* to find strategies businesses use to enhance their image. Make a list of the best strategies and compare with a partner.

5 Read the text again. How would you describe the attitude or stance of the writer towards the subject matter? Why? Find three pieces of evidence in the text to support your view.

Listening and discussion

6 🔊 1:17 Listen to the continuation of the article and answer the questions below.

1 Why could it be difficult for McDonald's to maintain its commitment to a greener way of operating? What challenges might it face?
2 How have the attitudes of McDonald's customers changed with regard to fast food? What is responsible for this change?

THE BIG
McMAKEOVER

A KHAKI GREEN café restaurant has quietly materialized in Hemel Hempstead. Under subdued lamp light, with the indie rock playing in the background, a lunching doctor sits on a curvy chair modelled on Arne Jacobsen's modernist classic. He could have chosen Rainforest Alliance-certified freshly ground coffee, with British organic milk, or a free-range egg, delivered by a lorry powered by biodiesel from recycled cooking oil, and a bag of carrot sticks or fresh fruit. (He couldn't have had a salad because Hemel has sold out.) But he has plumped for a Filet-o-Fish, fries and a fizzy drink.

Under its golden arches, and under our very eyes, McDonald's™ has been transforming itself. And today it announces the fruits of its labours: financial results for 2012 that are expected to be excellent around the globe and, in Britain, a triumph. The US-based chain is now selling more burgers than at any time since it arrived in Britain 38 years ago. Sales are growing almost as quickly as in the 80s boom, and this year will help fund a $2bn expansion around the globe.

Its popularity and profits signal a remarkable comeback. At the end of the 1990s, the company — founded when Ray Kroc teamed up with Dick and Mac McDonald to open the Des Plaines restaurant in 1955 — was in trouble. Following the McLibel case, in which two environmental activists were sued by the corporate giant and (in the end) won, its golden arches had become emblematic of all that was rotten in capitalism; an obesity crisis in the western world loomed large; there was disdain for the dead-end McJob; and Britain's BSE scare recruited an army of vegetarians. From 1999, annual UK sales stagnated at £1bn. In 2005, its profits collapsed by almost two-thirds, from £96.6m to £36.9m. Its restaurants seemed tired and its dwindling band of customers appeared embarrassed to be there. McDonald's was dying.

Two years later, it is hard to see what, in the wider world, has changed. Last year's headlines are a litany of potential PR pratfalls: 'Fast food "is almost as salty as the sea"', 'Prince says McDonald's should be banned', 'McDonald's accused of "piracy" by chair firm' are just three. Then there are the stories about a knife scanner fitted at a McDonald's in Tottenham, £125 parking fines for folk who don't finish their drive-through meals within 45 minutes, and

news from the US that McDonald's was offering Happy Meal coupons on school report cards while scientists found that pre-school children preferred the taste of food in McDonald's packaging to identical, unbranded meals.

But there was also an unobtrusive drip of positive stories. Last year it was reported that McDonald's now only sold sustainably farmed coffee certified by the international environmental charity Rainforest Alliance; it launched free, unlimited Wi-Fi in hundreds of its restaurants; it is turning its cooking oil into biodiesel to power its fleet of 155 lorries; is voluntarily raising what it pays for beef and pork by 5% above the market rate to help British farmers; and it only sells organic British milk (accounting for 5% of all supplies bought in Britain).

Then there are the new McDonald's replacing the old. Gone are the garish red signs, the strip lighting, the tacky plastic seats and sinister clowning Ronald. An appealing dark green log cabin-style building has popped up as a drive-through in Enfield's business park. From Eltham High Street in south-east London to Camberley in Surrey are sleek green McDonald's, all colourful retro modernism inside. By the end of last year, 140 outlets had been 'reimaged'. This year, another 200 will be given what McDonald's calls the 'less is more' treatment.

What is going on? Has McDonald's become a green-on-the-outside, green-on-the-inside modern restaurant, its record profits a sign that it has won back our trust? Or is its apparent reinvention one of the cleverest corporate scams of our time?

A young accountant from Watford and father of three, who loves cricket, Watford FC and quarter-pounders with cheese (in roughly that order), has some answers. Steve Easterbrook became Chief Executive of McDonald's UK in April 2006. He is widely credited with their change in fortunes and chuckles at the suggestion that McDonald's was like the Conservative party in its desperation to neutralize the negative perceptions clinging to its name. 'The business did stall at a time when the society around us was changing as fast as it has ever done,' he says. 'We had begun to look tired. We hadn't read all the signals that had been sent to us, that to do business in 2007, or more importantly in 2010 and 2020, you've got

to act in a different way; you've got to be more approachable.'

Traditionally, McDonald's bosses have been as likely to engage publicly with their customers as to open their suppliers' chicken sheds to the world, but Easterbrook has done both, marching on to *Newsnight* to debate fast food and allowing ordinary customers to inspect the company's supply chain. 'We haven't wanted to be too in your face with the communication of it,' he says. 'Hammering big corporate messages to people is boring. We've tried to have a more conversational tone ... [customers] don't want to be lectured or preached at, but they are interested.'

Easterbrook says McDonald's success is because of both its green moves and a back-to-basics focus on burgers. He argues that the restaurant has attracted more customers by extending its opening hours (to 6am in many places), improving core food (chicken breast in its chicken burgers and nuggets), switching from filter to freshly ground coffee and only using Rainforest Alliance-certified beans and British organic milk. 'At our core we're a burger business. But also we're a modern, contemporary business,' he says, 'and "reimaging" the restaurants is the most visible way to show customers that you are "with it".'

Back in a sleek 'reimaged' McDonald's in Chancery Lane, central London, young diners are both cynical and untroubled by their burger meals. Darren Collings, 20, is impressed by the new, 'Starbucksy' image. He and his friends are concerned by Jamie Oliver's exposé of battery chickens and want McDonald's to do more about its waste, but are still seduced by its convenience — and its burgers. 'The whole concept of McDonald's is burger, chips and Coke. That's what it is,' he says. No one is eating a salad, although Alex Roberts, 17, a student from Luton, reckons that McDonald's has moved with the times with its green initiatives. 'They are changing, but they are going to sell the stuff that sells, like Big Macs,' he says. 'It still makes you fat, doesn't it?'

> **'its golden arches had become emblematic of all that was rotten in capitalism'**

► CSR initiatives

► corporate PR

2.2 Vocabulary **Corporate social responsibility**

Glossary PAGE 153

cause-related
 marketing
community
 investment
corporate
 philanthropy
eco-efficiency

Discussion

1 Fill in the spaces in the quotations about corporate social responsibility (CSR) below with one of the following nouns.

brand   environment   hypocrisy   profits   responsibility

1 The business of business should not be about money, it should be about _____. It should be about public good, not private greed.
ANITA RODDICK, FOUNDER OF THE BODY SHOP

2 CSR has built-in incentives for _____ because when businesses face a conflict between making money and social responsibility, making money tends to prevail.
GEORGE SOROS, ENTREPRENEUR AND PHILANTHROPIST

3 Ethics is the new competitive _____.
PETER ROBINSON, CEO OF MOUNTAIN EQUIPMENT CO-OP

4 People are going to want, and be able, to find out about the citizenship of a(n) _____, whether it is doing the right things socially, economically and environmentally.
MIKE CLASPER, PRESIDENT OF BUSINESS DEVELOPMENT, PROCTOR AND GAMBLE (EUROPE)

5 There is one and only one social responsibility of business – to use its resources and engage in activities designed to increase its _____ so long as it stays within the rules of the game ...
MILTON FRIEDMAN, ECONOMIST

2 Compare your ideas with a partner before checking your answers on page 120. Which quotations are for CSR and which are against? To what extent do you agree with each one?

Listening

3 Some of the main activities big companies undertake in order to demonstrate CSR are listed below. What do you think each type involves? Try and complete the definitions.

1 **Eco-efficiency** was a phrase coined by the Business Council for Sustainable Development to describe the need for companies to ...
2 **Corporate philanthropy** – donating to charities is a simple and reputation-enhancing way for a company to ...
3 **Cause-related marketing** is a partnership between a company and a charity where the charity's logo is used in ...
   The charity gains money and profile and the company benefits by associating itself ...
4 **Sponsoring awards** – through award schemes, companies position themselves ...
5 **Codes of conduct** – corporate codes of conduct are explicit statements of ...
6 **Community investment** – many companies develop community projects in the vicinity of their sites, to ...

4 🔊 1:18–1:23 Listen and complete the definitions according to the speakers. How different are they from your own definitions?

5 Which specific CSR initiatives by large companies does the speaker mention? List the company names next to the fields of activity 1–6 above. Make notes of any additional information given about each initiative.

Reading

6 Read the extract from an article below about the negative aspects of CSR and match each word/phrase in **bold** in the text with its definition.

CSR:
Exposing
the fraud

If CSR is imposed from above, then we **run the risk** of reducing its role merely to a **tokenistic** PR exercise. CSR initiatives can simply create a **smokescreen**, and give companies the chance to **sidestep** their responsibilities of dealing with social and environmental issues. Many organizations **pay lip service** to CSR but only to meet legal requirements; few deliver on their promises. It's clear that they now need to move to implementing genuine CSR programmes. Off-shoring key business processes to countries with lower labour costs, for example, may be economically sound, but is it ethical? We have to learn how to **expose the fraud** of CSR.

1	run the risk	a)	to avoid something difficult or unpleasant
2	smokescreen	b)	something you do or say as a way of hiding your real feelings, intentions or activities
3	sidestep		
4	pay lip service	c)	to reveal something that is usually hidden and that is not what people claim it is
5	tokenistic		
6	expose the fraud	d)	doing something in order to make people believe that you are being fair, although this is not really true
		e)	to be in a situation where something bad could happen
		f)	when someone complies with a certain obligation or expectation but to the minimum possible extent

What examples of smokescreens, paying lip service and tokenistic PR exercises can you think of?

Discussion and presentation

7 Work in groups. Prepare a presentation on one of the CSR initiatives of the big multinational companies mentioned in Exercise 3 to give to the class.

1 Evaluate the effectiveness of the initiatives as you understand them. Do you think they are delivering real benefits both to the companies and to society? What are their strengths and weaknesses?
2 How do you think the companies in question could do more to avoid charges of 'tokenism' in their CSR policy? What suggestions would you make to improve and/or extend the initiatives and what benefits would these bring?
3 As a class, vote for what you think is the best existing CSR initiative.

Group A turn to page 114. Group B turn to page 116. Group C turn to page 119.

Internet research

Search for the keywords *FTSE4good.com* or *DowJones* or *BitC* to find the top CSR companies in the UK, the US or your country. Search for CSR policy and find out what other companies are doing.

2 | Corporate image

▶ future forms

▶ tentative language

English has no future tense, since the form of the verb cannot be modified to express future time. However, there are over 100 different alternative ways of expressing the future! These include using modal verbs, e.g. *will, may* and other constructions, e.g. *is bound to, is on the verge of.*

▶ **Grammar and practice** pages 124–125

2.3 Grammar The future, tentative and speculative language

Review of future forms

1 Work with a partner. Look at the *Did you know?* box and list as many structures as you can think of for talking about the future. Then exchange your ideas about the future events below.

1 your plans and intentions for work and study for the next few months (what *you're doing* and *going to* do)
2 what *you'll be doing* for Christmas/the summer holidays next year
3 a current news story and how you think it *will develop* in the future
4 the likely results of the next big political or sporting event in your country (what you think *will/won't* and *might* happen)
5 what you hope you *will have done* and *will have achieved* in your career and in your life by the time you reach retirement age

Recognizing longer future forms

2 The extracts below from journalistic texts contain examples of alternative future forms. Identify and <u>underline</u> the structure used to indicate the future. Mark the expressions as *C* (certain), *P* (probable) or *T* (tentative).

1 The disastrous results look <u>bound to</u> reinforce accusations that the US and British governments grossly underestimated the scale of the problem. ☐C☐
2 Mortgage rates seem unlikely to be cut any time soon. ☐
3 Until recently workers in far-flung manufacturing facilities were not asked what they thought of the companies they were supplying. That may be about to change. ☐
4 Sayako Industries, recently voted the smartest company on the planet, is poised to take over its long-time rival, Venezia. ☐
5 Following a spate of appalling sales figures and a brace of profit warnings, INN-signia, the hotels to pubs chain, appears on the verge of collapsing. ☐
6 Biggleswade Cereals is expected to announce a major acquisition later this week. ☐
7 Last week's potentially fatal flu outbreak should not affect full-year profits, the Dorchester Group announced yesterday. ☐
8 Newcomer South-West Retail could just overtake veteran Sell-By Jeans in the lucrative teenage-to-twenties clothing market. ☐
9 It's likely to be an old-style battle between old and new. ☐
10 Traverse may end their blockade soon. ☐

3 Decide on the degree of certainty indicated by the future forms in the box. Put each one into the correct column in the table.

> be poised to   will probably   be on the verge of   be on the brink of   may   be set to   should   be going to   be bound to   could   be certain to

Almost certain (8 expressions)	Probable (3 expressions)	Tentative (3 expressions)
be on the point of	*be likely to*	*might*

4 Replace the expressions in the sentences in Exercise 2 with an appropriate alternative future form from the table which expresses the same meaning.

Using future forms

5 Read the article below from a grocery trade magazine and fill in the spaces with a suitable form of the verb in brackets. To help you make an appropriate choice, consider how likely the event is to happen.

2.3 Grammar

INDUSTRY**NEWS**

Over the coming months look out for widespread changes across the grocery sector. Three of the major supermarkets appear to be planning image makeovers to woo back customers from the lower-cost retailers. Any time now FReSH Foodstores (1) _____ (unveil) its new-format stores featuring separate delicatessen and organic food 'pods'. With their new logos and signage and a contemporary colour scheme, the new-look FReSH stores (2) _____ (shake up) the competition.

Meanwhile, industry rumours suggest that market leader RightWays, (3) _____ (respond to) its rival's plans by launching its own revamped stores. The speculation is that it has its own image makeover planned. These plans (4) _____ (focus on) smartening up the stores and checkout areas as these were recently found to be in need of improvement. Although RightWays' efforts in this area haven't always been as successful as it might have hoped, this new strategy (5) _____ (just/work). Finally, market challenger My Grocer has its own plans afoot. We can't give you the details right now, but if all goes well it (6) _____ (close) the gap with RightWays. Competition watch out!

Tentative language

6 Read the *Did you know?* box about tentative language, then write the sentences below using the expressions in brackets so that they sound more tentative.

1 In today's modern business world far too much emphasis is placed on corporate image. (tend to)
In today's modern business world far too much emphasis tends to be placed on corporate image.

2 What? Leave the new marketing assistant in charge of the corporate rebranding initiative? I can't believe you're trivializing such a serious matter! (appear to be)
_____

3 The response to our survey showed that brand recognition in many of our target markets is poor and weaker than the competition. (seems to indicate)
_____

4 Given our image, it is going to be impossible to break into the American market. (may/prove challenging)
_____

5 Our consumers are going to demand more information about our carbon footprint. (appears likely)
_____

6 The Board have lost confidence in your abilities to lead the department. (have expressed concern/are concerned about)
_____

7 There are parts of the report on our CSR projects that need rewriting. (might/benefit from)
_____

Speaking

7 Work with a partner. Look at the situations below and take turns to break the news to your partner using tentative language. Take a few minutes to prepare and make notes about why the situation happened. Keep talking until you have ticked off and used at least *four* of the tentative expressions in the box.

☐ likely ☐ prove challenging ☐ seem to ☐ tend to ☐ appear to
☐ be concerned/express concern ☐ benefit from ☐ indicate

1 Explain why this year's sales results are so bad.
2 Tell someone that their contract is not going to be extended.
3 Explain why there has been a recent outbreak of food poisoning.
4 Tell someone that they will have to relocate to Alaska if they want to keep their job.

*There **appears to** have been a recent outbreak of food poisoning in our kitchens. Please don't be alarmed because the infection doesn't **seem to** be a serious one and those affected have **tended to** recover fairly quickly. However, the health and safety officers **expressed concern** with regard to the overall levels of hygiene in the kitchen premises.*

Did you know?

Tentative language is used in academic debate to present ideas as ideas rather than definite answers, e.g *This seems to indicate* (this is what I think my research proves) rather than *This proves*. Tentative expressions are also employed when the speaker wants to soften a message and present it as 'objective' rather than personal opinion, e.g. when giving criticism or bad news. Typical tentative language includes limiting words, e.g. *possibly* and *probably*, softening verbs, e.g. *appears* and *indicates* and modals, e.g. *could* and *may*.

► Grammar and practice pages 124–125

Internet research

Search for the keywords *tentative language* to read more about this. What seem to be the most common ways of sounding tentative?

Glossary   PAGE 153

carbon footprint
signage

2 | Corporate image

- ▶ prioritizing
- ▶ effective delegation
- ▶ roleplay: practise delegating and feedback

2.4 Management skills Time management

Discussion

1 Work with a partner. Tell the story in the cartoon. What points are made about managing the working week?

2 Research shows that our moods and aptitudes follow a pattern each week. Which days of the week do you imagine are best for doing the following?

- asking for a rise
- brainstorming
- getting important jobs done
- setting goals

- holding meetings
- doing sport
- finding a new job
- making redundancies

3 Work with a partner. Student A, read about Monday, Tuesday and Wednesday on page 114. Student B, read about Thursday, Friday and the weekend and holidays on page 116.

Share what you have learned, and compare it with the ideas you discussed in Exercise 2. Give examples from your own experience which support or contradict what you have read.

Prioritizing and delegating

Glossary   PAGE 154

brainstorm
delegate
Paired Comparison
  Analysis

4 Write a 'to do' list of at least eight tasks that you could do in the next week.

Decide which items on your list are urgent and important (A), urgent but not important (B), important but not urgent (C) or not important and not urgent (D).

(Urgent = tasks which have to be done as soon as possible.
Important = tasks which lead to achieving an important objective.)

	Important	Not important
Urgent	A	B
Not urgent	C	D

5 Use the Paired Comparison Analysis from Internet research to prioritize the urgent and important (A) tasks on your 'to do' list.

Discussion

6 Work with a partner. Discuss your 'to do' list. Think about the questions below.

1 Which items would you be reluctant to delegate?
2 Which items could you delegate to a trusted friend or team member?
3 Which items could you delegate to an inexperienced team member?
4 Are there items you could afford to ignore?
5 What are the advantages of delegation for managers and their teams? Brainstorm a list.
6 What are the reasons why many people are reluctant to delegate? Brainstorm a list.

Internet research

Search for the keywords *Paired Comparison Analysis* to learn how to use this decision-making tool to establish priorities.

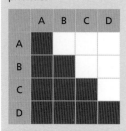

Listening

7 🔊 **1:24–1:28 Read the guidelines for effective delegation, and then listen to five extracts from a meeting.**

Margarita is delegating a cost-cutting project to Robin, a member of her team.

Match each extract with steps 3–7 in effective delegation.

Seven steps to effective delegation

① Define the task and check it is SMART (Specific, Measurable, Achievable, Realistic, Time-bound).
② Identify the person who can do the job.
③ Explain the reasons why you are delegating the task to them. ☐
④ State the results you expect. ☐
⑤ Discuss how they will do the job, and what resources are needed. ☐
⑥ Agree on deadlines, review dates and feedback strategies. ☐
⑦ Communicate details to other people who need to know. ☐

8 🔊 **1:24–1:28 Listen again and complete the sentences.**

1 I'd like you _____ _____ _____ ways of reducing our travel costs.
2 Is that something you'd be _____ _____ _____ _____?
3 Think about how much time you'll need, and _____ _____ _____ what you decide.
4 I suggest you _____ _____ _____ _____ every two weeks or so, OK?
5 I'll _____ Kim _____ you're _____ the project.
6 I'd appreciate it if you could _____ _____ _____ confidential.
7 I thought I'd _____ Estelle _____ _____ _____ some of your paperwork … _____ does that _____?
8 As a first step, could you _____ _____ _____ _____ with proposals we can _____ _____ Human Resources?
9 If they're happy, you can _____ _____ and _____ _____ new procedures.
10 Are you _____ _____ that?

9 **Work with a partner. You are assigning tasks to your team. Take turns asking and answering these questions.**

1 What do you want me to do?
2 Why me?
3 How do I know if I've done it right?
4 Does anyone else know about this?
5 Can I have someone to help me?
6 When do you want it for?
7 How much initiative can I take?
8 What should I tell my colleagues?

Roleplay

10 **In groups of three, take turns as A, B and C to practise delegating, using the seven steps from Exercise 7.**

Student A: Delegate one of the tasks from your 'to do' list in Exercise 4 to Student B.
Student B: Be yourself and react naturally. Ask questions if necessary.
Student C: Monitor the conversation and give feedback after the meeting. Point out effective delegating behaviour as well as giving constructive criticism.

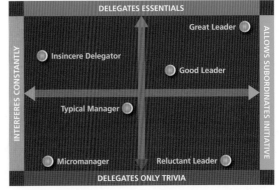

2 | Corporate image

2.5 Writing Newsletter articles

Discussion

1 Do the newsletter survey then compare and discuss your answers with a partner.

---

1 Newsletters are
a) thinly disguised propaganda that fools nobody.
b) old-fashioned and ineffective, a waste of time, energy, paper and money.
c) a cost-effective way to build relationships with customers, prospects, staff or stakeholders.

2 Newsletters should be published
a) regularly, because their benefits are cumulative.
b) irregularly, so as to provide an occasional pleasant surprise.
c) over a limited period, so as not to bore or annoy readers.

3 Newsletters should contain
a) real news about your organization, your staff or your products.
b) attractive pictures.
c) entertaining material that makes readers gasp, dream or laugh.
d) human interest.
e) a call to action.

Models

2 Read three versions of the same short newsletter article below and choose the most appropriate headline for each.

> You Love Trees   We Love Trees   Everybody Loves Trees

---

1 _____

Hamilton Hotels are proud to announce their new green initiative, in association with the United Nations Environment Programme's Billion Tree Campaign. Guests can now choose whether to have fresh towels each day or to reuse their towels, saving energy, water and reducing the use of detergents.

For every five reused towels, Hamilton Hotels have undertaken to plant a tree, which will help conserve fresh water, fix and maintain soil, combat global warming and encourage biodiversity. Guests at all 65 Hamilton Hotels have been invited to take part in the scheme since 1 January; over 3,000 trees have already been planted.

---

2 _____

On 1 January we proudly launched our new green initiative, part of the United Nations Environment Programme's Billion Tree Campaign. Hamilton Hotel guests can now choose to reuse their towels and help us save energy, water and reduce the use of detergents. In return, we will plant a tree for every five towels we don't need to launder.

By planting trees we aim to help conserve fresh water, fix and maintain soil, combat global warming and encourage biodiversity. We can help achieve the UNEP's goal of planting a billion trees a year by encouraging our guests to take part in the scheme at all of our 65 hotels; to date, we have already planted 3,000 trees.

---

3 _____

If you've stayed at a Hamilton Hotel since 1 January, then you'll already have heard about a great new way you can help reforest the planet! We've teamed up with the United Nations Environment Programme's Billion Tree Campaign so that you can not only save energy, water and reduce the use of detergents, but also play your part in the campaign to plant a billion trees a year.

Just hang your towel on the rail if you're happy to use it again, and we promise to plant a tree for you for every five towels you reuse. Every time you make the eco-friendly choice, you'll be helping conserve fresh water, fix and maintain soil, combat global warming and encourage biodiversity. So come and stay at one of our 65 hotels and help save the planet: you've already planted over 3,000 trees!

Analysis

3 Read the three versions of the article again and answer the questions.

1 Which version was intended for a) hotel staff b) guests c) other stakeholders?
2 List the difference in style between the different versions.
3 What objective is each version trying to achieve?
4 Which perspective (*I/we, you* or *it/they*) is likely to be most effective for the following types of communication a) expressing values or beliefs b) encouraging readers to take action c) making promises d) expressing attitudes, emotions, apologies?
5 Which perspective and style (*formal, informal*) are likely to be most effective in high (e.g. Asia) or low (e.g. USA) context cultures?
6 In version 3, which structures are used to contrast two sets of ideas and build a persuasive argument?

Language focus

4 Personalize these sentences by rewriting them using the *you* or the *we* perspective as appropriate.

1 The latest product catalogue is available on request.
  Please ask us for our latest product catalogue.
2 A free pair of prescription sunglasses with every pair of designer eyeglasses.
3 The open day is a unique opportunity to visit a state-of-the-art production line that should not be missed.
4 Everything possible is being done to ensure that all products are fully compliant in future.
5 Regrettably, this offer is now closed; no further applications will be accepted.
6 The Annual General Meeting is the opportunity for the Board to take shareholders' questions.
7 Only top quality ingredients guarantee the optimal fresh fruit juice consumer experience.

5 Rewrite the following pairs of sentences using the clues in brackets to combine ideas and build enthusiasm. Use the *you* perspective.

1 Early registrations will be given priority. More choices will be available too. (not only ... but also ...)
  If you register early, you will not only be given priority, but you'll also have more choice.
2 There are many regular visitors to our stores. They know there's always a bargain to be found. (if ... then ...)
3 We invite readers to complete our online survey. One reader will win the latest tablet PC. (just ... and ...)
4 Signing in to Carbux cafés attracts regular rewards. Each visit is worth ten loyalty points. (every time ... you ...)
5 We post daily updates on Twitter. Our special offers are not to be missed. (so that ...)
6 Pollution is reduced by car-sharing. In addition, petrol budgets are halved. (not only ... but also ...)
7 Project updates are released on a regular basis. We require a valid email address. (just ... and ...)

Output

6 Write a short article (150–300 words) for a newsletter about your English class, your institution or your organization. First, answer the following questions:

- Who is your audience?
- What news do you want to give?
- What do you want your readers to do?
- How will you address them?
- Given all of the above, what are the most appropriate style and tone to use?

7 Exchange articles with a partner. Edit your partner's article for style and accuracy. Give each other feedback including encouragement wherever possible and constructive criticism where necessary.

Internet research

Search for the keywords *how to write a newsletter* for tips on launching and maintaining your own newsletter. In groups, compile a list of dos and don'ts.

Glossary   PAGE 154

gasp
thinly disguised

2 | Corporate image

2.6 Case study   Pixkel Inc.

Discussion

1 **Think about the last time you bought an electronic device. How much did the factors below influence your choice? Number them in order of importance from 1 = essential to 7 = irrelevant.**

> price   quality and origin of components   quality of after-sales service
> quality of advertising   brand name and image   design
> manufacturer's reputation for social responsibility

Explain your answers to a partner.

Reading

2 **Caitlin Marks is the new Manager of Corporate Communications at Pixkel Inc., a California-based start-up which designs chipsets for digital cameras. Read her email and answer the questions below.**

⌷ | ⬇ INBOX | REPLY ◀ | FORWARD ➡

Did I tell you I'm working for my uncle Bill's firm? My job is to build a new image for Pixkel Inc. – and believe me, they sure need it! Pixkel is growing like crazy, but they're not really making any money; there are enormous delivery and cash flow problems, so you can imagine they're not winning too many friends either! Bill is an electronics wizard, but he's pretty much hands-off when it comes to management: he spends all his time in the lab, so everybody's doing their own thing – talk about a mess! I can't expect much help from Bill, so I really need to hit the ground running. Pixkel's largely a virtual company; only the design and admin. teams actually work here in Palo Alto. Everyone else seems to be out firefighting! I haven't even met most of the management team yet. I set up a conf. call to get their views on the situation, and now I'm trying to work out a strategy – but I'd really appreciate bouncing some ideas off someone I can trust. Any chance you could spare me some of your valuable time?

Glossary   PAGE 154

endorsement
firefighting
flavour of the month
hit the ground
    running
Intel Inside
real McCoy
swoosh

1   What sort of image does Pixkel have?
2   What constraints is Caitlin working under?
3   What sort of help would she like?

Listening

3 🌐 1:29 Listen to Caitlin's conference call with the management team and note what is said about the issues below.

1 teamwork
2 staff turnover
3 working environment
4 recruitment
5 reputation
6 competition
7 brand-building
8 cost control
9 visibility
10 objectives

4 🌐 1:29 After the meeting, the attendees each summed up their position with the expressions below. Listen again. Who said what, and what did they mean?

1 'We're not exactly flavour of the month, but brand-building doesn't come cheap.'
2 'Everybody's always blaming someone else; it's like herding cats.'
3 'The product's the real McCoy – sales and marketing just have to do their job!'
4 'The bottom line is we just don't know where we're going.'
5 'It's a jungle out there – the end user has never even heard of Pixkel.'

Discussion

5 In small groups, categorize the issues facing Pixkel and decide what Caitlin's priorities should be.

Listening

6 🌐 1:30–1:37 Listen to eight suggestions from the management team for improving Pixkel's corporate image. Make a note of the main points each member makes.

7 Work with a partner. Discuss how relevant, desirable or realistic each suggestion is for Pixkel.

Discussion

8 Caitlin has called you in to help. In small groups, draw up an action plan for Pixkel Inc.

Presentation

9 Present your plan to the class. The rest of the class should ask questions as the Pixkel staff. Hold a vote for the best action plan.

Internet research

Search for the keywords *BMW the hire viral* and watch the movies. Discuss how effective this type of brand-building is.

CARLA BUENAVENTURA, HR MANAGER

BEN RAINEY, MARKETING

JERRY WOO, SUPPLY CHAIN

LENA ZIMMER, SALES

ALEX O'DRISCOLL, FINANCE

2.6 Case study

Review 1

1 Match the beginnings with the appropriate endings to make phrases and collocations related to getting on in the workplace.

1	a potential	a)	run
2	steer well	b)	initiative
3	take	c)	minefield
4	get the credit	d)	waffle
5	a stimulating and challenging	e)	for it
6	meaningless	f)	from scratch
7	tightly	g)	clear of
8	learn everything	h)	environment

2 Fill in the spaces with the correct form of the verb in brackets, paying attention to tense, aspect and voice. Make sure you put any adverbs in the right place. One of the verbs is in the infinitive form.

Would everyone who loves meetings please stand up?

Corporate meetings and brainstorming sessions are extremely popular among executives and managers, who (1) _____ (clearly conduct) them for a long time. What is less clear (2) _____ (be) how useful they actually are. If people actually (3) _____ (prepare carefully) for meetings, and if the purpose of each meeting (4) _____ (think through properly), there might be some benefit in having them. The reality, however, is very different: employees (5) _____ (often ask) to attend time-consuming events that they (6) _____ (not think about) much beforehand, and which they (7) _____ (come away) from with little clear idea about what their purpose (8) _____ (be actually). (9) _____ (keep) them short, perhaps all meetings (10) _____ (should hold) with everyone standing up!

3 Match the behavioural competences 1–6 with their definitions a)–f).

1 self-development ☐
2 client orientation ☐
3 effective communication ☐
4 analysis ☐
5 flexibility ☐
6 innovation and entrepreneurship ☐

a) the ability to use the appropriate channel, means and style of communication with tact in a variety of situations
b) the ability to create something new (products or services) and to implement these in the marketplace
c) the willingness and ability to give priority to customers, delivering high-quality services which meet their needs
d) the ability to adapt with ease to a variety of situations; it is also about not being disconcerted by the unexpected
e) the ability to find opportunities to develop your skills and attributes through self-study, training, practical application, and/or support from others
f) being able to bring disciplined analytical thinking to data and situations, to see cause and effect and to use this to make effective decisions

4 Complete the sentences using the correct forms of the given words.

1 analyst
We need someone to _____ our data. They'll need financial experience and to be good at thinking _____. Our current _____ aren't detailed enough for planning purposes. Have we got that sort of _____ person on our staff?

2 communicator
We need somebody who is a naturally _____ person. They'll need to produce better internal _____ within our organization so that our message is conveyed more effectively.

3 innovator
We need somebody to think _____ in order to solve our existing problems. We don't want the same old solutions – we need _____ ones. This person will need to be able to _____ independently and then roll them out in waves.

5 Now put each word in the correct column below according to the number of syllables it has and its word stress pattern. One word has two possible stress patterns.

■••	•■••	■•••
analyst		

■••••	•■•••	••■••	•••■•

6 Make adjectives from the verbs in the box below and put them into the correct column according to their ending.

adapt   assert   care   cheer   confide   depend
energize   help   idealize   know   observe   power
reflect   respond   sense   sympathize   trust

-able	-ible	-ive	-ful

-ant	-ent	-worthy	-ic

7 Underline the word in each sentence below which does not collocate with the following noun.

1 I believe this applicant is not suitable because of their rather *introverted / irritable / frustrated / unconventional* nature.
2 I don't think we should hire that particular candidate – he doesn't have the right *qualifications / competencies / reputation / experience* for the job.

Review 2

Corporate image

1 In each group of five, match a beginning on the left with an ending on the right to make collocations about managing a company's image.

1 I'm impressed – she's made a quite remarkable
2 We're entering a whole new phase of dwindling
3 Provided they are certified
4 He's an environmental
5 I'm convinced they're all in it together – it's a corporate
6 With falling market share and stagnating
7 I would argue that it's the new legislation that brought about the profits
8 No, I'm all right really, just a health
9 I won't take it, it's a dead-end
10 So, what's next, a back-to-basics

a) activist through and through.
b) comeback after being out of the picture for years.
c) scam from top to bottom.
d) organic they can command a premium price.
e) resources, and we need to get used to it.
f) collapse – it's a case of cause and effect.
g) focus, or root-and-branch review?
h) job if ever there was one.
i) scare, nothing to worry about.
j) sales the last thing we should do is raise our prices.

2 Put the following sentences in order of likelihood, from the most likely to happen to the least likely.

1 The government seems highly unlikely to win the vote. ☐
2 Given an outstanding season, Contemporary Fusion looks bound to beat its profits forecast. ☐
3 They should reach the next bidding stage. ☐
4 At this stage it appears unlikely that they will get the contract. ☐
5 Now all that could be about to change. ☐
6 The convention is definitely going to be held in Bruges – I've seen it on their website. ☐

3 Replace the words in *italics* in each sentence with the expression from the box which is closest in meaning.

> is likely to   might possibly   is poised to   is sure to
> is expected to   probably won't

1 It's *bound to* affect sales – I've never known such awful publicity.
2 An investigation *will probably* be set up to find out what went wrong.
3 Brand recognition *is set to* rocket following the football sponsorship deal.
4 With the latest improvement in retail sales, consumer confidence *could just* be finally looking up.
5 Unless we focus more on visibility, interest in the product *is unlikely to* grow.
6 Well, version two really *should* deliver this time, now that we've ironed out the glitches from version one.

4 Fill in the missing verbs in the idioms and expressions in the sentences below. Some are in the *-ing* form.

1 Actually could you get it done now, or we might r__ __ the risk of missing the deadline altogether.
2 In the current environment we need to do more than just __ __y lip service to the equality legislation.
3 I am determined to __x__ __ __ __ the action for what it is – fraud.
4 Focus on what we've agreed on and stop s__ __ __ __ __ __p__ __ __ __ the issues.
5 In other words, all employees must now do their bit for the environment – 'individual eco-responsibility' to c__ __ __ a phrase.
6 The next step is for you to s__ __ goals for the coming three months, achievable ones.
7 As an alternative to penalties for failing to recycle we could o__ __ __ __ incentives for recycling more.
8 In short, we are f__ __ __ __ __ a conflict between what we need to do and what we need to say.

5 Fill in the spaces using an appropriate expression from the box.

> bouncing some ideas off   build a new image
> flavour of the month   hands-off approach
> hit the ground running   it's a jungle out there
> reluctant to delegate   the bottom line

McCay: Well, our main challenge here is to (1) _____ for our company – we're still seen as very old-fashioned and we need to change people's perceptions. If we could perhaps start by (2) _____ each other, and then we can perhaps evaluate these a little and move towards some kind of consensus. To fill in the background a little, times are changing. Fast. Actually (3) _____, the law business has gone global and our cosy firm is simply not attractive anymore.
Carew: 'Law business'? What are you saying exactly? What's (4) _____ here – are you telling us we've got to change?
McCay: As I see it, we're too inward-looking. Even though there's a lot of talent outside this little pool we're not using it, and most of us are (5) _____. We need a much more (6) _____.
Carew: So where does that leave us? I know I'm not (7) _____, but don't punish me by taking the best bits of my job away from me.
McCay: You don't understand. The market's changed, in fact there are new markets – we need to break into them, (8) _____ and make a real go of it.

▶ lift-out

▶ outsourcing in India

3.1 About business Outsourcing

Discussion

1 You have a weekend job serving drinks in a local café. The owner decides to outsource the staff to an employment agency: your job doesn't change, but now you work for Manpower instead of for the café owner.

In small groups, discuss whether your situation is better or worse than before, and why. Think about job security, working conditions, payment, training, opportunities, etc.

Listening

2 🔊 1:38 Listen to part of a presentation about lift-out to a group of HR managers, and answer the questions.

1 How and why does the speaker deliberately shock the audience at the beginning of the talk?
2 What is lift-out?
3 How has lift-out changed HR at BT?
4 What is the first change experienced by staff who are lifted out, and how is it explained?
5 What two advantages mean most people are happier?
6 Which risk of lift-out does the speaker describe, and how can it be reduced?

Reading

3 Read *The Indian Machine* and number the paragraph summaries in the order in which they appear in the article.

a) America *is about to* turn outsourcing to its advantage by freeing more people to invent new *miracle technologies*. 8

b) America's *online service jobs* are threatened by *inexpensive* Indian *knowledge workers*. 1

c) The computer *never became intelligent*: India is more frightening because the 'monster' is learning *incredibly fast*. ☐

d) Movies reflect how attitudes have *relaxed* as the *monster* that was the computer has become an everyday piece of office equipment. ☐

e) IT has transformed the *repetitive jobs* of the past with *the overall result* that today they are more strategic and more satisfying. ☐

f) Historical precedent *is reassuring*: lost jobs are disturbing but are eventually replaced by new ones. ☐

g) The shift from *products to data* has made India a key player on the global employment market. ☐

h) When computers promised productivity by *adding up numbers*, *printing documents* and *handling phone calls*, managers began to fear for their jobs. ☐

4 Find expressions in the article which correspond to the words in *italics* in the paragraph summaries.

5 Explain what the author means in these sentences from the article.

1 *The American cubicle farm is the new textile mill, just another sunset industry.* (lines 7–8)
2 *It's not a matter of blue collar versus white collar; the collar to wear is Nehru.* (lines 20–21)
3 *Then, as now, the potential for disruption seemed infinite.* (lines 29–30)
4 *We are now in the Desk Set period with India.* (line 58)
5 *... the next great era in American enterprise.* (line 73)

Discussion

6 In small groups, discuss the questions.

1 Would you rather be one of the 500 people left in BT's HR department, or one of the 1,100 consultants working for Accenture? Why?
2 Do you agree with Chris Anderson that computers have made us stronger? What about outsourcing?
3 Some countries have considered legislation to limit offshoring, supposedly to protect personal data: India has reacted angrily. Who is right?
4 Many companies hoped to cut costs by offshoring but have experienced negative reactions from customers. In your view, do the benefits of outsourcing outweigh the disadvantages?

Internet research

Search for the keywords *benefits of outsourcing* and *outsourcing backlash*. Make a list of arguments for and against outsourcing.

THE Indian Machine

Computers threatened our jobs, but ultimately made us stronger. So will outsourcing.

by Chris Anderson

WORRIED about India's practically infinite pool of smart, educated, English-speaking people eager to work for the equivalent of your latte budget? Get used to it. Today's Indian call centers, programming shops, and help desks are just the beginning. Tomorrow it will be financial analysis, research, design, graphics – potentially any job that does not require physical proximity. The American cubicle farm is the new textile mill, just another sunset industry.

The emergence of India is the inevitable result of the migration of work from atoms to bits: bits can easily reach people and places that atoms cannot. India's geography is no longer a barrier to development: cheap optical fiber and satellite links have liberated an army of knowledge workers. Never before have we seen such a powerful labor force rise so quickly.

There is some solace in history. Agricultural jobs turned into even more manufacturing jobs, which decades later turned into even more service jobs. The cycle of work turns and turns again. Neat. Of course, there's another part of the cycle: anxiety. It used to be that factory workers worried, but office jobs were safe. Now, it's not clear where the safety zone lies. It's not a matter of blue collar versus white collar; the collar to wear is Nehru.

For US workers, the path beyond services seems uncertain. But again, history provides a guide. Thirty years ago, another form of outsourcing hit the US service sector: the computer. That led to a swarm of soulless processing machines, promoted by management consultants and embraced by profit-obsessed executives gobbling jobs in a push for efficiency. If today's cry of the displaced is 'They sent my job to India!' yesterday's was 'I was replaced by a computer!' Then, as now, the potential for disruption seemed infinite. Data crunching was just the start. Soon electronic brains would replace most of the accounting department, the typing pool, and the switchboard. After that, the thinking went, the modern corporation would apply the same technology to middle management, business analysis, and, ultimately, decision-making.

Computers have, of course, reshaped the workplace. But they have also proved remarkably effective at creating jobs. Bookkeepers of old, adding columns in ledgers, are today's financial analysts, wielding Excel and PowerPoint in boardroom strategy sessions. Secretaries have morphed into executive assistants, more aides-de-camp than stenographers. Typesetters have become designers. True, in many cases different people filled the new jobs, leaving millions painfully displaced, but over time the net effect was positive – for workers and employers alike.

At the same time, we learned the limits of computers – especially their inability to replace us – and our fear of a silicon invasion diminished. The growing détente was reflected in 40 years of Hollywood films. *Desk Set*, from 1957, was about a research department head who keeps her job only after a battle of wits with a computer (the machine blows up). By 1988, the computer had moved from threat to weapon: In *Working Girl*, Melanie Griffith has both a stock market terminal and a PC on her desk and uses her skills and knowledge to move from secretary to private office. By the time Mike Judge made *Office Space* in 1999, the PC had faded into just another bit of cubicle furniture.

We are now in the Desk Set period with India. The outsourcing wave looks awesome and unstoppable. Like the mystical glass house of the 1970s data processing center, India's outsourcing industry thrums with potential and power, as if it were itself a machine. Today, the outsourcing phenomenon is still mostly in the batch-processing stage: send instruction electronically, receive results the same way the next morning. But the speed at which the Indian tech industry is learning new skills is breathtaking. Some US firms now outsource their PowerPoint presentations to India, a blow to the pride of managers everywhere. From this perspective, India looks like an artificial intelligence, the superbrain that never arrived in silico. No wonder workers tremble.

But the Melanie Griffith phase is coming, as is the Mike Judge. It's not hard to see how outsourcing to India could lead to the next great era in American enterprise. Today, even innovative firms spend too much money maintaining products: fixing bugs and rolling out nearly identical 2.0 versions. Less than 30% of R&D spending at mature software firms goes to true innovation, according to the consulting firm Tech Strategy Partners. Send the maintenance to India and, even after costs, 20% of the budget is freed up to come up with the next breakthrough app. The result: more workers focused on real innovation. What comes after services? Creativity.

© "The Outsourcing Institute"

- supply chain
- strategic decision stages
- reverse logistics

Discussion

1 Work with a partner. Do the logistics quiz below.

AMAZING LOGISTICS STATISTICS!

1 How long does it take to make a can of soda, including everything from mining aluminium ore in Australia to delivering the can to your fridge?
a) 39 days   b) 193 days   c) 319 days
2 How much of that time is spent on manufacturing, as opposed to logistics?
a) 3 hours   b) 3 days   c) 3 weeks
3 How many people are involved in the process of shipping a single container by sea?
a) 10   b) 30   c) 100
4 General Motors employs 280,000 people. How many people are employed by UPS?
a) 84,000   b) 248,000   c) 428,000
5 What is the annual cost of returned goods in the USA?
a) $100 million   b) $1 billion   c) $100 billion

Check your answers on page 120.

2 Match the questions 1–9 with the strategic decision stages a)–i) in the supply chain.

1 Which plant will make the new yoghurt? ☐
2 Where can we get a regular supply of milk? ☐
3 How much finished product do we need in the warehouses to meet demand? ☐
4 Have you audited the dairy farm? ☐
5 How many flavours are we going to offer? ☐
6 How do we get the milk from the farms to the factory? ☐
7 Who's going to deliver to the retailers? ☐
8 Can we avoid stocking packaging? ☐
9 Which warehouses are we going to use? ☐

a) source raw materials
b) validate vendor quality
c) define production location
d) define product quality
e) source transportation channels
f) consider using JIT (Just-In-Time)
g) decide inventory levels
h) decide location of distribution centres
i) choose logistics provider

Listening

3 As a hypermarket manager, how could a logistics provider help you with large stocks of the following?

a) yoghurt which is not what you ordered
b) yoghurt which is an unpopular flavour in your region
c) yoghurt which is past its sell-by date

🔊 1:39 Listen to an extract from a presentation by USF Processors, the market leader in reverse logistics, to find out.

Glossary   PAGE 154

JIT
reverse logistics

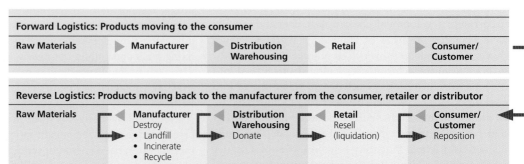

Forward Logistics: Products moving to the consumer				
Raw Materials	▶ Manufacturer	▶ Distribution Warehousing	▶ Retail	▶ Consumer/ Customer

Reverse Logistics: Products moving back to the manufacturer from the consumer, retailer or distributor				
Raw Materials	◀ Manufacturer Destroy • Landfill • Incinerate • Recycle	◀ Distribution Warehousing Donate	◀ Retail Resell (liquidation)	◀ Consumer/ Customer Reposition

Internet research

Search for the keywords *Just-In-Time*. Make a list of its advantages and disadvantages. Discuss whether Just-In-Time would be beneficial in manufacturing the product you chose in Exercise 5.

4 Fill in the spaces in this extract from the presentation in Exercise 3 using the words in the box.

> consumer finished goods goods manufacturer outlets retail organization
> raw materials recycled repositioned salvage supply chain warehouses

In simple, forward logistics, goods, information and financial transactions move from one end of the supply chain to the other. As you can see in the top half of the slide, traditionally (1) _____ are moved to the manufacturer, where they are transformed into (2) _____. These then move forward via (3) _____ and distribution centres to retail (4) _____, and then on to the (5) _____.

The goal of reverse logistics is to maximize the value of all (6) _____ which, for one reason or another, are removed from the primary distribution channel. This is achieved by moving them beyond the expected end point of the (7) _____. So in the bottom half of the slide, you can see that goods can be moved back from the consumer toward the (8) _____. Products can be (9) _____ and sold to customers in a different geographical location or in a different (10) _____; they can be returned to distribution for (11) _____ or, for example, for donation to charity, or they can go back to the manufacturer to be destroyed or (12) _____.

🔊 1:39 **Now listen and check.**

Discussion

5 Work in small groups. Choose a manufactured product you are familiar with, or one that you would like to make. Discuss the strategic decision stages a)–i) in Exercise 2 for this product, and consider what role reverse logistics might have. Then illustrate your supply chain in a large, coloured flow diagram. Finally, present your project to another group.

Listening

6 🔊 1:40 Listen to a second extract from the presentation in Exercise 3 and match USF Processors' value propositions 1–7 with the outcomes a)–g). The first one is done for you.

Value Propositions

1. Use technology, especially *a system where the supplier owns the goods until they are scanned at the point of sale*
2. Reposition product
3. Manage date codes proactively
4. Manage in-store inventory
5. Recall management
6. Handle *faulty products which the customer sends back to the manufacturer* efficiently
7. Provide accurate and objective data

Benefits

a) avoid having *products which have passed their sell-by date*
b) monitor the supply chain *from beginning to end*
c) avoid *situations when no supplies of a product are left*
d) reduce legal responsibility
e) promote understanding and better deals between partners in the supply chain
f) anticipate and move *products which the retailer cannot sell*, for instance to *shops run by charitable organizations*
g) avoid wasting money

7 Unscramble the words and phrases used in the presentation and match them with one of the paraphrases in *italics* above.

1. acnS-abdes adginrT
2. enRrstu
3. aelSst
4. aCdelr-ot-aeGrv
5. ckoouSstt
6. aabeellnssU
7. fhirTt eortSs

Discussion

8 Work in small groups. Discuss which category of problem is being described, and how you would use reverse logistics to deal with each case. How could you avoid these problems in future?

1. A mail order customer opens her new mobile phone to find it has been damaged in the post.
2. A supermarket receives an anonymous warning that cyanide has been put in its yoghurts.
3. A fashion store has a stock of 50 pairs of jeans in last year's colours.
4. A hypermarket has 2,000 cans of soda in stock with a sell-by date of 08.08.12.
5. A toy manufacturer is selling dolls outsourced from the Far East which contain lead paint.
6. A music retailer has more Christmas music CDs than it can sell.

3 | Supply chain

▶ building noun phrases

▶ defining relative clauses

3.3 Grammar   Noun phrases

Noun phrases

1 Work with a partner. Read the *Did you know?* information about noun phrases then look at the sentences below. <u>Underline</u> the head noun in the long noun phrase. 'Unpack' and explain the noun phrase to your partner.

1 Can I have the eastern region outage log <u>summary</u>, please?
   a document with a summary of the recorded or logged statistics for power outages in the eastern region
2 We are going to consider the basic service problem statistics per 1,000 customers.
3 Unfortunately, our advanced database handling system is not very reliable.
4 Many of the staff have complained of significantly higher overall transport costs as a result of the move.
5 Doctors fear that smoking-related heart disease is on the increase again.
6 Traditional industrial design engineering is what interests him the most.
7 He needs to complete the US Air Force aircraft fuel systems equipment mechanics course.
8 We are making progress thanks to government-sponsored cancer research programmes like this one.

2 In each group of five, match the phrases on the left with those on the right to make meaningful noun phrases.

1 a chain of high street   a) distribution centre
2 different modes   b) coffee retailers
3 the person   c) who grow 70% of the world's coffee
4 a major regional   d) responsible for overseeing each stage in the supply
5 those smallholder producers   chain process
                                   e) of transport

6 minimum standards   f) commodity
7 a bewildering choice   g) the growers and harvesters
8 each stage   h) of personal and environmental welfare
9 those at the bottom: i) in the supply chain process
10 a single tradable   j) of coffee brands

3 Now use the complete noun phrases to fill in the spaces in the text below.

FREE TRADE *or* FAIR TRADE?

Faced with (1) _____, today's consumer would do well to investigate a little deeper in order to make their choice more informed. The cup of coffee they are enjoying in any one of (2) _____ has almost certainly been imported – most of the world's coffee is grown by a small number of countries, such as Brazil, or in Africa: Burundi, Kenya and Ethiopia. At each step of the way, despite being (3) _____, its value has increased dramatically. Involving (4) _____ and necessitating transportation across continents and oceans, this product has a surprisingly complex supply chain. (5) _____ is the Logistics Manager, who needs to handle the entire process. This manager's job involves overseeing the transportation of the coffee from (6) _____ to a port, from where the commodity is shipped abroad for processing, packaging and local distribution by one of the large roasting companies. Here the product is sorted and redirected to the next place in the supply chain. The key point is that the industry is largely vertically integrated; in other words, a small number of powerful operators control (7) _____ after the coffee is initially purchased from the grower. And most likely to receive the least money in the chain are (8) _____.These include in particular (9) _____, which they do on tiny farms of less than 25 acres. If the coffee is certified fair trade, however, (10) _____ apply, meaning those powerful operators are less welcome. Buyer beware!

Defining relative clauses

4 Using information from the text, write definitions for the noun phrases below using relative clauses with the correct relative pronoun or adverb (*that, which, who, whom, when, where, why, how*).

A 'vertically integrated industry' refers to an industry which has only a few powerful operators controlling all or most of the steps of the supply process.

1 a complex supply chain
2 a distribution centre
3 a smallholder producer
4 the fair trade policy

Building noun phrases

5 Work with a partner. Rewrite each of the brochure descriptions below into one information-rich sentence. Pay particular attention to the noun phrases.

1 At the moment we run 20 depots. They are regional and national. Each one is managed autonomously.
  We currently operate 20 autonomously managed regional and national depots.
2 We source all our coffee ethically. It is of the highest quality. You will love it.
3 We are flexible. We are smart. We can offer a solution every time. It is always the right solution.
4 Our brand is strong. It is recognized all over the place. People trust it.
5 We offer specialized equipment for medical purposes. We have a huge range. It is hard to beat.
6 Heathrow Airport is a hub for global air transport. It has thousands of flights every day. It is expanding fast.
7 Logistics is a military term, originally. It offers solutions for transportation. These are integrated. They are also at the right price.

Describing products and systems

6 Work with a partner. RDC Solutions is a supply chain management organization. Use the pictures and phrases to compose a short introductory text (150–200 words) for the company brochure presenting the company and its services. Pay special attention to the noun phrases and clauses you use.

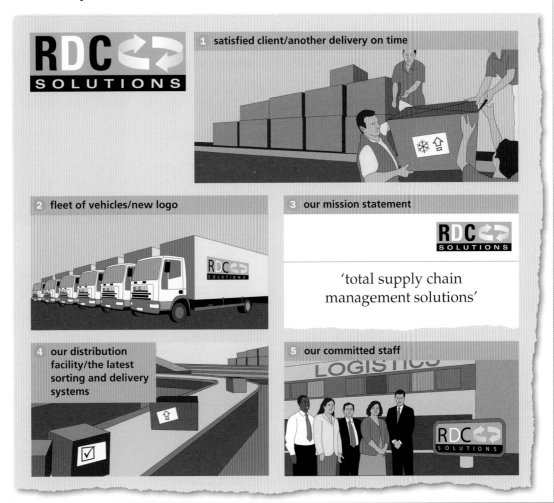

Glossary   PAGE 155

vertically integrated

- ▶ force field analysis
- ▶ cleft sentences
- ▶ roleplay: presentation of a change management plan

Discussion

1 Work in small groups. Discuss what you would change about one of the following in order to deliver better services to customers.

> your city or country's public transport system
> your country's professional sports league
> your country's system of medical care
> your own idea

2 As a task force, turn some of these problems into opportunities.

1 Using the SMART criteria (Specific, Measurable, Achievable, Realistic, Time-bound), define the objective(s) that you would like to reach, and write a mission statement.
2 Compare your mission statement with those of other groups. Do they match the SMART criteria? Which ones inspire you most? Why?

Listening for gist

3 🔊 1:41 Listen to an interview with Goran Radman, a Change Management Consultant. How does he help retail companies?

Listening for detail

4 🔊 1:41 Listen again and complete the summary and the force field analysis chart below.

1 Goran Radman helps retailers to move towards an _____.
2 At the top of every retailer's wish list is the ability to _____ in real time.
3 This system aims to eliminate _____, stockouts and returns.
4 CPFR stands for _____.
5 To design an ideal system all the partners need to _____.
6 After performing a force field analysis, Goran's job is to _____.

Internet research

Search for the keywords *JM Fisher's Process of Transition*. Discuss how well this description fits your own experiences of change.

DRIVING FORCES			RESTRAINING FORCES		
strong	moderate	weak	weak	moderate	strong
increasing (7) _____			(9) _____		
			(10) afraid of _____		
	(8) better _____				
			(11) not _____		
			(12) not _____		

Glossary   PAGE 155

CPFR
force field analysis
think outside the box

Discussion

5 Work in small groups. Discuss possible driving and restraining forces for companies considering the changes below.

> upgrading computer software   adopting JIT (Just-In-Time)
> outsourcing business processes like HR and IT   offshoring production

6 In your groups, identify the driving and restraining forces for the goal you defined in Exercise 1, and draw a force field analysis chart for it. Score each force one (weak), two (moderate) or three (strong).

Add up the total score for each side of the chart. How likely is your plan to succeed? Discuss how you could strengthen the driving forces and weaken the restraining forces.

Listening

7 🎧 1:42–1:49 In his book *The Heart of Change*, John P. Kotter advocates eight key steps to successful change. Listen to eight extracts from Goran Radman's conversations with Maria Castillo, a client whose sports equipment stores are underperforming. Match each extract with the corresponding step.

STEP 1: increase urgency ☐	**STEP 5:** empower action ☐
STEP 2: build the guiding team ☐	**STEP 6:** create short-term wins ☐
STEP 3: get the vision right ☐	**STEP 7:** don't let up ☐
STEP 4: communicate for buy-in ☐	**STEP 8:** make change stick ☐

Cleft sentences

8 Look at these sentences Goran used. How are these cleft sentences different from the simple forms in *italics*? Why are they used?

The thing that people need to take on board is that this is really urgent.
People need to take on board that this is really urgent.
What you should do is get all the staff on board.
You should get all the staff on board.

🎧 1:42–1:49 Listen again to find a(nother) cleft sentence in each extract.

9 Reformulate these sentences using the words given.

1   We all need to stop burying our heads in the sand and step back so we can see the big picture.
    What we _____.
2   You should encourage staff to tackle problems themselves.
    What you _____.
3   You have to catch them doing something right.
    The thing _____.
4   Some people will dismiss CPFR as just the flavour of the month.
    What _____.
5   It's really important that they buy into making this thing work.
    What _____.
6   We should roll out the changes in waves to build momentum.
    The reason _____.
7   We need to engage their hearts and minds.
    It's _____.
8   What counts most is getting into the habit of winning.
    It's _____.

10 In groups, prepare an action plan to reach the goal you defined in Exercise 1. Take account of your force field analysis and Kotter's eight steps to successful change.

Presentation

11 Present your action plan to the class using cleft sentences to emphasize important points.

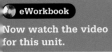

eWorkbook

Now watch the video for this unit.

3 | Supply chain

3.5 Writing   Emails

Discussion

1 Are you a telephone or an email person? Does it depend on the situation? Give examples of when you would use each. Do your friends and family make the same choices?

Model

2 Read the exchange of emails below, starting at the bottom with the email dated 7 April. How would you describe the relationship between the correspondents on a) 5 April b) 13 April c) 21 April and d) 3 May?

✉ | ⬇ INBOX | REPLY ⬅ | FORWARD ➡

Dear Ian,
Thank you for returning the non-standard parts. As you requested, I have negotiated a discount of 12% on this order to compensate for the inconvenience caused to you and your company. However, to qualify for the initial 3% discount for payment within 10 days, we should have received your bank transfer by yesterday, 2 May. I am sure this was just an oversight, but I would appreciate it if you could settle our invoice, less the further 12%, as soon as possible. Thank you again for your patience; I look forward to working with you again soon.
Best regards,
Dani

Dani Simmons wrote on 21 April:

Ian,
This is just to confirm what we agreed by phone. Although we are confident the 40 micron coating would be sufficient, we recognize that you did indeed specify 60 microns, and we apologize for the inconvenience this mistake has caused. As agreed, we will ship a first batch of replacement parts this afternoon by FedEx, and the remainder with our usual forwarder, who will also pick up the parts sent in error. Please accept our sincere apologies for this mistake; I can assure you that it will not happen again.
Best wishes,
Dani

Ian Banks wrote on 21 April:

Dani,
The goods finally arrived this morning, but our tests showed the coating is only 40 microns, so the parts are non-standard and we can't use them. This puts me in a very difficult position. Please call me as soon as possible.
Ian

Dani Simmons wrote on 20 April:

Hi Ian,
As I said by phone, I'm really sorry to hear you haven't received the goods. The forwarder has assured me the truck has now cleared customs and should arrive at your factory within 12 hours. Please let me know immediately if the goods have not arrived by tomorrow morning.
Sorry again for the inconvenience.
Dani

Ian Banks wrote on 20 April:

Hi Dani,
As of this afternoon, your shipment has still not arrived. Production are getting nervous as we only have two days' stock. Could you look into this and get back to me asap?
Thanks,
Ian

Dani Simmons wrote on 13 April:

Dear Ian,
Thank you very much for your order. I'm pleased to confirm we can ship the parts on the 15th.
Kind regards,
Dani

Ian Banks wrote on 13 April:

Dear Dani,
This is just to confirm the order we discussed by telephone today for the following parts:
200 FD140 mm, 300 GJ150 mm and 1,000 FD 240 mm, all with the 60 micron coating. Please find attached the details for your invoice. Can you confirm the goods will be shipped no later than the 17th?
Rgds,
Ian

Dani Simmons wrote on 10 April:

Dear Mr Banks,
Further to our telephone conversation today, our R&D department assure me that the 60 micron coating will be more than adequate for your requirements. We have shipped the samples this afternoon by FedEx and look forward to hearing the results of your tests.
Best regards,
Dani

Ian Banks wrote on 9 April:

Dear Ms Simmons,
Thank you for your email and price list. As I mentioned in Hannover, we would need to test your fastenings before placing an order; would you be kind enough to send samples of your galvanized steel range? Could you also confirm that you can supply all references with a 70 micron zinc coating? Thank you for your help.
Ian Banks

Dani Simmons wrote on 7 April:

Dear Mr Banks,
We met two days ago at the Hannover Trade Fair. As promised, I am attaching full details of our prices. As discussed, I am pleased to confirm that we can offer a discount of 7.5% on orders over 500 pieces. Please feel free to contact me for any further information.
Yours sincerely,
Dani Simmons

3 **With a partner, roleplay the telephone conversations that took place on 10, 20 and 21 April.**

- Decide who makes the call (Dani Simmons or Ian Banks).
- Begin the call with a greeting, identify yourself and make small talk, as appropriate.
- State the reason for the call and discuss your business.
- End the call in an appropriate way.

Analysis

4 **With a partner, answer the questions.**

1 Which of the emails from Ian and Dani could *not* have been replaced by a phone call? Why did they choose email rather than the telephone for the others?
2 Complete the table to show how greetings and salutations/sign-offs illustrate changes in the business relationship.

	Formal	Neutral	Friendly	Direct
Greeting				
Salutation/Sign-off				

Language focus

5 *As discussed ...* Find six more expressions in the emails beginning with *As*. Which one has a different meaning from the others?

6 **Even if the general tone of business emails is often informal, polite or indirect expressions are still important. Highlight or <u>underline</u> polite equivalents in the emails for the more direct expressions below.**

1 call me if you need more details
2 the answer is yes
3, 4 see attachment (two expressions)
5 can you let me have samples of ...
6 re: our phone conversation today,
7 let me know what's happening
8 sorry about that
9 I'm not at all happy about this
10 we're really sorry we got it wrong
11 we're sorry this is a nuisance for you
12 we won't do it again
13 thanks for understanding our problem
14 I hope you will order from us again
15 please send your payment
16 you probably just forgot

Output

7 **Work in groups of two (or four) to write and reply to business emails using appropriate style.**

Student A: look at page 117.
Student B: look at page 118.

Student A: look at page 117.
Student B: look at page 118.

Glossary PAGE 155

batch
coating
fastening
galvanized
micron

3.5 Writing

3.6 Case study   WEF Audio

Discussion

'Family businesses are like family weddings – and we all know how difficult they can be.' –
Sir Gerry Robinson

1 **Work in small groups. Discuss the following questions.**

1 Which business sectors favour family businesses?
2 In which cultures are family-run businesses common?
3 What are the advantages and disadvantages of family businesses?

Reading and discussion

2 **Read the extract from WEF's website and answer the questions.**

> **INTERNET**
>
> ▶ HOME | PRODUCTS | REVIEWS | DISTRIBUTORS | FAQ | SITE MAP
>
> WEF Audio was founded in 1958 by Franz Theiner, a physicist and opera lover, with the goal of bringing audio perfection to the discriminating audiophile. For half a century the company has enjoyed a reputation for the highest quality and workmanship under the leadership first of Herr Theiner, and now of his daughter Eva and son-in-law Karl Hoffmann. Every loudspeaker WEF has ever sold has been built by hand here in the Vorarlberg region of Austria from the finest materials and components available. In addition to meeting the steady demand for its world-famous 'Emotion' family of traditional loudspeakers, WEF is now applying its know-how to developing new high-quality audio products incorporating the latest technology, ranging from noise-cancelling headphones to in-car systems and home cinema.
>
> ▶ **Franz Theiner** Founder and President
>
> ▶ **Eva Theiner-Hoffmann** General Manager
>
> ▶ **Karl Hoffmann** Operations Manager

1 What image does WEF try to project? What are its USPs?
2 When did WEF start to diversify its product portfolio?
3 Why do you think this decision was made?

3 **In small groups, discuss the questions below about WEF's scorecard.**

WEF scorecard (10 = best, 1 = worst)		Two years ago	Last year	This year
Customer	Quality	9	9	8
	Delivery times	7	6	5
	Customer satisfaction	8	7	6
Internal	Efficiency	6	5	5
	Inventory	5	2	3
	Innovation	3	6	7
Financial	Sales	7	8	9
	Cost of sales	3	4	7
	Profitability	6	3	2
Employee	Competitive salaries	7	9	9
	Employee satisfaction	6	7	5
	Employee turnover	10	6	5

1 Which indicators have improved/deteriorated/remained unchanged over the last two years?
2 What possible explanations can you suggest for these trends?
3 What should WEF's priorities be now?

Listening

4 🎵 1:50 Listen to a conversation between Bettina and George, two middle managers at WEF. What would a) George b) Bettina c) Eva Theiner-Hoffmann like to do?

5 🎵 1:50 Listen again and complete the tables.

Changes	Explanations
The food has really improved.	- It's a strategy to reduce staff turnover.
Sales are rising.	- (1)
New products only contribute 10–12% of profits.	- With traditional methods, margins are too small.
More and more cash is tied up in stock.	- (2)
They can't keep skilled staff happy.	- (3)

Proposal	Advantages	Disadvantages
Just-In-Time	Cut production costs Increase (4) _____ Cut delivery times	Franz would never agree to it Would quality levels be maintained? Suppliers' (5) _____ would push costs up
Outsource	Contractors can produce (6) _____ Contractors would (7) _____ returns Forget staffing headaches	Franz and Karl wouldn't trust them with quality and (8) _____ risky, it could (9) _____ Already invested in production in Austria
Relocate	Can (10) _____ cheaply Salaries are far lower Eva wants to (12) _____	Logistics would be complicated The (11) _____ would go ballistic Franz is keen to keep Eva and Karl together

Simulation

6 Work in four groups to prepare a board meeting to decide what strategy WEF should choose. Read your instructions, then prepare your arguments for the meeting.

Group A turn to page 115.   Group C turn to page 118.
Group B turn to page 116.   Group D turn to page 121.

7 Form new groups of four with one student from each group, A, B, C and D. Hold meetings to discuss the agenda below. When you have finished, compare your outcomes with other groups.

WEF

AGENDA

1 Apologies for absence: FT, EH, KH.

2 New production strategy – for decision.

3 Resources and action required to implement new production strategy – for discussion.

4 AOB

3.6 Case study

4 | Managing conflict

▶ management styles

▶ managing conflict

4.1 About business Management style

Discussion

1 In small groups, discuss these questions.

1 What are the qualities you value most in these 'managers'?

> a parent   a teacher   a sports coach   a driving instructor

2 What experience do you have of managing other people?
3 What sort of manager are you or would you be?

Reading

2 Before you read, discuss the questions with a partner. Then read *Managers from hell* and compare your answers with the ideas in the article.

1 What are the characteristics of the manager from hell?
2 Why do people become bad managers?
3 What can you do if your boss is the manager from hell?

3 Read the article again. Explain what is meant by the following phrases:

1 *the carrot and the stick* (lines 7–8)
2 *rabbits caught in the headlights* (line 25)
3 *Dr Jekyll or Mr Hyde* (line 33)
4 *to move the goalposts* (line 59)
5 *the moral highground* (line 80)
6 *a slanging match* (line 82)

Glossary PAGE 155

gunslinger
hell for leather
meat and drink

Listening

4 🔊 1:51–1:55 Listen to five extracts from a presentation on models for management and conflict styles by Mary Walbright, a professor at the University of Bolton-Milwaukee. Match the charts with the people who devised them.

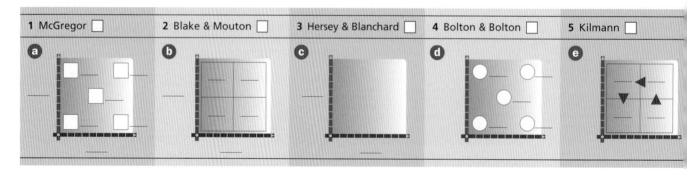

| 1 McGregor ☐ | 2 Blake & Mouton ☐ | 3 Hersey & Blanchard ☐ | 4 Bolton & Bolton ☐ | 5 Kilmann ☐ |

5 🔊 1:51–1:55 Listen again and label the charts.

Discussion

6 In small groups, discuss the questions.

1 How realistic is Dr Housego's suggestion that 'the team has to manage the boss'? Which parts of her advice do you agree or disagree with?
2 Which of Hersey & Blanchard's management styles would be appropriate for a) a supervisor with personal problems b) an enthusiastic management trainee c) an experienced staff member who has made a serious mistake?
3 What do you think happens when there is a conflict between a) a Driver and an Amiable b) an Expressive and an Analytical c) a Driver and an Expressive?
4 What is the difference between collaborating and compromising?
5 Which of the models in Exercise 4 do you find the most interesting, and why?

Internet research

Search for the keywords *management style questionnaire*. Test your own management style and report back to the class on your results.

MANAGERS FROM HELL

Like Sergio Leone's gunslingers, managers come in three categories: the good, the bad and the ugly. In an average career, most of us will encounter one or two genuinely charismatic leaders, a fair number of mediocre bosses, and the occasional
5 manager from hell. Most people in positions of authority genuinely want to be fair and objective, even if only a few consistently succeed. Some will admit to using both the carrot and the stick, a kind of 'good cop, bad cop' management style. Only a very few set out to achieve results by making other
10 people's lives a misery; these are the real managers from hell.

The symptoms are easily recognizable: a chronic lack of trust in staff, blaming other people for their own mistakes and a tendency to let problems fester rather than taking decisive action. Nightmare managers are poor communicators, often
15 preferring to send emails rather than face discussion and disagreement. Should team members dare express a different opinion, the manager from hell resorts to screaming and shouting to avoid being proven wrong.
20 The team's self-confidence is constantly undermined by a refusal to allow creative thinking, initiative or autonomy; changing objectives and deadlines without consulting the people involved quickly leaves staff terrified of making
25 mistakes, frozen in inertia like rabbits caught in the headlights.

Surprisingly in an age of political correctness, team-building and people skills, some office workers claim that they actually prefer a direct, no-nonsense approach. 'At least with a straight-talking disciplinarian, you know where you are,' says Dr Jane
30 Housego, a behavioural psychologist at the University of East Anglia. 'But there's nothing worse than coming to work every morning wondering whether you're going to be dealing with Dr Jekyll or Mr Hyde.' Inconsistency is meat and drink to the manager from hell: leaving people guessing what you're going
35 to do next is fundamental to any 'divide and rule' strategy.

Often this kind of behaviour is completely unconscious, Housego explains. 'Most ineffective managers don't realize just how destructive they are. More often than not, they've been promoted to management because they were good
40 salespeople, engineers, chemists, or whatever. But because they've never been trained to manage, they reproduce bad models received from their own bosses.' Driving a team hell for leather can actually be a successful strategy in the short term,

so initial successes reinforce these patterns of behaviour. But
45 the higher up the corporate ladder they go, the less likely they are to succeed. 'Inevitably, slave drivers make enemies,' says Housego. 'Sooner or later an ex-slave will get themselves into a position where they can take revenge. What's more, senior managers are political animals who don't much care to share
50 the top floor with a monster.'

In the meantime, however, co-workers still have to live with the manager from hell. How can they limit the damage? 'You and your boss get paid for doing the same thing: meeting corporate objectives,' Housego continues. 'When a boss is
55 unable or unwilling to manage the team properly, the team has to manage the boss. First of all, make sure all objectives, deadlines and deliverables are written down in black and white.

Not only does that make it much harder for the boss to move the goalposts further down
60 the line, it also provides an objective measure for your own performance. Similarly, put any information that might reflect badly on the manager's decisions, skills or judgement in writing: refer to the facts impersonally and
65 objectively, avoiding personal opinions; give the boss the opportunity to take corrective action without losing face. Don't get into arguments with the boss in meetings; when other people are present, there's only ever going to be one winner.'

70 Housego also recommends keeping a diary with all the evidence you may need if you have to justify yourself. If your boss blames you for not doing tasks you were never assigned, schedule weekly meetings where you review the coming week together, then confirm everything immediately after
75 the meeting in a friendly email. And if the worst comes to the worst and the situation becomes untenable, always have a plan B. If you have to leave, make sure you leave on your own terms: go when you're ready to go, not just when your boss gives you no alternative.

80 One final piece of advice is to occupy the moral highground. 'Whatever happens,' says Housego, 'you should always resist the temptation to get into a slanging match. Criticizing your boss can only damage your own reputation. Sooner or later the manager from hell will be found out. When top management
85 finally realize your boss is impossible, make sure you are seen as part of the solution, not part of the problem.'

> **'managers come in three categories: the good, the bad and the ugly'**

4 | Managing conflict

▶ office conflicts

▶ conflict management strategies

Glossary   PAGE 155

get somebody's goat
harassment

4.2 Vocabulary   Managing conflict

'Conflict is inevitable,
but combat is optional.'
MAX LUCADE

Discussion

1   With a partner, unscramble the verbs in **bold**, then rank the collocations from least to most desirable in the workplace.

> **aidov** conflict   **akprs** conflict   **deefsu** conflict   **eelorsv** conflict   **aaeeclts** conflict

Listening

2   1:56–1:63 Listen to eight items of office gossip and identify the problems.

a) a buyer is not going to put up with a supplier's mistakes ☐
b) a management trainer got someone's back up ☐
c) an intern got off on the wrong foot with his supervisor ☐
d) an assistant is fed up with her boss ☐
e) an employee who gets on her manager's nerves ☐
f) someone flew off the handle with a customer ☐
g) someone is fed up with an auditor ☐
h) two colleagues don't get on ☐

3   Fill in the spaces in the questions about the office gossip with words from the box.

> ballistic   blinkered   cheese   fussy   sick   straw   tether   voice   way   word

1   Who went _____ in the workshop?
2   Who is at the end of his _____?
3   Whose trainee rubbed him up the wrong _____?
4   Who is persuaded to take their business elsewhere by the last _____?
5   Who is _____ and hard to manage?
6   Who likes the sound of his own _____?
7   Who always has to have the last _____?
8   Who are like chalk and _____?
9   Who is _____ and always goes by the book?
10   Who said argumentative people made them _____?

How good are you at passing on office gossip? What can you remember about Dave, Lin, Nisha, Pavel, Mr Jarlberg, Jo, Ed and Katrina? The questions will help you.

Internet research

Search for the keywords *workplace harassment*. Be prepared to discuss definitions of what does or does not constitute harassment, how companies can eliminate it, and what to do if it happens to you.

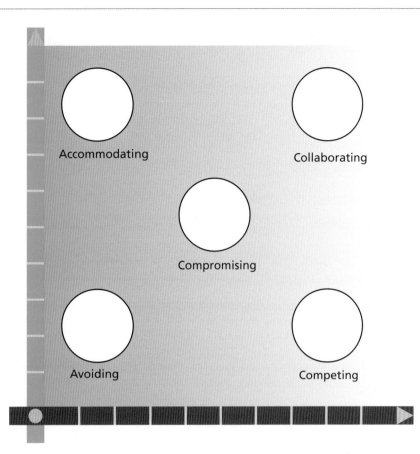

Accommodating

Collaborating

Compromising

Avoiding

Competing

4 Sort two pieces of advice into each of the five conflict management strategies.

1 Competing   2 Collaborating   3 Compromising   4 Accommodating   5 Avoiding

a) Don't let them get away with it – stand up for yourself! ☐
b) Take my advice: keep your head down and wait for it to blow over. ☐
c) If I were you, I'd just throw in the towel. ☐
d) If there's really no room for manoeuvre, my advice is just to agree to disagree. ☐
e) I think you should both lay your cards on the table, and just try and clear the air. ☐
f) See if you can get some movement from both sides and work out your differences. ☐
g) Say you need to mull it over; they'll have forgotten all about it by next week! ☐
h) Try and talk it through calmly and rationally – but stand up for your rights. ☐
i) Why don't you just face up to the inevitable? Admit defeat and smooth things over. ☐
j) Don't take it lying down – make sure you get your own way. ☐

Collocations

5 Fill in the spaces in this conversation with collocations from Exercise 4.

Dave: Look, Ed, we can't just wait for this thing to (1) _____ over; I think we should both lay our (2) _____ on the table, and try and clear the (3) _____.

Ed: All right, I'm happy to try and (4) _____ out our differences, but don't imagine I'm going to just throw in the (5) _____! I won't let you get (6) _____ with it!

Dave: Ed, it's perfectly normal to (7) _____ up for your rights – but I think there's room for (8) _____. If we talk it (9) _____ calmly and rationally, I'm convinced we can reach an agreement.

Ed: OK, but you're going to have to face up to the (10) _____; you're not going to get things all your own (11) _____!

Roleplay

6 Work with a partner. Hold conversations about the problems in Exercise 2.

Student A: Explain the problem, and how you feel.
Student B: Advise your colleague on how to deal with the situation.

4 | Managing conflict

▶ subordinators

▶ coordinators

Did you know?

Conjunctions include coordinators and subordinators. Coordinating conjunctions join words or groups of words that are equal in rank grammatically. The main coordinating conjunctions are *and, but* and *or*. *And* is more frequent than all the other coordinators put together. In texts it accounts for one word in every 40. Subordinating conjunctions introduce a clause that is dependent on the main clause. Some common subordinating conjunctions include *although, as, before, until, when* and *while*.

▶ **Grammar and practice**
pages 128–129

4.3 Grammar   Conjunctions

Subordinators and coordinators

1 Work in small groups. Read the *Did you know?* information, then play the *if, and, but* game. Two people start discussing one of the topics below. They aren't allowed to use the words *if, and* or *but*. The person who says any of these words is 'out' and another person from the group takes their place to continue the conversation or start a new one.

- How I deal with conflict
- Why it is important to be assertive
- The importance of apologizing

2 Complete the sentences with an appropriate conjunction from the box.

> and   as   as if   but   in case   or   provided   so   supposing   though
> unless   whereas   while

1. _____ you are partly to blame, I won't make an issue of it on this occasion.
2. We need you to take the initiative _____ sort the problem out yourself.
3. I'll tell you what we could do – kill two birds with one stone: deal with Fernando _____ we are in Madrid.
4. Don't – whatever you do – use that door, _____ there's a real emergency.
5. OK, you can take the day off tomorrow _____ you make up the time later in the week.
6. _____ no one ever mentioned it I assumed it wasn't important.
7. The difference is, James has apologized for being out of order, _____ you have behaved _____ you haven't done anything wrong.
8. I'd love to be able to tell you what went wrong, _____ I'm telling you I've got absolutely no idea.
9. There's no real reason for you to be at the meeting, _____ you might as well take the afternoon off.
10. What I'm saying is we need to get all the documentation together _____ the inspectors turn up.
11. You can resolve the issues between you _____ you can take the consequences – it's up to you.
12. _____ she doesn't agree, what should we do then?

Expressing meanings through subordinators

3 Jack and Adele are discussing a conflict at work. Read their conversation. For each of the examples 1–10 cross out the subordinator that *can't* be used.

Jack: Did you manage to talk it through with those two?

Adele: What, Marc and Maria? Well, I wanted to check out the legal side of things first (1) *so that / in case / in order that* we know exactly where we stand.

Jack: OK, but we don't want to leave it too long. They need to know we're on to their case, (2) *since / because / unless* they might turn the tables on us otherwise.

Adele: I know what they're like. And (3) *once / while / as soon as* Hulya's come up with the right procedural stuff I'll talk to them.

Jack: I'm sure we'll be on solid ground, (4) *as / provided / as long as* they don't get nasty.

Adele: Yeah, you never know. Ever since Ruth left, Maria's been behaving (5) *as though / as if / even though* she's in charge.

Jack: I know. I don't like it. I guess it was Maria who actually went for the top job, (6) *supposing / whereas / while* Marc just complains without actually doing anything about it.

Adele: OK, but it's Marc who's always there for you (7) *as soon as / as long as / the minute* anything goes wrong. Well, for me anyway.

Jack: I wish I could agree. (8) *Whether / Whenever / When* I need him I can't track him down. Anyway, it's Maria who needs our support, (9) *although / because / since* she's the one who puts in the real work.

Adele: (10) *Rather than / Just as / Like* I thought – you always did back Maria!

4 Work in small groups. Use an appropriate conjunction to join the groups of sentences in each section to make a coherent text.

SECTION 1

Two employees, Lee and Jasmine, are chosen to work on a special project.
They are given their brief.
It includes a two-week deadline to come up with a business plan for their new target market.
They are from different departments.
They do not know each other.
They are expected to quickly work together.

SECTION 2

When the boss is in the room they seem to get on well.
In private they are suspicious of each other.
Jasmine is an outgoing person.
Lee seems to be a rather private person.
Jasmine's key idea is to focus on a persuasive 'hearts and minds' strategy to organically grow sales.
Lee's plan involves an 'in-your-face' TV-led campaign aimed at growing sales fast.
Jasmine argues that Lee's plan would be prohibitively expensive and too unsubtle.

SECTION 3

Halfway through the first week, communication has apparently broken down.
The two employees cannot find any common ground to move forward.
Jasmine insists on discussing their differences.
Lee is more concerned with the deadline.
He wants to quickly get on with the task itself.
They agree to work independently on separate plans.

SECTION 4

Things come to a head in the middle of the second week.
Jasmine argues that Lee is being too secretive.
Jasmine thinks Lee is not sharing his ideas.
Lee responds by accusing Jasmine of trying to control him all the time.

SECTION 5

Lee, meanwhile, argues that Jasmine's plans will not work.
Her plans to build brand recognition organically through local initiatives would take too long.
Her plans probably wouldn't work.
Eventually Lee persuades Jasmine to go with his plan.

SECTION 6

The day of the deadline comes.
Lee realizes that their plan is actually quite weak.
The television network is too fragmented.
The advertisements would not easily reach the target consumers.
It is too late to change anything.

SECTION 7

The Marketing Director arrives.
She takes one look at the plan.
She realizes the plan is nowhere near ready.
She blames both participants.

SECTION 8

The Marketing Director leaves the room.
The participants launch into a heated argument over who is to blame.
The Marketing Director returns to collect her papers.
She witnesses the employees shouting at each other.
She gives them each a written warning.

Internet research

Search for the keywords *causes of communication breakdown*. Make a list of five common causes and compare with a partner.

Glossary   PAGE 156

hearts and minds strategy
turn the tables on somebody

Discussion

5 Work in small groups. Discuss the following questions about each stage of the conflict.

1 Who is responsible for the conflict?
2 How could the conflict have been avoided?
3 What steps should be taken to resolve the situation?

Roleplay

6 With a partner, roleplay a conversation between yourself and the Marketing Director where you defend either Lee or Jasmine's role in the process. Try to persuade the Marketing Director that the other person should take the blame.

4 | Managing conflict

4.4 Management skills   Assertiveness

Your **assertive** rights in the workplace

- The right to hold your own opinions.
- The right to a fair hearing for those opinions.
- The right to need and want things that may differ from other people's needs and wants.
- The right to ask (not demand) that others respond to your needs and wants.
- The right to refuse a request without feeling guilty or selfish.
- The right to have feelings and to express them assertively if you want to.
- The right to be wrong sometimes.
- The right to have others respect your rights.

from Assertiveness at Work, by Ken and Kate Back

Discussion

1 Work with a partner. Discuss which of your assertive rights are contravened by these comments.

1 'When I want your opinion, I'll ask for it!'
2 'What do you mean, you can't work late tonight? Don't you have any sense of loyalty?'
3 'I don't care how you feel about it, just get on with the job!'
4 'I will not tolerate mistakes, do you hear me?'

2 Which answers would you choose?

1 a) Sorry, I didn't mean to interrupt you.
   b) I think exchanging views will help us move forward.
   c) You're so opinionated, why don't you ever listen to me?
2 a) Oh, all right then, I'll do it.
   b) Yes, I do, but unfortunately I've got family commitments tonight. I'm happy to reschedule the work though.
   c) You should've planned ahead, I knew this would happen!
3 a) Never mind, it doesn't matter.
   b) I realize you're worried that it's urgent, but as I said, I feel there are more important jobs I should be doing.
   c) Why don't you do some work for a change?
4 a) It won't happen again.
   b) That seems a bit unfair to me.
   c) Calm down, it's no big deal.

3 Work with a partner. Answer the questions.

1 Which of the answers above are aggressive, non-assertive/passive, assertive?
2 What kind of body language would you associate with each type of behaviour?
3 What kind of outcomes are aggression and non-assertiveness likely to lead to?
4 How do perceptions of what constitutes aggressive or passive behaviour vary between countries and cultures?

Listening

4 1:64–1:67 Linda is a supervisor in an open-space office in a merchant bank. Listen to her handling four difficult situations. For each case, identify the problem and tick (✓) the assertiveness techniques Linda uses to resolve it.

Assertiveness techniques

1 Acknowledge the other person's position, but make sure your views are heard. ☐☐☐☐
2 Ask for more time to respond. ☐☐☐☐
3 Just say no – don't apologize or justify yourself. ☐☐☐☐
4 Offer an acceptable compromise. ☐☐☐☐
5 Use *I* statements to express your feelings: avoid arguments and blaming with *you* statements. ☐☐☐☐
6 Use the 'broken record' technique – repeat your position as many times as necessary. ☐☐☐☐

Glossary   PAGE 156

have a bone to pick with somebody
hearing

5 🔊 **1:64–1:67 Listen again and complete the useful expressions in the checklist.**

Useful expressions: Handling conflicts

Asking for time

Can I _____ _____ to you later on?
Can we work _____ _____ this afternoon?
I need some time to _____ it _____.
I'm not in a position to give you an answer right now.

Acknowledging and being heard

I understand that you _____ _____, but I'd much rather ...
I realize that this is maybe not the _____ _____, but ...
I appreciate that you have your _____ _____, but ...
I'd love to talk about this later, but right now I ...

Offering compromise

What would be an _____ _____?
I'd be happy to ...
I'd much prefer to ...

Expressing feelings

I hesitate to _____ _____ this, but ...
The way I _____ _____ is like this ...
I feel guilty about saying no, but ...
I think we should ...
That seems a bit unfair to me.

Saying no

I appreciate _____ _____, but no, thanks.
No, thanks.
I'm afraid not.

Speaking

6 Work with a partner. Reformulate and continue these conversations more assertively.

A: Can we talk? You never gave me an answer about taking Wednesdays off.
B: Some other time, OK? I'm in a hurry now.
A: You always say that. You never listen to what I say anyway.
B: Nonsense! Of course I do. I've just got bigger issues to deal with at the moment, that's all.
A: ...

C: Lend me €50, will you, I'll pay you back next week.
D: Oh, €50? Well, all right then, but I wanted to buy a pair of shoes after work ...
C: What do you need more shoes for? You've got hundreds of them already!
D: Yeah, but ... the thing is, you're always asking to borrow money!
C: ...

E: I thought I'd already told you about wearing jeans to work!
F: Look, you don't understand! These are designer jeans, right? Jean-Paul Gaultier.
E: I don't care if they're Gaultier, Gucci or 24-carat gold-plated! No jeans, d'you hear?
F: It's not as if the customers ever actually see me, is it? No video on our phones, is there?
E: ...

Roleplay

7 With a partner, roleplay conflict situations in the workplace.

Student A turn to page 114.
Student B turn to page 116.

Internet research

Search for the keywords *how to read body language*. Make lists of body language associated with aggression, passivity and assertiveness in your culture and report back to the class.

eWorkbook

Now watch the video for this unit.

4 | Managing conflict

4.5 Writing Letters

Model

1 Read the three letters below and choose the best greeting and salutation/sign-off for each from the box.

> Dear Roger,   Sincerely, Jo Finn, Purchasing Manager   Dear Mrs White,
> Yours faithfully, P. Mitchell, CEO   Dear Sirs,   Yours sincerely, Pavel Cwiklinski

❶ It has come to our attention that you have made unauthorized use of our company's logo on your website www.2manydiscounts.com. You neither asked for nor received permission to use our logo. We therefore believe you have wilfully infringed our rights and could be liable for statutory damages.
We demand that you immediately cease to use the logo and that you desist from this or any other infringement of our rights in future. Unless we receive an affirmative response from you within one week indicating that you have fully complied with these requirements, we shall consider taking legal action.

❷ I am writing to inform you that I have a grievance relating to non-payment of overtime which I would like you to investigate. The main issues are as follows:
1. On two separate occasions, 11 March and 7 May, due to inaccurate information supplied by the customer, I was required to work until 8.30pm and 11pm respectively re-installing milling machines on Custom Labs' premises.
2. Having remonstrated with Custom Labs' Production Manager on the second occasion, I received an official warning further to a complaint from the customer.
3. Although I do not contest the fact that I overreacted, I feel strongly that the overtime incurred through no fault of my own should be paid.
I trust you will arrange a grievance hearing as soon as possible. I understand that I am entitled to be accompanied by a colleague or a trade union representative at the hearing.
I look forward to hearing from you.

❸ I am writing to request your help in improving your shipping department's service to us. Over the last quarter, the number of delivery errors has reached an unacceptable level (see enclosed summary). These recurrent mix-ups are a source of delay, extra work and additional cost.
Whilst your product quality is very satisfactory and we have no wish to go elsewhere, we cannot continue to overlook so many mistakes. We would urge you to review your procedures; if the situation does not improve we will be left little choice but to make alternative arrangements.
I look forward to hearing from you as soon as possible.

Analysis

2 With a partner, answer the following questions.

1 Which letter mostly uses the first person/second person/third person?
2 Which letter is the most diplomatic/the most aggressive/the most assertive?
3 Summarize each letter in one sentence. Is each summary diplomatic, aggressive or assertive?

Language focus

3 Match the sets of expressions on the left (1–5 and 6–10) with those with similar meanings on the right (a)–e) and f)–j)). How is the tone different from the original? Is it more diplomatic, more aggressive or more assertive?

1	We demand that you immediately cease …	a)	You know you have a legal obligation to …
2	… desist from this … in future.	b)	Would you please stop … now.
3	… I would like you to investigate.	c)	It is the company's responsibility, not mine.
4	… I feel strongly that the overtime incurred through no fault of my own should be paid.	d)	I insist that you reconsider.
5	I trust you will …	e)	Please don't do it again.

6	We are increasingly concerned about the tight schedules.	f)	Prove you can deliver on time.
7	We would urge you to … if the situation does not improve we will be left little choice but to …	g)	We'll sue you if you don't do as you're told.
8	Unless we receive an affirmative response … we shall consider taking legal action.	h)	Don't forget that I can escalate the problem.
9	I understand that I am entitled to be accompanied by a colleague or a trade union representative at the hearing.	i)	I expect an immediate answer.
10	I look forward to hearing from you as soon as possible.	j)	Do what we're asking, or else …

4 Rewrite the following sentences using the words in brackets, as in the example.

1 Please return the completed form at your earliest convenience. (look forward)
I look forward to receiving the completed form as soon as possible.
2 It would be really nice if you could promise never to do anything like this again. (demand, desist)
3 According to the company rules, you're supposed to tell me about any changes to my schedule. (trust)
4 Don't you think it would be a good idea to obtain ISO certification? (urge)
5 Don't forget, if I'm laid off you have to pay a month's salary for every year of service. (understand, entitled)
6 I didn't cause the damage, so I shouldn't have to pay. (held responsible, incurred, no fault)
7 Do you think you could possibly stop this harassment? (insist, cease, me)
8 If you don't agree, we'll sue you for every penny you've got. (affirmative response, little choice, action)
9 We know you have deliberately used our copyright material without permission. (attention, infringe)
10 We are reluctant to change suppliers but will do so if necessary. (wish, elsewhere, alternative arrangements)

Output

5 Write a suitable letter for one of the following situations.

1 A series of workshops given for your team by a consulting firm has been very disappointing so far; in particular, the trainer has failed to listen to and take participants' opinions into account. Another series of workshops is planned for next year, but unless things improve you are inclined to work with another firm.
2 Your manager, Linda Hall, has cancelled your holidays three times in the last year, supposedly because the department is short-staffed. You have twice lost your deposit on holidays you had booked, and would like to be compensated. Conversations with Linda and her superior, Jerry Richards, have failed to produce a satisfactory outcome, so you have decided to raise a grievance with the HR Director, Felicity Knott.

Internet research

Search for the keywords *thank you letter* to find sample letters to send after a job interview, an internship or a recommendation. Compare your findings with a partner and save the most helpful or appropriate templates for future use.

Glossary PAGE 156

grievance
infringe
remonstrate
statutory
wilful

- ▶ qualities of a good manager
- ▶ conflictual relationships
- ▶ resolving conflicts

Glossary PAGE 156

concern
to go over
   somebody's head

4.6 Case study Olvea Brasil

Discussion

1 Work with a partner. Imagine your ideal team leader. What would they do in the following situations?

> you need help   you make a big mistake   you do something really well
> you do your job with no problems   you have personal problems

Reading

2 Read the background to the case and answer the questions.

1 What are Eliana's concerns?
2 What kind of management style does the company encourage?
3 Why does Eliana like to hear both sides of the story?

ELIANA SCHAEFFER, Director of Human Resources at Olvea Brasil, stood at her window and stared out pensively at the mountains rising above the city. On her table were four employee files; each had been put in the 'concerns' category at last Friday's six-monthly staff review. Eliana knew very well that although a 'concern' tag was supposed to be an early warning, all too often it meant that a crisis was just waiting to happen.

Olvea Brasil is the Brazilian subsidiary of an international group which supplied components for the automobile industry. Aware that they relied heavily on the skills and creativity of their engineers for survival, Olvea's management encouraged a culture that was officially firmly people-orientated. At the same time, Eliana understood that in a field where competition was fierce, and customers more and more demanding, productivity was crucial; results often took precedence over people's feelings.

It was going to be a tough morning; Eliana had made appointments with each of the four 'concerns' in turn. After reading their manager's comments in their files, she liked to hear the employee's side of the story before reaching any conclusions. 'More often than not it's the manager who's the real concern!' she thought as she sat down at the table to review the four files.

Internet research

Search for the keywords *how to manage your boss*. Take a class vote to find your top tips.

3 Work in small groups. Read the employee files opposite and answer the questions below. What do they suggest about the relationship between each employee and their manager?

Which members of staff:
1 have changed their attitude?
2 do not communicate well?
3 are disappointing or disappointed?
4 are being unreasonable?
5 have a limited future with the company?

Listening

4 🔊 1:68–1:71 **Listen to Eliana's interviews with the four members of staff, and take notes.**

Discussion

5 **In small groups, discuss the questions.**

1 How are the employees' stories different from their managers' versions? Who should you believe?
2 What are Carla Hartmann, Vitor Martins, Isabel Correia and Antony Middleton's management styles?
3 What strategies do you feel would be most effective in managing Wilson Holden, Susan Shipley, Luigi Tarantini and Natasha Gomes in future?
4 How should Eliana manage the managers?

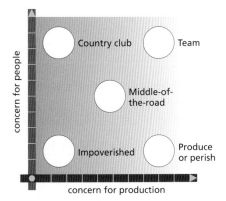

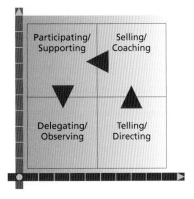

Presentation

6 **In your groups, draw up an action plan covering all the issues. Present your plan to the class and take questions.**

NAME: Wilson Holden
AGE: 26
POSITION: Moulding Engineer
MANAGER: Carla Hartmann
MANAGER'S COMMENTS: Young graduate engineer. No problems in first year, but uncommunicative. Three months ago he started suggesting changes to procedures. I explained it was not his job to make changes; if changes are needed I will make them. Since then he has consistently disregarded procedures and encouraged other colleagues to do the same. He refuses to follow instructions; last week he refused to work on Saturday, even though all the engineers agreed to do one Saturday per month. He is insolent, arrogant, frequently uses foul language and cannot accept criticism.

NAME: Susan Shipley
AGE: 38
POSITION: Project Manager
MANAGER: Vitor Martins
MANAGER'S COMMENTS: Susan is very experienced and autonomous (13 years with Olvea), but she seems unhappy. No obvious problems – her work is satisfactory, but people in the department say she's miserable and demotivated. Isabel Correia, my boss, said she asked to speak to her, so I thought I'd better bring it to your attention.

NAME: Luigi Tarantini
AGE: 48
POSITION: Head of R&D
MANAGER: Isabel Correia
MANAGER'S COMMENTS: Luigi does a great job for us, we've always worked well together. But just recently he's become colder, not his normal friendly self. With my engineering background, I enjoy working with Luigi in the lab, but he has become almost secretive about his work – when I offer to look at the latest test results with him he keeps suggesting I have more important things to do.
No complaints about the quality of his work, everything is fine – he just doesn't seem to want to share with me the way we used to.

NAME: Natasha Gomes
AGE: 23
POSITION: Administrative Assistant
MANAGER: Antony Middleton
MANAGER'S COMMENTS: Natasha is pleasant and compliant. However, she lacks initiative and seems frightened of making mistakes. She seems unable to make decisions herself; she phones me several times a day to ask for instructions when a little common sense is all that is necessary. Her work is acceptable but never excellent. Although she is much more willing than the rest of my department, I am not sure that she possesses the qualities we expect in an administrative assistant.

Review 3

1 Fill in the spaces in the noun phrases below with a suitable word from the box.

> backdrop chains consumers difficulties power
> reform supply suppliers

Smaller food suppliers are being hit hard, a report by the National Grocers Commission reveals today. The report shows that it is the larger suppliers who are best placed to benefit from (1) the increased buying _____ of the major supermarket players. (2) The _____ of groceries is increasingly being concentrated in the hands of a few very large suppliers. (3) _____ caused by increasing supermarket domination together with (4) a worsening economic _____ mean that smaller suppliers are being doubly squeezed. Worst hit are (5) those _____ who have only one customer. (6) Wider _____ of the agricultural industry has hardly helped. Today's (7) complex supply _____ favour the larger and more technologically advanced operators, who in turn are able to pass savings on to their customers. Some good news at least for (8) beleaguered _____ with less and less money to spend!

2 Correct the mistakes in the noun phrases in *italics* in the following sentences.

1 It remains unclear *what particular countries are affected*.
2 The report focuses particularly on *retailers of coffee whom meet the refreshment needs in cities worldwide of office workers*.
3 Our aim is to find *a practical solution offering software piece which is inexpensive*.
4 *The reason which here are gathered so many great team leaders today* is to celebrate the life and achievements of Santiago Gabrielli.
5 Your key job responsibility involves promoting and achieving *personal and social welfare high standards*.
6 Dr Stephen James is *a successful outstanding manager who educated at Harvard*.

3 Choose the correct verb from the box to fill in the spaces in the description of a logistics supply process.

> choose consider decide source validate

When planning a new food-processing business, first of all, (1) _____ just one logistics provider to cover all areas of the operation, thereby reducing unnecessary financial outlay. Be sure to (2) _____ the quality of the product being supplied, paying particular attention to the consistency of high standards of quality. It is generally recommended to (3) _____ produce from farms with the highest standards of animal welfare. To reduce costs further, you may want to (4) _____ using a single-sized container for all deliveries. Use a range of cost-determining techniques to define the location of the main production facility and (5) _____ on the exact number of regional distribution centres that you will require.

4 Make instructions and action plans by matching a beginning with an ending.

1 Phase one involves completely upgrading ☐
2 We should also consider outsourcing ☐
3 If we adopt ☐
4 We should give some serious thought to offshoring ☐
5 We require a written quotation to be provided ☐
6 Authority for any systems upgrade must first be sought ☐
7 I would like to emphasize ☐
8 The equipment has been delivered, but it has not yet been authorized ☐
9 Above all we should maximize ☐

a) production to a low-cost manufacturer in China.
b) the company's computer software systems.
c) Just-In-Time practices we could drastically reduce our inventories.
d) business processes including accounts and recruitment.
e) for use in this facility.
f) in writing.
g) from department heads.
h) the value we extract at all levels of our operation.
i) the need for clarity and brevity in any internal communication.

5 Rewrite the sentences beginning with the words in brackets to make them more emphatic.

1 We are trying to project an image of timeless quality. (The image)

_____

2 We have recently diversified our product portfolio because we want to appear more cutting edge. (In order to)

_____

3 The decision to offshore our production facility to the Far East was due mainly to a desire for cost savings. (The reason)

_____

6 Fill in the missing letters in the sales of goods terms, and match these with their meanings a)–f).

1 R__t__ __ __ __ __ ☐
2 St__ __ __ __s ☐
3 U__s__l__ __ __ __ __ __ __ ☐
4 __to__ __ __ut__ ☐
5 S__ __n-b__ __ __ __ __ t__ __d__ __ __ __ ☐
6 C__ __d__ __ -to-g__ __ __ __ ☐

a) products which the retailer cannot sell
b) from beginning to end
c) faulty products which the customer sends back to the manufacturer
d) products which have passed their sell-by date
e) a system where the supplier owns the goods until they are scanned at the point of sale
f) situations when no supplies of a product are left

Review 4

Managing conflict

1 Match the idioms and expressions in sentences 1–8 with their meanings a)–h).

1 I would have gone, but it wasn't really my cup of tea. ☐
2 At the end of just one week working with him I was at the end of my tether. ☐
3 Basically, he was rubbing me up the wrong way. ☐
4 I would have liked to help him, but I always go by the book whenever there's money involved. ☐
5 And when he said 'Where were you?' I'm afraid I completely flew off the handle. ☐
6 Well, it's probably because I got off on the wrong foot with him. ☐
7 Anyway, after about six months there I threw in the towel. ☐
8 I don't understand why, because I laid my cards on the table from the outset. ☐

a) I followed procedures.
b) I gave up.
c) I started badly.
d) I ran out of patience.
e) I was annoyed.
f) I was open and frank.
g) It wasn't to my taste.
h) I got angry.

2 Rewrite each sentence using the subordinator given, making any changes necessary.

1 You need to keep a backup copy because the original could get mislaid.
(in case)
_____

2 Some tasks are too difficult – with others it's just that they're weird.
(while)
_____

3 I can only assess your work if you meet the deadline.
(unless)
_____

4 Step up on the podium and then immediately reach for the mic and start speaking.
(as soon as)
_____

5 The reason why I missed the deadline is that I didn't actually know about it.
(because)
_____

6 You can take Friday off, but you must make up the time next week.
(provided)
_____

7 Despite having flu and being run-down, Simone managed to give an excellent presentation.
(although)
_____

8 He thinks he owns the place, and behaves like it too.
(as if)
_____

3 Complete the expressions by filling in the spaces with an appropriate word.

1 I'm afraid I'm not in a _____ to give you an answer at the moment.
2 I do feel _____ about saying no, but on this occasion I really must refuse your request.
3 I _____ your telling me about your legitimate concerns, but …
4 I _____ to ask you this, but could I take next Monday off?
5 Would that be an acceptable _____ for you?
6 I quite _____ that you have had personal setbacks, but the deadline must still stand, I'm afraid.
7 I'd _____ to talk about all this later on, but actually right now I've got my own deadline to meet.
8 On balance I think I would _____ to let you work it out amongst yourselves.

4 Put one of the verbs from the box into the first gap, then think of the correct particle (adverb or preposition) to fill the second (and third) gaps in each sentence.

face   get   mull   put   smooth   stand   talk

1 Right, that's it, I won't _____ _____ _____ any more complaints – just get on with it from now on.
2 He's actually broken the law, I really don't think he should be allowed to _____ _____ _____ it.
3 My advice in this place is that you must _____ _____ _____ yourself, since no one else will.
4 No problem, if you're not sure just _____ it _____ for a day or two and get back to me.
5 Basically, he needs to _____ _____ _____ the facts and recognize that it's unacceptable.
6 I'm sorry you're feeling that way, but if you want to _____ it _____ with someone I'm more than happy to listen.
7 I'll ask Michelle, she'll manage to _____ things _____ in the office and by tomorrow we'll all have forgotten there was ever a conflict.

5 Match a beginning with an appropriate adverbial ending to make tips for giving bad news.

1 Lay out the facts
2 Get straight
3 Give the background to the situation
4 Arrange a meeting
5 Approach the issue
6 Tell those involved
7 Couch the bad news
8 Offer some suggestions

a) to the point.
b) before stating the bad news.
c) to discuss the matter.
d) clearly and succinctly.
e) in positive terms to try and soften the blow.
f) sensitively and slowly.
g) to overcome the bad news.
h) face to face.

5 | Marketing and sales

5.1 About business Strategic marketing and partnering

Discussion

1 Work with a partner. Which market segment(s) do these pairs of businesses target? What qualities and strengths do they market themselves on? Are they similar or different?

- a bus service and a taxi company
- an opera house and a cinema
- a public university and a private business school
- a hairdresser and a tattoo shop

Skimming

2 Read *A recipe for success – how to develop a strategic marketing plan* quickly. Three well-known companies are used to illustrate particular strategic marketing skills. Which companies are they and which skill does each one illustrate?

Scanning

3 Scan paragraphs 3, 4 and 5 for the words and phrases in the box and complete the five rules for developing a strategic marketing plan below.

> be up to   follow up   growth   identify   identify   keep an eye on
> make adjustments   plan   polish   profit   understand   volume

1 … and … your customers
2 … what the competition …
3 … opportunities for …, … or …
4 … and … your message
5 … results and …

Reading for detail

4 Work with a partner. Read the article again and mark these statements *T* (true) or *F* (false).

1 Businesses are often panicked into marketing campaigns when customers are buying too slowly. ☐
2 Tactical choices, like launching a low-cost product, must be consistent with the long-term plan. ☐
3 Renault allied with international partners to deliver more low-cost models than GM and VW. ☐
4 Kingfisher's image in the beverage market gave it a competitive advantage over cheaper airlines. ☐
5 Consistent branding and messaging provide opportunities to increase growth, profits and volume. ☐
6 Using networking, direct mail, websites, brochures, etc. are examples of tactical marketing. ☐
7 Toyota initially overestimated American consumers' appetite for new technology. ☐
8 Toyota's current strategy downplays the hybrid's low emissions, focusing on its celebrity image. ☐

Internet research

In groups, list what you think are the most valuable brands in the world, from one to ten. Search for the keywords *top ten brands*. Which group got the most right?

Glossary PAGE 156

air time
be up to something
M&A
sign on the dotted line
testimonial
workhorse

Listening

5 🔘 2:01 Listen to an interview with Ari Maas, a Marketing Consultant and specialist in business partnering, and answer the questions.

1 Why is the cocktail party host a better analogy for what Ari does than the marriage bureau?
2 What are Apple® and Nike's core markets, and what do they have in common?
3 What products did they decide to promote together, and what were the benefits for customers?
4 How did Apple® and Nike use the Internet to provide additional benefits?
5 Which type of businesses are most interested in adopting Apple® and Nike's model?
6 What criteria does Ari suggest businesses use to test the suitability of the partnering model?

Discussion

6 Work in small groups. Think about companies which are currently successful. What do you consider to be their marketing strategies? How do their strategies differentiate them from their competitors? Who could they partner with and what new benefits could they offer consumers by using digital tools, such as social media?

A recipe for success
how to develop a strategic marketing plan

The basic purpose of marketing is to persuade prospects to sign on the dotted line as quickly as possible. A slowdown in the sales cycle is so dangerous for a company's cash flow that many businesses make the mistake of frantically buying air time and advertising space without any clear overall strategy. Relying on tactical marketing to run a business is like opening a restaurant on the strength of your chocolate cake alone: the cake may be world-class, but if you haven't thought about what else your customers like to eat and drink, where and when they like to dine out, and how much they're prepared to pay, then you have a recipe for disaster!

Strategic marketing begins long before the first ad hits the street. It involves putting yourself in your customers' shoes, understanding who they are, what they buy and why they buy it. It's about gathering and interpreting information in order to develop a coherent, long-term plan, setting goals that are understood by everybody in the organization, and then ensuring that every tactical choice is consistent with the overall strategy. Automobile maker Renault S.A. provides a striking example. As long ago as 1999, Renault realized that establishing and maintaining a global presence would require a product offering covering the full range of vehicles, from basic low-cost workhorses to high-end luxury models. Over a decade, it entered into strategic alliances with Japan's Nissan, China's Dongfeng Motor and Russia's AvtoVAZ (Lada); the alliance now delivers over eight million vehicles per year, placing it behind only General Motors and Volkswagen.

So how do you develop a strategic marketing plan? First and foremost, by identifying and understanding your customers. You need to know where they live, what they do, what inspires them, which media they engage with, and what kind of messages resonate with them. Next, you need to keep an eye on what the competition are up to: what kind of strategy are they pursuing, which market segments are they targeting, and what are they doing better or worse than you? India's Kingfisher Airlines looked at new low-cost competitors as well as the established market players, and identified that the low end of the market offering, whilst undeniably cheap, was falling below customers' expectations. Leveraging the young, dynamic image of the group's Kingfisher beer, they launched a new flying experience in 2005 with modern, comfortable single-class aircraft, in-flight meals and entertainment. Calling these budget services 'Funliners' and offering prices that were still comfortably below those of the established market leaders, Kingfisher Airlines took 6% of the market in their first six months and would go on to own the second largest share in India's domestic air travel market.

A strategic marketing plan also requires careful opportunity analysis. Businesses need to identify opportunities for growth, for profit or for volume, and to plan the measures needed to pursue them. Similarly, the message sent out to customers must be planned, refined, polished and then protected against dilution or deviation: consistent branding and messaging are essential to keeping a clear message in customers' minds. Only then should marketers start considering the most effective tactics to employ to implement their strategy: the media plan, networking, direct mail, website, brochures, testimonials, etc.

Finally, as in any continuous improvement process, results must be followed up closely so that any necessary adjustments can be made. Toyota's pioneering hybrid vehicle, the Prius, provides a good example. First marketed in the US in 2000 as a green vehicle with low emissions, the car failed to convince American ecologists who found it underpowered and overpriced. Toyota listened to consumers and redesigned the car with more space and power. The new Prius was repositioned with an emphasis on comfort, economy and safety, downplaying its ecological virtues. Finally, as the car acquired iconic status with celebrities, Toyota was able to adjust its strategy once again. Today's message is one of high customer value achieved without compromise: Prius owners get comfort, performance and safety, *and* help save the planet.

'Strategic marketing involves putting yourself in your customers' shoes, understanding who they are, what they buy and why they buy it.'

5 | Marketing and sales

Glossary   PAGE 156

Generation Y

5.2 Vocabulary Marketing

Discussion

1 **Work in small groups and discuss the questions.**

1 What differences are there in the products that you and your parents or grandparents aspire to own and the way you buy them?
2 In what ways are your attitudes to advertising and brands different from those of your parents' or grandparents' generations?
3 Give examples of how marketers could make their brands more attractive to your own generation's concerns, aspirations, goals and lifestyle choices.

Collocations

2 **Which collocation in each group of four would you not expect to find in an article about brand strategy?**

1 brand ownership   brand endorser   brand position   brand new
2 to greet a brand   to tailor a brand   to devise a brand   to recommend a brand
3 a flaming brand   a potent brand   a youth-orientated brand   an emotionally driven brand
4 to develop a brand   to detect a brand   to buy a brand   to support a brand

Reading

3 **Work with a partner, read the article and answer the questions.**

1 What are the characteristics of Generation Y consumers (people born between 1979 and 1994)?
2 How can marketers connect with them?

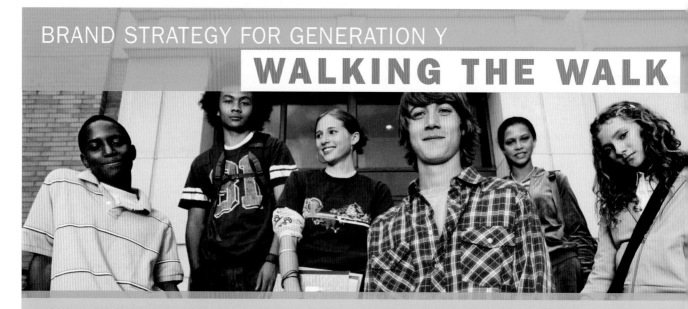

BRAND STRATEGY FOR GENERATION Y
WALKING THE WALK

THE MOST MARKETING-SAVVY segment a business will ever target is undoubtedly Generation Y. With no illusions about how much manufacturers covet their disposable income, the children of the eighties scrutinize any new brand on the block with icy cool. It's not enough just to talk the talk: only genuinely youth-orientated brands can also walk the walk.

So just how do top Gen-Y brands like Converse (shoes), Ben & Jerry's (ice cream) and JetBlue (air travel) succeed where so many others fail? Their secret lies in establishing an emotional connection with their customers, a powerful, psychological attraction that allows these emotionally driven brands to nurture a special relationship and motivate purchase intent.

What are the brand-building strategies to help your business walk the walk? In every market segment, a strong brand not only attracts an initial purchase but also brings longer-term benefits like customer loyalty and premium pricing. But Gen Y-ers are especially influenced by brands that project an emotional appeal they can share in and exploit. For these consumers, a brand is a form of self-expression that communicates an identity to their peers. This emotional investment means that Gen Y-ers will support and recommend the brands they use; they willingly become brand endorsers, creating the kind of buzz that can make market share rocket.

To build an emotionally potent brand, first consider Gen Y-ers' values, and what benefits buying your brand will bring them. Then, fine-tune your brand by positioning it so as to satisfy your target customers' emotional needs: in particular, try to own the all-important 'lifestyle empowerment' brand position. Finally, learn from the Converses and Ben & Jerry's of this world by creating a sense of brand ownership – every truly successful brand in this market manages to foster the impression that it belongs to Gen Y-ers, and to them alone.

4 Read the article again and <u>underline</u> all the collocations with the word *brand*.

Which ones refer to action by brand managers, which to consumers or their reactions, and which ones describe the brands themselves?

5 Write examples or definitions for five collocations, then test a partner.

6 Choose the best equivalent for the words in **bold** from the article.

1 the most marketing-**savvy** segment   a) shy   b) keen   c) knowledgeable
2 **covet** their disposable income   a) desire   b) lose   c) target
3 to motivate purchase **intent**   a) desire   b) enthusiasm   c) indifference
4 customer loyalty and **premium** pricing   a) inflated   b) low   c) high
5 communicates an identity to their **peers**   a) superiors   b) associates   c) friends
6 creating the kind of **buzz**   a) intoxication   b) excitement   c) rumours
7 **own** the all-important 'lifestyle empowerment' brand position   a) occupy   b) buy   c) capture
8 **foster** the impression   a) adopt   b) promote   c) protect

Internet research

Search for the keywords *Converse, Ben & Jerry's* and *JetBlue*. How do they create a sense of brand ownership, and foster the impression that the brand belongs exclusively to Gen Y-ers? Find other examples of Gen-Y brands which use this strategy and report back to the class.

Discussion

7 Work with a partner. Discuss how you could apply the ideas from the article to tailor your brand to Generation Y consumers in one of the markets below.

> banking services   golf courses   public transport   garden centres   public libraries

Listening

8 2:02–2:07 Two teams of students from Oxford and Cambridge are competing on TV's *Marketing Challenge*. Listen to six questions and try to answer correctly before the participants.

9 2:02–2:07 Listen again and label each diagram with the name of the marketing technique from the quiz that it illustrates.

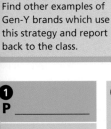

1 P_____
2 P_____
3 P_____
4 P_____
5 P_____

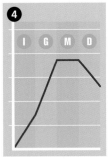

Discussion

10 In small groups, talk about examples of how the marketing terms above apply to brands and markets you are familiar with.

5 | Marketing and sales

▶ dependent prepositions

▶ prepositional phrases

5.3 Grammar Prepositions

Dependent prepositions

1 Complete the phrases 1–8 with the correct preposition from the box. Then match each with the correct ending a)–h).

about against by ~~for~~ into of on with

1 The UK accounts _for_ ☐
2 Individual local markets are mainly characterized _____ ☐
3 Right, could you two stop arguing _____ ☐
4 Listen, I'm not questioning the importance _____ ☐
5 Oscar, could you possibly ask Louise to comment _____ ☐
6 At all costs we need to defend _____ ☐
7 I'm afraid I strongly disagree _____ ☐
8 As for our target consumers, they are divided _____ ☐

a) threats to our market share.
b) the proposal and get back to us by lunch? I'd really value her comments.
c) four different types according to their perceived tastes and socioeconomic groups.
d) controlling costs – what I am saying is we mustn't lose sight of our sales targets.
e) you on that one.
f) differences in their local culture and behaviour practices.
g) procedure and actually talk to each other about strategy?
h) nearly 60% of our gross profits, and that's risky.

Reformulating

2 Look at the phrases in *italics* that come after the preposition in each sentence. Rewrite them using the pronouns given in brackets to create a new sentence that means the same as the original.

1 I'm not interested in *your views.* (what)
  I'm not interested in *what you've got to say.*
2 Could you give me more details of *your itinerary?* (where)
3 As long as you get it done on time he doesn't care about *the methods you use.* (how)
4 That door must not be used except *in emergencies.* (when)
5 We need to organize these strategies according to *their main purpose.* (what)
6 Could you tell us more about *the reasons for his departure*? (why)
7 I need you to come up with something like *a preliminary list of our new markets.* (where)
8 We need to focus more on *the actual job itself.* (exactly what)

Modifying meaning

3 Fill in the spaces with words from the box to modify the prepositional phrases.

almost   at least   entirely   only   particularly   rather   right   straight

1 I'm happy to say that these allegations are _____ without foundation.
2 I envy her – she seems to succeed _____ without trying.
3 I'm sorry, but I've been feeling _____ out of it recently; it's a real struggle concentrating.
4 His promotion looks a bit suspicious: he went _____ to the top.
5 Just look at how strong their campaign is so far, _____ in terms of promotional literature, not to mention visibility, sales – you name it.
6 Hold off on the price hikes for the moment, _____ until we can be sure the market is holding up.
7 It's not just these sales figures that are disappointing, we've had a terrible financial year _____ across the board.
8 I need results, and that means not _____ with regard to sales, but customer satisfaction as well.

Did you know?

Prepositions are unpredictable in form, and can consist of one, two, three or four words: *in reading style manuals, due to adverse conditions, with reference to your enquiry, in the light of what you said.* There are about 200 prepositions in English and no other language uses the same prepositions in the same ways.

▶ Grammar and practice pages 130–131

Internet research

Search for the keywords *marketing failure* to find an example of a company that has experienced one. Take notes and then tell a partner.

Listening for gist

4 🔊 2:08 **Listen to the informal presentation by Dimitri Karras, Marketing Director of Rainbow Software Solutions and answer these questions.**

1   Which part of the world is Dimitri Karras focusing on?
2   What is the main purpose of his presentation?
3   Do you think he is successful in achieving his aim? Why? Why not?

Listening for detail

5 🔊 2:08 **Now listen again and fill in the spaces in the extracts below with the idiomatic prepositional phrases used by the speaker.**

1   _____, what we need more than anything else is a joined-up strategy.
2   _____, we all need to be focusing on the same strategy, whatever part of the business we're working in.
3   So, we can then, _____, capture the whole market _____.
4   _____, have you all managed to have a look through the strategy document?
5   The strategy is, _____, pretty straightforward – _____ focus on the new customer, convince them that they need us, and all that stuff; _____, well, I'll come on to that in a minute.
6   I should emphasize that we need to be careful with customers _____. They can be a bit demanding so _____ just fall back on the 'customer is king' thing.
7   I don't really foresee anything _____ that can go wrong.
8   _____ it's just like what we've been doing in eastern Europe, though on a bigger scale, _____.
9   We must all avoid mentioning that glitch in the software, _____.
10   _____, make sure you all keep quiet about the temperature thing _____.

6 **Work with a partner. Explain the meaning of the idiomatic prepositional phrases from Exercise 5 in your own words and suggest synonyms where possible.**

Speaking

7 **Work in threes. Senior personnel at Rainbow Software Solutions are holding a meeting to discuss why the North American marketing operation failed so badly. Choose one of the roles below and hold the meeting. Each person has five complex prepositions to use. The person who uses all their phrases first wins.**

Student A you are Regional Marketing Negotiator (North America), turn to page 115.
Student B you are the Marketing Director, Dimitri Karras, turn to page 120.
Student C you are the Managing Director of Rainbow Software Solutions, turn to page 119.

Glossary   PAGE 156

joined-up strategy

- active listening techniques
- asking questions
- roleplay: discussion with active listening

5.4 Management skills Active listening

Discussion

1 Work in small groups. Discuss the questions.

1   What percentage of what we communicate do you think is transmitted by a) words b) tone of voice c) body language?
2   Think of some examples of good communicators. What do they have in common?

Reading

2 Fill in the spaces in the article with the words from the box.

closed   leading   multiple   open   supplementary   trick

Let your customer do the talking

You know your product is the best on the market, but how do you sell it to your customer? Just stop talking, listen actively, and give your customer a chance to tell you!

Active listening is a life skill which can improve communication in all sorts of situations, not only on sales calls. Once you know exactly what it is that your customer, your boss, your co-worker or your partner needs, wants, thinks and feels, it becomes much easier for you to provide solutions.

The first step is to ask the right questions. There are a whole range of question types to choose from, and all too often, we don't stop to ask ourselves which ones are most suited to the task in hand. Most people will be familiar with (1) _____ questions which use words like *who, what, when, why,* etc. to invite the customer to follow their own agenda. They can often be followed up with (2) _____ questions, to focus on a particular point in more detail, or

to get the other person talking about their feelings. (3) _____ questions, on the other hand, require only a yes or no answer; they are useful for confirming what you have heard, and for redirecting the conversation.

Other question types should be used with care: (4) _____ questions can be useful to help a customer who is finding it difficult to express their ideas or feelings, but a barrage of options is likely to produce an unfocused response. (5) _____ questions encourage the customer to give a response that the seller wants to hear: later on, they can be a powerful tool in closing the sale, but remember, in the early stages, we want to elicit the customer's view of what they want, not to sell them our own convictions. Finally, (6) _____ questions are no-win questions: whatever answer the customer gives, they fall into your trap. This kind of question is very risky, and is probably best avoided.

3 Match these sample questions with the question types in Exercise 2.

1   Could you tell me more about the opportunities you just mentioned?
2   What would you say if I told you we hacked into your IT system in less than two minutes?
3   How do you see your networking needs developing in the future?
4   I think that we should organize a demonstration – when would be the best time?
5   So, do you think you'll still buy off-the-shelf software packages in future?
6   Tell me about your IT staff. How do they feel about a change of platform? Do you think you can bring them round to the idea, and how long will it take?

Simulation

4 Work in groups of three. Student A is a market researcher for an online store which sells books, music and software. Interview Student B about new products or services they might be prepared to pay for. Student C should monitor the question types used, and give Student A feedback at the end of the conversation.

Brainstorming

5 With a partner, brainstorm examples of behaviour from your culture which shows you are *not* listening: think about body language in particular. Then write a checklist of recommended behaviour for active listening.

Internet research

Search for the keywords *reading body language*. Report back to the class on your favourite findings.

Listening for gist

6 🔊 2:09 Listen to a conversation between Irina, an estate agent and Mr Garcia, a potential customer and answer the questions.

1 What are Mr Garcia's reasons for wanting to move?
2 What obstacles will Irina need to overcome to make a sale?
3 How does Irina show she is listening actively?

Listening for detail

7 🔊 2:09 With a partner, complete the useful expressions from the conversation in Exercise 6. Then listen again and check your answers.

Useful expressions: Active listening

Paraphrasing what the other person has said

If I understand _____, you're saying that _____ you'd like …
If I've got this right, the main issue is …

Reflecting what the other person feels

I see. My _____ is that it'll be a wrench for you to leave, am I right?
It sounds to me as if …

Clarifying what the other person has implied

I'm not too _____ about this. What sort of time frame do you have in _____?
I don't quite see what you're getting at. Can you be more specific about …

Echoing what the other person has said

(That's probably too soon.) Too _____?

Not saying anything or just making encouraging sounds

(Well, there's the financial side to think of as well.) _____?

Summarizing what the other person has said

OK, do you mind if I recap? What we've _____ so far is that …
Let's just recap on what you've told me so far.

Focusing on the next step

Now then, what I would _____ is that we start by … Shall we tackle … first?

8 Work with a partner. Suggest improvements to the marketer's responses to a focus group.

A: I have no idea what it is, what it's supposed to do, or why anyone would buy it.
Marketer: (1) Oh, so you like it, but I haven't explained it very well?
B: And with these sharp edges, it's not something you'd want your children to get hold of.
Marketer: (2) You're obviously a neurotically overprotective parent.
C: It's certainly aesthetically uncompromising.
Marketer: (3) You what?
A: To my mind, it's much too expensive.
Marketer: (4) What are you talking about? Don't be ridiculous!
C: Have we helped you gain any valuable insights, then?
Marketer: (5) What, apart from the fact that you think it's poorly explained, dangerous, ugly and overpriced?
B: So, what's next, or have we finished?
Marketer: (6) Certainly not. You can have a bathroom break, then I want you back for more tests.

Discussion

9 Work in groups of three to discuss one of the topics below. Student A should speak about the topic; Student B should facilitate and listen actively; Student C should monitor the conversation and give feedback afterwards.

brands versus no-name products   premium versus no-frills services   quality versus price
market share versus profit   design versus function   marketing versus sales

5.4 Management skills

5 | Marketing and sales

▶ structuring a proposal

▶ reason, purpose and
  concessive clauses

▶ writing a proposal

5.5 Writing   Business proposals

Discussion

1 In groups, decide what sort of proposal you would write for the people below. In what form would you send it and what documents might it contain?

> email   memo   letter   report   contract

> price   work schedule (proposed dates and times)   references   research data   CV
> methodology or proposed plan of action   other attachments (what?)

1 Your boss, after chatting in the canteen about your suggestions for a team-building day for your department.
2 A conference organizer, after reading a call for papers.
3 A customer, after a phone call requesting assistance with technical problems in their workshop.
4 The Ministry of Education, after reading a call for proposals for a research grant.

Model

2 Read the proposal below, and choose the best heading for each section.

> Conclusion   Credentials   Deliverables   Introduction   Objectives   Value

1 _____

As public interest in Paralympic sports has declined in recent years, the National Paralympic Association (NPA) wishes to raise awareness of its activities. Building brand awareness will on the one hand encourage more disabled people to get involved and on the other, boost attendance at Paralympic events.

5 **2** _____

While the NPA's communication budget remains modest, its goal is to reach as wide a public as possible through a viral video campaign, with a view to attracting both participants and spectators. Even if commercial virals have become increasingly common in social media, K2U Video believe the objective is eminently achievable.

10 **3** _____

K2U Video will deliver a three-minute viral video of spectacular moments from Paralympic sports, with the intention of capturing the widest possible audience. The clip will focus on athletic prowess and sporting drama so as to support the message that Paralympic sport is every bit as engaging as able-bodied events. The video will launch in early December so that audiences will peak in time for the summer programme. For
15 the purpose of forecasting attendance and evaluating return on investment, K2U will monitor performance and supply weekly metrics over the period from December to June.

4 _____

Given that visual impact is crucial, we are delighted to confirm that the film will be directed by award-winning Bollywood Director Rajiv Khan. The project will be managed by K2U's founder and Director Philip Boston. Our
20 considerable experience in comparable projects such as flu vaccination and recycling means our proposal offers every guarantee of success. (see attached DVD)

5 _____

The cost of the project will be €525,000. Of this total, half will be met by grants from the regional and national sports councils; a further 20% will be financed by advertising revenues from the NPA website.
25 Although the remaining investment is still significant, our financial proposal demonstrates that the project will more than double revenues from forthcoming events. In other words, the campaign will not only pay for itself, but also trigger improved income over several years. (see appendix C)

6 _____

In conclusion, we recommend this viral campaign as the most cost-effective method of adding value to the
30 Paralympic brand. Spectacular sports like wheelchair rugby and ice-sledge hockey are still relatively unknown to the general public and will have an immediate impact on event attendance; by the same token, we expect numbers of participants to rise steadily as brand awareness improves.

Search for the keywords *how to write an RFP* and compile a list of essential points to include in a request for proposal.

Glossary PAGE 156

concessive clause
credentials
metrics
prowess

Analysis

3 Which section of the proposal explains the following?

1 return on investment
2 project scope and action plan
3 analysis of the current situation
4 key personnel and expertise

4 Which of the phrases a)–c) below demonstrates the following essential messages:

1 **compliance** (satisfying the client's needs)
2 **capability** (the supplier's ability to deliver)
3 **value** (the reasons why this is a good investment)?

a) *The clip will focus on athletic prowess ... as engaging as able-bodied events.* (lines 12–13)
b) *... the campaign will not only pay for itself, ... improved income over several years.* (lines 26–27)
c) *Our considerable experience in comparable projects ... every guarantee of success.* (lines 19–21)

Now identify at least one further example of each in the model.

Language focus

5 Complete the checklist of useful expressions with adverbials from the model.

Reason clauses

because viral videos increase brand awareness, ...
since the sports councils will only fund part of the project, ...
_____ public interest in Paralympic sports has declined ...
_____ that visual impact is crucial, ...

Purpose clauses

in order to optimize return on investment, ...
_____ attracting both participants and spectators.
_____ capturing the widest possible audience.
_____ support the message that ...
_____ audiences will peak in time for the summer programme.
_____ forecasting attendance ...

Concessive clauses

Even though TV coverage of Paralympic sport has increased, ...
_____ the NPA's communication budget remains modest, ...
_____ commercial virals have become increasingly common in social media, ...
_____ the remaining investment is still significant, ...

Output

6 Work with a partner. Write and exchange RFPs (requests for proposal) for one of the situations you discussed in Exercise 1. Then write a proposal answering your partner's RFP, demonstrating compliance, capability and value.

5.5 Writing

- ▶ consumer groups
- ▶ branding and promotion
- ▶ formulating a strategic marketing plan

5.6 Case study **Presnya Taxi**

Discussion

1 In small groups, try to agree on a definition of the characteristics of taxi users.

Within this group of consumers, which sub-categories do you consider are the most attractive for a taxi company to target?

2 Read the advertisement for Presnya Taxi. In your groups, discuss how effective you think it is.

PRESNYA TAXI

Travel in comfort and style with Presnya Taxi!

Fast, reliable transport anywhere in Greater Moscow
Airport transfers a speciality
Friendly English-speaking drivers
Mon – Fri 0600 – 2300
Call (495) 101-52-57

'WE DO BETTER'

Listening

3 🔊 2:10 Listen to a conversation between the owner of Presnya Taxi, Volodya Vasilyev, and his Scottish daughter-in-law, Ally, and answer the questions.

1 Why is Volodya worried?
2 What are the threats to Presnya Taxi's business?
3 What does Ally get Volodya to agree to?

Discussion

4 Work with a partner and discuss the questions.

1 To what extent do you think Presnya Taxi's problems are specific to their market?
2 Do taxi companies in other cities and countries experience similar difficulties?
3 What solutions have they developed?
4 What do you think Ally will suggest?

Reading

5 Read Ally and Andrey's notes and add your own suggestions, comments and answers to their questions. Student A look at Ally's ideas on page 115. Student B look at Andrey's notes on page 117.

Discussion

6 With a partner, share Ally's, Andrey's and your own ideas. Sort them into Strategy options, Branding decisions, Partnering decisions and Promotion options, and discuss how feasible and effective each would be.

Strategy options			
Branding decisions			
Partnering decisions			
Promotion options			

Simulation

7 In groups, hold meetings to discuss the agenda below and decide on a strategy for Presnya Taxi. Remember to use active listening techniques to ensure that everybody's ideas are given a fair hearing.

PRESNYA TAXI

AGENDA

1 *Marketing Strategy.* A new strategy is needed to address a steady fall in turnover in increasingly difficult market conditions.

2 *Branding.* The company's brand no longer offers customers an attractive promise.

3 *Partnering.* The company wishes to explore opportunities for mutually beneficial partnerships.

4 *Promotion.* To support its new strategy and branding, the company requires new promotional ideas.

5 *Any Other Business.*

Internet research

Search for the keywords *limobikes* to find out how this service works. Discuss with a partner how successful it would be in your country.

Presentation

8 Present your group's strategy to the class and answer questions.

6.1 About business Crisis management

Discussion

1 Work in small groups. Do the quiz. Then turn to page 118 to check your answers.

What would you do in these crisis situations?

1 A psychopath puts cyanide in your company's paracetamol capsules; several customers die, and you have to recall 31 million bottles of the product worth over $100 million.
a) relaunch the product under a new name
b) scrap the product and the brand
c) relaunch the brand with tamper-proof packaging

2 A customer complains they found a human finger in your company's chilli con carne.
a) recall the product immediately
b) pay the customer compensation
c) deny any responsibility

3 A host on your company's provocative radio show makes racist remarks.
a) have him make a public apology, but let him continue to host the show
b) fire him and cancel the show
c) fire him, but continue the show with a new, less provocative host

4 A company which is obviously guilty of wrongdoing asks your PR company to help.
a) take the contract
b) refuse the contract
c) take the contract, but charge double your normal fee

Reading

2 Read the extracts from Dezenhall's book, *Damage Control*. Answer the questions.

1 What did the crises cost:
   a) a leading cell phone manufacturer   b) Merck   c) Perrier   d) Audi
   Why does Dezenhall refer to them?
2 How does Dezenhall argue these concepts are relevant for crisis survivors?
1 *strong leaders*	4 *self knowledge*	7 *guarantees*
2 *climate shifts*	5 *luck*	8 *baby steps*
3 *pain thresholds*	6 *feel-good gurus*	9 *the little guy*
3 According to Dezenhall, how has the way we judge a crisis changed?
4 What is the political model of crisis management?
5 How does Dezenhall see the media in general and TV in particular?

Glossary PAGE 156

canard
feel-good guru
pit bull
whistle-blower

Listening for gist

3 🔊 2:11 Listen to an interview with Jack French, journalist at *The Spin Monitor*. According to French, is Eric Dezenhall's reputation in the PR industry justified?

Listening for detail

4 🔊 2:11 Listen again and answer the questions.

1 Explain the meanings and connotations of the following descriptions: *a colourful character, the pit bull of public relations, brass-knuckled, Machiavellian.*
2 As well as PR, what else is Dezenhall known for?
3 Did Dezenhall attack or defend the following? The chemicals industry, the precautionary principle, Greenpeace, the Open Access movement, Exxon Mobile, the Publishers' Association.
4 What does French tell us about Qorvis Communications and Sitrick & Co.?
5 How successful is Dezenhall's damage control strategy, according to French?
6 What two reasons does French give to explain Dezenhall's discretion about his work on behalf of his firm's clients?

Internet research

Search for the keywords *bad crisis management.* Share your stories and vote for the best example of how not to handle a crisis.

Discussion

5 In small groups, discuss the questions.

1 *In our culture, whoever attacks, wins, whoever defends, loses.* Is this a sad indictment of American culture, a more global phenomenon, or a misleading exaggeration?
2 Do you think there are circumstances in which PR firms should defend companies that pollute the environment, exploit workers or market defective products?

DAMAGE CONTROL

Crisis management, while a rare corporate discipline, is nevertheless a fundamental one because the future of the enterprise is on the line. A grieving widower appeared on Larry King Live in 1992 and speculated that his wife's
5 terminal cancer was caused by a cellular telephone: a leading cellphone manufacturer saw its stock drop by 20 per cent in the following days. Merck's recall of its arthritis drug Vioxx cost the company roughly $750 million in the fourth quarter of 2005 alone. A Merrill Lynch stock
10 analyst estimated that damages against the company could run between $4 billion and $18 billion. Perrier was toppled from its perch atop the best-selling bottled water mountaintop after the chemical benzene was found in its product. And when the Audi 5000 was accused of 'sudden
15 acceleration', its sales evaporated and the Audi brand essentially vanished from the US market for a decade.

WHO SURVIVES?

Companies (and individuals) that survive crises tend to have certain features in common, features that are often
20 evident in the first moments of an engagement.
- *They have strong leaders* who have broad authority to make decisions.
- *They question conventional PR wisdom* and do not worship at the altar of feel-good gurus who espouse
25 'reputation management', the canard that corporate redemption follows popularity.
- *They are flexible*, changing course when the operating climate shifts (which it usually does).
- *They commit significant resources* to the resolution of a
30 crisis with absolutely no guarantee that these resources will provide results.
- *They have a high threshold for pain*, recognizing that things may get worse before they get better.
- *They think in terms of baby steps*, not grandiose
35 gestures, which explains Rome's success, after all.
- *They know themselves*, and are honest about what kinds of actions their culture can – and cannot – sustain.

- *They believe that corporate defence is an exercise in moral authority*, and that their critics are not necessarily
40 virtuous simply because they purport to be standing up for 'the little guy'.
- *They are lucky*, often catching unexpected breaks delivered by God, nature, fortune, or some other independent factor.

45 Enterprises and individuals under siege need all the help they can get these days. Since the tech bubble burst and corporate scandals have come to fill the media vacuum once occupied by lionizing of messianic CEOs, it seems as if no one's exempt from hostile scrutiny. Crises are now
50 judged not only by financial (Did the company recover?) and ethical (Was the public welfare served?) standards, but by whether the company handled its crisis effectively in the eyes of Wall Street, Madison Avenue, the plaintiff's bar, and twenty-four-hour-a-day cable news. Inevitably, the
55 airwaves are filled with experts from various fields who will opine that the crisis is being mismanaged. (Saying 'all's well' doesn't make for very good TV.)

We endorse a political model of crisis management versus the more conventional public relations approach.
60 The fundamental difference is that the political model, which is practiced in our hometown of Washington, D.C., assumes the threat of motivated adversaries while the public relations model tends to view crises as organic and resolvable through good communications. In real crises
65 there are often opponents – a mirror image of your own crisis management team – that want to torpedo you. That opposing team consists of competitors, plaintiffs' lawyers, the news media, politicians and regulators, short-sellers, multi-million dollar non-governmental organizations
70 (NGOs), corporate stalkers, whistle-blowers and bloggers. These opponents don't care whether you 'do the right thing'; they care about defeating you.

'Companies that survive crises tend to have certain features in common.'

6 | Risk management

6.2 Vocabulary **Risk management and digital risk**

'Risk is good. Not properly managing your risk is a dangerous leap.'
EVEL KNIEVEL

Glossary **PAGE 157**

cease and desist order
ERM

Brainstorming

1 Work with a partner. You have opened a small coffee shop next to a university. Brainstorm a list of possible risks that you may need to manage. Try to sort your list into categories.

Reading

2 Read the article and answer the questions.

1 Does the article refer to any risks you didn't think of in Exercise 1?
2 What four categories of risk are mentioned?
3 What three strategic advantages of Enterprise Risk Management (ERM) are discussed?

Enterprise RISK Management

by Joanne Sammer

Although most companies have their bases covered should they meet with fire, theft or flood, such hazards represent only a small portion of the myriad risks they face. A survey of the Fortune 1000 found that 58% of companies that suffered a stock drop traced it to strategic risks, most commonly competitive pressures and a customer shortfall. Operational risks accounted for losses at 31% of the companies, and the remaining 11% attributed their losses to financial risks. None of the businesses cited hazard risks as the reason for their losses.
To begin dealing proactively with financial, operational and strategic risks, organizations can adopt enterprise risk management (ERM). In a nutshell, ERM allows organizations to examine all the risks they face, measure the potential impact of those risks on the long-term viability of the company, and take the appropriate steps to manage or mitigate those risks. In general, the range of risks most businesses face includes hazard risks, such as property damage and theft; financial risks, such as interest rate and foreign exchange fluctuations; operational risks, such as supply chain problems or cost overruns; and strategic risks, such as misaligned products. The key to ERM success is to address all those risks in an integrated fashion. ERM is a compelling tool for a number of reasons. First, the process of identifying, quantifying and prioritizing risks makes them more prominent and real to executives and managers who may not have given risk management significant thought before. Second, a holistic approach to risk management takes the entire concept beyond the traditional parameters of what is insurable. It greatly expands the company's definition of risk to include anything that threatens the organization's continuity. This approach also divides the concept of risk into those risks that can help a company grow and those that will only lead to loss. Risk identification at the level of granular detail is not necessary and can even be detrimental to a thoughtful ERM effort. 'If a risk does not impact company performance, don't look at it,' says a risk management consultant. 'If someone smashes a company car, it is probably not material to business performance.'

3 Read the article again and <u>underline</u> all the risks it mentions. Sort them into hazard risks, strategic risks, operational risks and financial risks.

4 Unscramble these verbs from the article which collocate with the noun *risk*.

1 acef	2 adel hitw	3 aeeimnx	4 aaegmn
5 aegiimtt	6 defiinty	7 afinqtuy	8 eiiioprrtz

Describing risks

5 Mark these verbs and expressions from the article *a*, *b* or *c* according to their function.

| a) linking losses to risks   b) characterizing risk   c) taking action |

1 to trace to ☐
2 to take the appropriate steps ☐
3 to threaten the organization's continuity ☐
4 to account for ☐
5 to have one's bases covered ☐
6 to impact company performance ☐
7 to cite as the reason for ☐
8 to identify risk at the level of granular detail ☐
9 to be material to business performance ☐
10 to attribute to ☐
11 to measure the potential impact ☐
12 to have an impact on the long-term viability of the company ☐

6 Use words and expressions from Exercises 4 and 5 to fill in the spaces in the text.

All techniques for (1) _____ with risk belong to one or more of Dorfman's four Ts:

TOLERATE: a viable strategy for small risks which are not (2) _____ to business performance. It may also be appropriate if their probability can be quantified as very small, or if insurance would (3) _____ for such high expenditure that it would impact company performance more than the risk itself.

TREAT: this means identifying methods that (4) _____ the severity of the loss, and taking the appropriate (5) _____ to reduce any impact on the long-term (6) _____ of the company.

TERMINATE: avoiding risk completely can be (7) _____ as the reason for choosing not to enter a market or accept an order; however, if this also means not earning profit, it may in fact threaten the organization's (8) _____ more than (9) _____ an acceptable level of risk.

TRANSFER: some risks may be transferred to another party, for example, by insurance. However, companies that may think they have their (10) _____ covered by outsourcing business processes need to measure the potential (11) _____ of new risks they may (12) _____ as a result.

Listening

7 What specific risks do you think e-businesses are vulnerable to? Brainstorm a list.

8 🔊 2:12 Listen to an interview with Steve Leach, Managing Director of Brand Intelligence and answer the questions.

1 What are 'passing off', 'cybersquatting', 'hacking' and 'protest issues'?
2 How does Brand Intelligence stop this type of abuse?

9 Use words from the box to fill in the spaces in the paragraph.

| abuse   desist   issue   litigate   monitor   perpetrators   pursue   reversal |

When they locate areas of brand risk, damage and (1) _____, Brand Intelligence track (2) _____, initiate (3) _____ and then (4) _____ progress. When necessary, they will (5) _____ 'cease and (6) _____' orders, and in the worst cases, (7) _____ for damages or (8) _____ criminal and civil action.

10 You also heard these words in the interview. Which does not belong in each group?

1 masquerading, freeloading, trading, defacing, cracking
2 boycott, infringe, bombard, scan, pirate
3 open, exposed, malicious, vulnerable, defenceless

Discussion

11 Work in small groups. You work for Imports Unlimited, a Web-based company that imports low-cost popular consumer goods from China.

Consider the various strategic, operational, financial and digital risks you face, and the strategies and techniques you would employ to manage them.

Present your plan to the class.

6 | Risk management

6.3 Grammar Perspective and stance

Listening for perspective

1 🔊 2:13 Listen to an interview with Li Bai, an expert on risk management. <u>Underline</u> the perspectives below which are explicitly mentioned. Are any other perspectives implicit?

> economic cultural political financial business global individual banking ethical human psychological historical managerial philosophical environmental

2 🔊 2:13 Listen again for expressions which indicate the speaker's perspective, and fill in the spaces with their exact words.

1 Risk management is the attention that organizations must pay _____ to things that can and do go wrong.
2 _____, if somebody is a bad risk, you would not lend them money.
3 _____, they never studied the likely behavioural responses.
4 _____, some of the banks saw the problem coming.
5 So _____ this affected everyone?
6 _____, you can see the logic.

Reading for stance

3 Work with a partner. Read the texts opposite and identify the writer's stance, choosing from one or more of the possibilities in the box below.

> tentative confident optimistic pessimistic apologetic subjective objective critical sarcastic sceptical

Identifying stance expressions

4 Work with a partner. Read the texts again and <u>underline</u> the language which indicates the writer or speaker's stance. Match each expression with one or more of the attitudes in the box above.

In text A, *seem likely to continue* is fairly tentative, but *across the board* is essentially confident ...

TEXT A:

> **OPINION**
>
> Prices of commodities seem likely to continue rising across the board in the foreseeable future. In the current climate of rising inflation generally there remains little doubt that the impact on households' real wealth, not to mention their rapidly deteriorating mood, will be wholly unpleasant. In my view, the government's reputation for economic competence is now in tatters.

TEXT B:

To make matters worse for the beleaguered Minister, it now emerges that the tough new business regulations she is now promoting so forcefully were originally proposed not by her own government but by the opposition. Surely that is an example of hypocrisy, is it not? It is little wonder that voters are increasingly confused over where the latest feel-good policy is coming from.

TEXT C:

On balance, it could be argued that the likelihood of the enterprise succeeding seems somewhat limited. While there are some grounds for optimism with regard to the technology actually functioning correctly, considerable doubts remain over the ability of the project to withstand the probable risks which may lie ahead.

CONFIDENTIAL

TEXT D:

While the company makes every effort to ensure that our products reach you in perfect condition, on this occasion we recognize that our standards clearly fell short of your expectations. We therefore have no hesitation in offering you a full refund plus a voucher which you may use in part-payment for a future purchase. We remain confident that you will be completely happy with our products in future.

Expressing stance

5 Rewrite the sentences below to express the stance given in *italics*.

1 Investing in emerging markets is rewarding. *Tentative*
   In certain circumstances investing in emerging markets can be rewarding if you have a healthy appetite for risk.
2 Your risk management plan is arguably full of holes. *Confident*
3 In fact, the strategy has been exceptionally successful. *Tentative*
4 Prices are definitely going to rise. *Tentative*
5 If I may say so, you could have paid more attention to the risks involved. *Critical*
6 On the whole, there are good reasons to suppose that the product is beginning to take hold. *Confident*
7 I would doubt the likelihood of the same thing happening twice. *Objective*
8 Arguably mistakes were made, but some useful lessons have been learned. *Subjective and apologetic*
9 For the most part, we seem to have maintained a reasonable level of sales, although we cannot be certain about the immediate future. *Confident, objective and* pessimistic

Speaking

6 In small groups, take turns to improvise a one-minute presentation on a risk of your choice, choosing an identifiable stance. At the end of one minute, the others have to identify your stance.

Glossary PAGE 157

property ladder

6 | Risk management

6.4 Management skills Communicating in a crisis

Discussion

1 You organized a New Year's party and several guests have been injured by fireworks and taken to hospital. How do you deal with the press?

Mark this advice ✓ = I agree, ✗ = I disagree or ? = it depends.

1 When journalists phone you, say you are too busy to speak to them. ☐
2 Smile for the cameras as you walk to your car; after all, nobody has died. ☐
3 At the press conference, emphasize how successful the party was in raising money for charity. ☐
4 When a journalist says local fire regulations were ignored, tell her she is mistaken. ☐
5 When journalists claim guests threw fireworks from table to table, ask them who told them that. ☐
6 When asked how much compensation the injured guests will receive, give an optimistic figure. ☐

Work in small groups and compare your answers.

Reading

2 Read the article and choose *Do* or *Don't*. Which pieces of advice apply to the situation in Exercise 1?

'It will never happen to me'

The first myth to strangle at birth is that crises only happen to other people. Like so many other business skills, the essence of communicating in a crisis is preparation; if you're convinced it's not going to happen, you're unlikely to have prepared for the worst. Admittedly, you may never find yourself being questioned on prime time TV about why your government is doing nothing to stop refugees starving to death, or why your company allowed toxic chemicals to leak into the water supply. But sooner or later, you almost certainly *will* find yourself facing questions about why your project is behind schedule, or why you can't deliver your customer's order. In every case, following a few simple dos and don'ts can make life a lot easier.

1 Do/Don't prepare – for the questions you want to answer, those you can't answer, and especially for the ones you really *don't* want to answer. Find out what your opponents are saying, and prepare an answer for that too. Have an answer ready for everything.
2 Do/Don't be led where you don't want to go: as long as you provide relevant information, there is no need to answer leading or trick questions.
3 Do/Don't build bridges from questions you don't want to answer so that you can give the answers you want to.
4 Do/Don't use sound bite techniques: indicate that you are going to summarize the essentials, leave a brief pause to focus attention, then deliver your key message in 20 seconds or less.
5 Do/Don't be drawn into speculating about outcomes for which there is no evidence.
6 Do/Don't formulate your ideas in negative terms; always use positives.
7 Do/Don't use alliteration and groups of two or three words to reinforce your key messages.
8 Do/Don't use analogies or stories to explain difficult or technical concepts.

Listening

3 🔊 2:14–2:21 Listen to extracts from eight interviews in crisis situations. What situations are being discussed, and which of the tips in Exercise 2 are, or are not, being applied?

4 🔊 2:14–2:21 Listen again and complete the key phrases.

1 Running a business without risk management _____ _____ walking a tightrope.
2 It's a _____ question, but I think the bigger _____ here is really …
3 Even more _____ _____ _____, the new machines will improve precision, productivity and profitability.
4 Let's _____ on the _____, shall we?
5 The really _____ thing to _____ is that talks are underway.
6 Let's not _____ that _____ _____ there is no evidence of patients suffering any ill effects.
7 Let me _____ _____ _____ the current position.
8 We are _____ _____ that the commission will report that there was no wrongdoing.

Alliteration

5 Find suitable words to complete these examples of alliteration and grouping.

1 The new factory will be bigger, brighter and _____.
2 Holidaymakers will always come to our islands in search of sea, sand and _____.
3 Our goal is to become Britain's best _____.
4 The company intends to fulfil its obligations to shareholders, suppliers and _____.
5 We believe better people make better _____.
6 Our restaurants use only the finest and freshest _____ available.
7 We aim to give every child a _____ home, a healthy family and a hopeful future.
8 The company is making every _____ to reduce _____.

Analogies

6 Match the two halves of these analogies.

1 Life is like an onion,
2 Starting a business is like bungee jumping,
3 Running a company is like playing tennis,
4 Job interviews are like dating,
5 An insurance policy is like old underwear,
6 Managing a crisis is like playing a musical instrument,

a) except they keep moving the net and changing the slope of the court.
b) the gaps in its cover are only shown by accident.
c) you peel it off one layer at a time, and sometimes you weep.
d) the more you practise, the better you get.
e) everybody oversells themselves.
f) only one isn't certain if the cord is short enough.

7 With a partner, suggest your own ideas for these analogies.

1 Learning English is like ...
2 Giving a media interview is like ...
3 Deadlines are like ...
4 Crises are like ...

Speaking

8 Work in pairs. Prepare to be interviewed about one of the crisis situations below.

- Try to foresee the questions you will be asked, and how you will answer them.
- Prepare what you will say in response to questions you cannot answer.
- Prepare the main message you would like to convey, and formulate a 20-second sound bite.
- Try to think of an analogy and/or alliteration to use which will make it more memorable.

1 A cook at your restaurant has been taken to hospital with a suspected tropical disease.
2 Police have raided your football club to investigate rumours of financial irregularities.
3 Some of the futuristic office chairs your company makes have collapsed, injuring users.
4 Your building company has not paid 50 immigrant workers' salaries for the last three months.
5 Your airline has cancelled all flights due to bad weather. Thousands of angry customers are stranded.
6 Your nightclub is said to refuse entry to certain people on the grounds of their physical appearance.

9 Work in small groups. Take turns to be interviewed by the rest of the group about the crisis you have prepared for.

- ▶ structuring a report
- ▶ key expressions for corporate reports
- ▶ making recommendations

Discussion

'In an age of mobile communications and video conferencing, when 160 characters are considered sufficient to convey the majority of important messages, a written report printed out on paper no longer serves any conceivable useful purpose.'

1 Do you agree? How many good reasons can you think of for writing a report rather than making a multimedia presentation?

Model

2 Read the extracts from a report below and answer the questions.

1 What problem is Chocsome Inc. facing?
2 What is the risk a) to consumers and b) to the company?
3 What are the pros and cons of each of the three options considered in the report?
4 What are the report's key conclusions and recommendations?

To: AL REYNOLDS, PRESIDENT, CHOCSOME INC.
From: CARLY STROSS, VINGE CONSULTING
Subject: RESPONSE TO LINDANE ALLEGATIONS

This report was commissioned by the Board of Chocsome Inc., in response to media reports that 'Spiral' chocolate bars could contain traces of the pesticide Lindane. Based on extensive scenario modelling, the report's purpose is to recommend a marketing strategy taking into account potential risks, costs and benefits. (...)

Research conducted jointly by Chocsome laboratories and the Jasinski Hospital clearly demonstrates that the tiny traces of Lindane found in Spiral pose absolutely no risk to health. Although an international ban on the agricultural use of Lindane has been in place since 2009, it seems likely that a limited number of West African cocoa farms are still using residual stocks. Unfortunately, focus groups left little doubt that, should public awareness be raised by the current wave of media attention, the impact on sales, on the brand and on Chocsome's image could be severely detrimental. (...)

We therefore identified three main scenarios for research. In scenario A, we posit the immediate recall of all stock and withdrawal of Spiral from the market. Scenario B would issue a categorical denial of any public health risk and launch a legal counterattack on prominent media channels for libellous allegations. In scenario C, we study the effect of gradually phasing out Spiral and rebranding the product. (...)

In the light of the above findings, we reached the following conclusions. Although scenario A is the only option that could satisfactorily terminate the risk, the opportunity cost is extremely high for very few other benefits. We therefore have no hesitation in ruling out this strategy. On the basis of the evidence presented above, strategy B, assuming it was successful, would present the greatest benefits in terms of preserving the brand and the current revenue stream. However, the risk of public opinion turning against us is unacceptably high, and would appear to be impossible to treat or transfer; reluctantly, we have little choice but to reject this hypothesis. This leaves option C, which has the potential to be a successful strategy, provided we can minimize claims against Spiral and successfully introduce the replacement brand; our cost/risk/benefit studies suggest that, on balance, it offers the best compromise. (...)

We therefore recommend that option C be implemented as quickly as possible. A task force comprising representatives from marketing, sales, production and supply chain should be set up immediately in order to update and validate existing plans for rebranding and phasing out Spiral. The next step is to persuade consumers to switch to the new brand without losing sales. Clearly timing is critical, but we remain confident that, in the medium to long term, this strategy will maintain or even improve Chocsome's market share. (...)

Analysis

3 Number these sections in the order they appear in the report:

☐ Conclusions ☐ Findings ☐ Recommendations ☐ Introduction

4 The phrases in the box convey the writer's *stance* towards the things they are writing about (i.e. how they feel about them). Match the phrases with the things they refer to 1–5.

> we have no hesitation in   it seems likely that   we remain confident that
> we have little choice but to   left little doubt that

1   where the traces of Lindane come from   3   strategy A   5   strategy C
2   how consumers might react   4   strategy B

Can you modify the phrases so that they show a different stance towards the fact or event reported?

It seems unlikely that …

Language focus

5 Complete the checklist of key expressions from the model. Choose a heading from Exercise 3 for each group of phrases.

Useful expressions: Corporate reports

_____

This report was _____ by the Board of Chocsome Inc. _____ on extensive scenario modelling, …
the report's _____ is to recommend a marketing strategy

_____

In the light of the above findings, we _____ the following conclusions.
On the _____ of the evidence presented above …
which has the _____ to be a successful strategy, provided we can …

_____

Research conducted … clearly _____ that …
the _____ on sales … could be severely detrimental
We therefore _____ three main scenarios …

_____

We therefore _____ that option C be implemented …
A task force … _____ be set up immediately
The next _____ is to persuade consumers to switch to the new brand

6 Choose the best option to complete each sentence.

1   _____ we face similar problems in the future, we would withdraw the product. (must, should, need)
2   Our second option _____ the existence of a new, unexploited market niche. (doubts, claims, posits)
3   The CEO _____ a categorical denial of covering up risks to human health. (issued, expressed, made)
4   Scrapping the product launch would effectively _____ the risk. (treat, transfer, terminate)
5   New, stricter legislation means we have to _____ this option. (rule out, cut out, strike out)
6   Unless we can treat the risk we will be forced to _____ this hypothesis. (deny, decline, reject)
7   On _____, this option offers the best compromise. (average, balance, whole)
8   We recommend this strategy _____ immediately. (to implement, implementing, be implemented)

Output

7 In small groups, discuss the situations below. What are the possible risks? What options do you have and what are their advantages and disadvantages?

1   Your pharmaceutical firm has been accused of overpricing drugs in developing countries. In fact, you charge less than 50% of Western prices.
2   A newspaper report claims your football club's stadium is not safe for more than 20,000 people. You regularly have attendances of over 40,000 fans. In fact, you have an excellent safety record.
3   Your film studio has been accused of cruelty by animal rights campaigners. In fact, you take great care of any animals that appear in films; any dangerous scenes are computer generated.

8 Choose one of the situations in Exercise 7; write a short report in which you introduce the situation, invent details of your findings and options, explain your conclusions and recommend a solution.

Internet research

Search for the keywords *risk matrix* to learn how to use this tool to assess potential risks. Draw up a risk matrix for any risky activity you are involved in and write a short report making recommendations for managing the risks.

Glossary   PAGE 157

libellous
opportunity cost
posit

6.6 Case study Périgord Gourmet

Foie gras, or fattened goose liver, is a traditional French delicacy which is exported all over the world. However, it is a subject of controversy, since geese are force-fed in the last two weeks of their lives. Animal rights campaigners claim this is cruel to the birds, and the production of foie gras (though not its sale) is banned in countries like the UK, Germany, the Czech Republic, Finland, Luxembourg, Norway, Poland, Sweden, Switzerland, Denmark and Israel.

Discussion

1 In small groups, discuss how you would feel about working for the companies below.

- a pharmaceuticals laboratory that conducts animal tests
- a kangaroo-leather sports shoe manufacturer
- a circus with performing animals
- an egg farm with battery hens
- a pet shop
- a 'foie gras' distributor

Reading

INTERNET

Périgord GOURMET

Order your favourite treats direct from south-west France
Foie gras, Pâtés, Snails, Frogs' legs, Mushrooms, Truffles, Chestnuts, Jams

All our products are sourced from free-range organic farms and cooked to traditional Périgord recipes.

Delivery worldwide
Click here to order
All major credit cards accepted

PG'S MARKETS:
- France 48%
- Far East 23%
- North America 17%
- Europe & Russia 12%

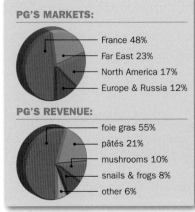

PG'S REVENUE:
- foie gras 55%
- pâtés 21%
- mushrooms 10%
- snails & frogs 8%
- other 6%

... no longer tolerate this deliberate and unashamed cruelty to geese and ducks! Unless you withdraw all foie gras products immediately, we will not hesitate to take direct action against you, your suppliers, contractors or customers in order to protect these defenceless animals.

| **Farms:** breeding and fattening | ▶ | **Slaughterhouse:** (additional livers imported from Hungary) | ▶ | **Processing plant:** cooking, packing, labelling | ▶ | **Warehouse:** stock and shipping | ▶ | **Forwarder:** express courier to customer |

2 Work with a partner. You work for Périgord Gourmet's (PG) new Risk Management Department. Read the documents about PG's operations, and a message received from an anonymous animal rights group. Discuss whether the statements are *T* (true), *F* (false) or *N* (neither).

1. PG produce foie gras by force-feeding geese. ☐
2. Customers in the UK and Germany cannot buy PG's foie gras. ☐
3. Most of PG's customers are in Europe. ☐
4. The extremist animal rights group is threatening to sabotage production of foie gras. ☐
5. The most vulnerable link in the production chain is the processing plant. ☐
6. Withdrawing foie gras completely would mean making half of PG's staff redundant. ☐

Discussion

3 Work in small groups. Brainstorm the potential risks for the company. Consider the impact each risk might have on the company's long-term future, and decide how to react to each risk.

	Risk	Impact	Tolerate	Treat	Terminate	Transfer
Hazard risks *e.g. fire*						
Financial risks *e.g. exchange rates*						
Operational risks *e.g. supply chain problems*						
Strategic risks *e.g. changes in legislation*						

Compare your ideas with other groups.

Internet research

Search for the keywords *animal enterprise terrorism act*. List the arguments for and against this type of legislation, and hold a class debate.

Listening

4 🌐 2:22 One month later, Pierre-Yves Gaget, PG's founder and owner, receives a call from the US. Listen to the conversation and answer the questions.

1 Who does the caller work for?
2 What has happened?
3 What two questions does she ask?
4 What is the suspected cause of the problem?

Discussion

5 Work in groups. Discuss the implications of what you have learned; consider the notes Pierre-Yves Gaget has made, as well as your own ideas. How should Périgord Gourmet handle the crisis?

> *poisoned foie gras, or some other food or drink?*
> *isolated incident? coincidence, or first case in a campaign?*
> *warn customers or wait for more information?*
> *try to keep it quiet, or pre-empt with a press conference?*
> *recall all products, only foie gras, or none?*
> *stop shipments, or all production?*
> *accuse animal rights group without proof, or wait for police investigation?*
> *give in and stop selling foie gras, or fight?*

Listening

6 🌐 2:23 Listen to a voicemail message from Pierre-Yves Gaget and answer the questions.

1 What is the good news?   2 What is the bad news?   3 What does he want you to do?

7 In your groups, prepare your statement.

- Prepare the main message you would like to convey, and formulate a 20-second sound bite.
- Try to foresee the questions you will be asked, and how you will answer them.
- Prepare what you will say in response to questions you cannot answer.

Simulation

8 Each group should make its statement and take questions from the rest of the class (in the role of journalists).

Take a vote to decide which group handled the crisis best.

6.6 Case study

Review 5

1 Put the words in the right order to make meaningful questions.

1 comes do from branding you think where
2 you what seems marketing less than whose can strategy attractive offer
3 competition your brand differentiate strategy how from you does the
4 define or characteristics group socioeconomic which a demographic
5 power is you when what strategy say do you mean
6 than strategic firefighting is why a choice better thinking
7 compete to you are how supposed then
8 you that succeed what can you would do ensure

2 Fill in the spaces with an appropriate preposition from the box.

> across   except   in accordance with   in the light of
> on account of   until   without   with regard to

1 The next step in our restructuring process is to make changes right _____ the board.
2 Trading conditions had been beginning to pick up, _____ recently that is.
3 Your concerns over safety, let me reassure you, are entirely _____ foundation.
4 You shouldn't use company premises, _____ to conduct company business.
5 Our regional offices are to be closed _____ the increasingly dangerous civil war there.
6 Your role is to make sure we operate strictly _____ current regulations.
7 I propose we now redesign our brochures _____ the recent logo and website changes.
8 _____ the latest sales figures, exactly how bad do you think they are?

3 Find six matching pairs of words from the box below which have similar meanings.

> adapt   additional   concerns   constitutes   create
> devise   forms   hikes   increases   supplementary
> tailor   worries

4 Choose the word or phrase from the box which collocates with all the words in each set. Two words are not needed.

> a brand   an impression   appeal   a solution   prices
> question   text

1 tailor   market   endorse   develop   _____
2 give   foster   create   make   _____
3 premium   inflated   all-inclusive   competitive   _____
4 emotional   youth   national   financial   _____
5 supplementary   closed   trick   leading   _____
6 coherent   academic   promotional   predictive   _____
7 find   evaluate   provide   develop   _____

5 In each group of five match the sentence beginnings with the correct endings.

1 OK, ladies and gentlemen, step one is to elicit ☐
2 And the ultimate aim, of course, is for you to close ☐
3 When formulating a strategy, choose the one which is best suited ☐
4 At some stage during the conversation you should confirm ☐
5 If possible without them realizing it, bring ☐
6 Along the way keep thinking of ways of overcoming ☐
7 One useful technique which can prevent misunderstanding later is to paraphrase ☐
8 You may not wish to, but you may have to compromise ☐
9 By listening more effectively you can gain ☐
10 You may find your potential customers recommending ☐

a) your customers round to the idea that they need your product or service, even if they don't.
b) to the desired purpose.
c) from the customer their perception of your brand.
d) that what you believe you have been told is what the other person actually believes they said.
e) the sale on the best possible terms.

f) on price, especially in the toughest markets.
g) what the person has said using your own words.
h) that the product be modified.
i) a valuable insight into your client's mindset.
j) the main obstacles to closing the deal.

6 Match each response technique 1–7 with its function from the box below.

> clarifying   echoing   focusing on the next step
> not saying anything   paraphrasing
> reflecting what the other person feels   summarizing

1 I'm not too clear about this. What sort of revision did you have in mind?
2 As you say, too quickly, too carelessly and too pointlessly.
3 If I understand correctly, you're saying that basically we've got the strategy wrong.
4 OK then, what I would say is that we now go for a whole new marketing plan.
5 I see. My guess is that you'll find joining even harder than leaving.
6 Right, could I just recap? What we've established so far is that you're unhappy with your line manager.
7 Mmm. Uh-huh. Yeah.

Review 6

Risk management

1 Cross out the verb in each set of four which does not collocate with the noun on the right.

1 *relaunch refuse take cancel* the contract
2 *recommend adopt follow recover* a new strategy
3 *apply fight reduce double* your fee
4 *recall relaunch occupy damage* the product
5 *refer deny take on delegate* responsibility
6 *survive exploit practise manage* the crisis
7 *defend influence speculate see* the media
8 *guarantee commit defend improve* results

2 Complete the text with the words in the box.

> based on   commissioned   conclusion   demonstrate
> identified   impact   purpose   recommend   respond
> rule out   terminate

This confidential report on our response to the discovery of tiny traces of lycomethane sulphate in our 'Pure Source' water has been (1) _____ by our Board of Directors. Its (2) _____ is to decide the future of the brand and (3) _____ a post-crisis marketing strategy. We have (4) _____ three possible ways forward. The first is that we keep the product on the market and continue as before. (5) _____ extensive testing and research, we have incontrovertible proof that such minute traces of lycomethane pose absolutely no danger to health. However, the (6) _____ on sales since media coverage of the discovery began has been devastating. The fate of other brands who have suffered similar PR scares in the food and beverage industry, for example the Chocsome Lindane scandal (7) _____ what is likely to happen if we fail to (8) _____ to public opinion. We are therefore obliged to (9) _____ the option of keeping 'Pure Source' brand on the market. The choices remaining to us are either to rebrand 'Pure Source' and re-launch it in due course or to (10) _____ the product line altogether. Due to the disappointing sales of Pure Source even before the crisis, we have reached the (11) _____ that the latter option – that of discontinuing the product – is the best course of action.

3 Match the sentence beginnings with the correct endings.

1 The company's problems can be ☐
2 What we must now do is take ☐
3 She cited ☐
4 In my view, our success is directly attributable ☐
5 It would be very difficult to measure ☐
6 Of paramount importance is that we have our bases ☐
7 You have got to guard against anything that threatens ☐
8 OK, step one, identify the major ☐

a) risks and assess their levels of seriousness.
b) conflicting advice as the reason for failing to act appropriately.
c) the impact such a policy might have on perceptions of our brand.
d) to our planning and commitment to strategic growth.
e) traced back to the period two years ago when insufficient checks and balances were in place.

f) covered at all times to prevent damage.
g) drastic steps to reduce our exposure to that market.
h) our company's good standing in the eyes of our clients.

4 Put an appropriate word from the box into each space to complete the following text.

> abuse   bombarded   damage   identify   impact
> monitor   resources   strategy   tolerate   vulnerable

In a world where consumers and companies are often (1) _____ with advice on risk, we would all benefit from a clear-headed examination of what really constitutes risk and what is simply scaremongering and fear. Some parties, notably insurance companies and special policies sales people, have been known to (2) _____ the position of trust that they have with the consumer. Such unscrupulous operators prey on (3) _____ people such as the elderly. This is unfortunate, for we all have to (4) _____ a certain degree of risk or we would simply never get out of bed in the morning, and if one thing is certain it is that we cannot insure against every eventuality. What, then, is to be done? First of all, it is wise to have a clear (5) _____. Just as companies (6) _____ potential risks and put in place ways of dealing with them, individuals too can take steps to work out low-cost strategies to deal with risk. A key consideration here is to closely (7) _____ one's situation: things can change as we get older, and different situations require tailored solutions. A singer, for example, depends on their voice for their livelihood more than most professions, and would be well advised to insure against any (8) _____ to their voice. Such an eventuality would severely (9) _____ on their earning potential. Given limited (10) _____, prioritizing this particular insurance product might have to take precedence over more conventional insurance needs such as property.

5 Decide whether the adverb in each of the following sentences is a typical collocation or not. Mark the sentences as either correct or incorrect.

1 On the issue of individual accountability for personal decisions taken I tremendously agree. ☐
2 While I am abroad I expect you to keep me fully informed of any important developments. ☐
3 As we now know she is wholly innocent of any wrongdoing, we owe her a formal apology. ☐
4 I am beginning to believe that what they told me about their market share was necessarily misleading. ☐
5 At least he's honest – he openly admits to having had a part in the deception. ☐
6 'Acts of God' are simply believed to be unpreventable, but in some cases it can be the actions of humans that contribute to their devastating effect. ☐
7 In actual fact it is not explicitly obvious what your main argument is. ☐
8 The company remains forcefully committed to outstanding service. ☐

- ▶ investment banking
- ▶ free vs. regularized markets

7.1 About business   Investment banks

Discussion

1 Your bank might use your money in different ways. Which of the following are you happy with? Why? Why not?

1 lending to private individuals
2 lending to businesses
3 lending to other banks
4 lending to the government
5 lending to other countries
6 trading in foreign currencies
7 trading in gold and other commodities
8 speculating on the stock market
9 speculating on the property market
10 buying and selling debt from and to other banks

Scan reading

2 Read *Investment banks – heroes or zeroes?* quickly. Which paragraphs answer the following questions?

1 What is the popular image of what investment bankers do?
2 Why have investment banks become controversial?
3 Do investment banks use private individuals' money to speculate?
4 Why are investment bankers paid huge bonuses?
5 Which part of investment banks' activities are many people uncomfortable with?
6 How do investment banks assist large companies?

Reading for detail

3 Read the article again. What are the banks' counter-arguments to the following criticisms?

1 Investment bankers are just brokers who take unjustifiably large cuts on investment in industry.
2 Investment banks charge enormous sums for just giving advice on a few balance sheets.
3 It is unethical for investment banks to speculate on commodity, exchange and derivatives markets.
4 Investment banks should be spun off from retail banks to avoid access to individual customers' cash.
5 No individual, however competent, should be paid millions when taxpayers are involuntary shareholders.

Listening

4 🔘 2:24 Listen to an interview where Barry Elliot, a financial journalist, talks about why a free market doesn't work for banks. Why does Barry feel greater regulation is needed?

5 🔘 2:24 Listen again. What does Barry say about the following?

1 how business deals work in a free market
2 why such deals usually work well
3 paying salesmen on the number of sales made
4 the role of banks and bankers in the sub-prime crisis
5 what happened if debtors couldn't pay
6 bankers personal risk
7 why salesmen are not in fact paid on the number of sales made
8 letting banks go bankrupt

Discussion

6 In groups, discuss the following points.

1 Heroes of investment and growth, or zeroes of greed and selfishness? What is your view of investment banks and bankers?
2 Should politicians weigh in and force universal banks to sell off their investment banking divisions?
3 In your opinion, are there individuals in any field whose skills really justify 'Himalayan' pay packages? Should there be salary caps, disincentives for companies that pay excessive bonuses, or a 'millionaire' tax on incomes above a certain ceiling?

Internet **research**

Chinese Walls are used in many other contexts than finance. Search for the keywords *Chinese Wall* and *information firewall*. Present an example to the class, explaining why it is or is not desirable.

Glossary   PAGE 157

bail out
call the shots
fat cat
going rate
grind to a halt
market volatility
weigh in

Investment banks
heroes or zeroes?

Ever since Lehman Brothers hit the headlines in 2008 with the largest bankruptcy filing in US history, investment banks like Goldman Sachs, Barclays and UBS have been a subject of controversy. Seven-figure payouts
5 have attracted criticism from media and government, prompting top bankers to forgo or even be stripped of their bonuses. So just how do investment banks make profits and pay salaries that are so much higher than in other industries, and how do they justify awarding
10 their executives, in the words of the Bank of England, 'Himalayan' pay packages?

Investment bankers are famous for working long days, longer nights, weekends and holidays too; but do they provide an essential service to business and economic
15 growth as providers of capital, as they would have us believe, or are they just fat cats, creaming off profits as simple middlemen between users and investors? To begin to make any kind of judgement, we need to consider exactly what investment banks do.

20 Traditionally, the role of the investment banker has been to help corporate clients by providing independent and objective financial advice. Corporations might require the banks' expertise in order to raise capital on the bond markets, to help float a business on the stock market,
25 or to consult, facilitate and possibly finance mergers and acquisitions. As a supposedly impartial adviser, the bank might be asked to provide a fairness opinion on any transaction. Critics might say that the fees charged for delivering such services and opinions are out of all
30 proportion to the time spent examining a few financial statements. The banks, on the other hand, would argue that their charges are in proportion to the serious risks involved in providing financial guarantees and meeting the potentially major costs should things go wrong.

35 Where investment banks have stirred up far more controversy, though, is in the second side of their business, the markets division. Many observers see a potential conflict of interest in investment banks not only enjoying privileged access to confidential information on their
40 customers' businesses, but also themselves trading directly on the financial markets. In theory, a 'Chinese Wall' separates the advisory and markets divisions, but in many countries there are calls to force banks to make these two businesses completely independent. Recently,
45 investment banks have made extremely large profits on the derivatives market. These are complex financial instruments which, essentially, allow the bank to make profits by buying and selling future debt repayments. Derivatives have been accused of encouraging speculative
50 risk-taking and increasing market volatility; by leveraging a country's future repayments, they make it more difficult for the economy to service its debt. The banks, however, see foreign exchange, commodities and derivatives trading as a natural extension of their advisory services: they argue
55 that these activities are essential tools in managing their customers' growth and the financial risks involved.

Investment banks, in theory, are not involved in retail banking; understandably, after the Leeson and Kerviel affairs, most individual customers would feel
60 uncomfortable with the idea of their savings being used to finance their bank's trading activities. However, like Merrill Lynch with Bank of America and JP Morgan with Chase, almost all of the major players are partnered with high street banks, a fact which has also brought calls from
65 around the world for more transparency or preferably a complete split-up of these universal banks. The economy has gone global, say the banks, and if their international networks did not detect opportunities and match supply and demand for capital, industry would grind to a halt.
70 Raising capital has a cost, and investing has a risk; without investment banks' expertise in optimizing capital to cost and return to risk ratios, global industry would be starved of investment and growth, and pension funds would be unable to protect their members' futures.

75 Notwithstanding their undeniable skills and hard work, how can any one banker's work be worth several million pounds per year, ask the critics, especially when the banks in question have recently been bailed out using taxpayers' money? Surely shareholders and investors
80 should come first? Pay peanuts, and you get monkeys, the banks reply; if you don't pay the going rate, top bankers will take their talent elsewhere. Ultimately, unless the politicians weigh in, it's the markets that call the shots; for the moment at least, it seems the heroes will get to
85 keep their zeroes.

'Are they just fat cats, creaming off profits as simple middlemen between users and investors?'

▶ types of investment

▶ investment jargon

7.2 Vocabulary   Investment choices

Discussion

1 Work with a partner. You have €50,000 to invest. Decide which one of the following investment choices you would make. Discuss your choices and say why.

1   Use the money as a deposit for a house to start building a property empire.
2   Invest in yourself, by doing an MBA at a top business school in the USA.
3   Take a year out, without working, to come up with the ultimate business plan.
4   Put all the money into stocks and shares and aim to double it within three years.
5   Buy works of art, jewellery, gold and vintage wine and hope for the best.
6   'Downshift' by moving to an inexpensive region so your money goes further.

Reading

2 Read the interview with actress Felicia Turner from the money pages of a weekend newspaper and complete the text with words and phrases from the box.

Glossary	PAGE 158

buy-to-let
downshift
eighth age of man
quids in

bricks and mortar   buy-to-let   companies   diversify   entails   equities
exposed   portfolio   recession   recoup my losses   risk-averse   value

From receptionist to actress – an investment journey

How did you end up where you are now?

Actually, I didn't set out to become such a well-known actress living in a plum property in the most beautiful county in England. But I've always had my head screwed on when it comes to making my investment decisions.

What was the best investment decision you ever made?

This house, definitely. I bought it near the end of the bear market of the 90s and since then it's tripled in (1) _____.

And the worst?

When I was quite young I was persuaded to put all my eggs in one basket. One financial basket: the stock market. I used all my spare cash to buy (2) _____, mainly in blue chip (3) _____. But they still plummeted in value very soon afterwards, when the markets crashed and the (4) _____ set in.

Did that put you off investment?

No. Quite the opposite. I was determined to (5) _____, so I started over. That's when I started out in property and over a period of 12 years I've built up a(n) (6) _____ of 12 flats and houses around London and the south-east which I rent out. Little did I know I would wind up as the (7) _____ queen I am today, or so I have been described.

Do you see yourself as a risk-taker?

In life you mean? But seriously, no, I don't. I actually see myself as a cautious investor. Indeed, my financial adviser describes me as (8) _____, which given my personal life always amuses me. But that does not stop me from taking difficult decisions. One of my mantras is (9) _____ or die. In other words, make sure you have several different types of investment, so if one sector goes pear-shaped, you're not ruined.

So where else, apart from property, is your money invested?

Without going into too much detail, I make sure I'm (10) _____ to investments in several different currencies. Of course, this strategy (11) _____ risk, but the other side of the coin is that this risk pays off: whenever sterling takes a tumble, I'm quids in.

Finally, do you have any sound advice for the younger investor?

Work hard, and whenever you're spending money, never forget how hard you worked for it. That'll make you spend less, and save more. Oh, and don't put it under the mattress: (12) _____ are your best bet – with property you can't lose!

Internet research

Search for the keywords *property investment* and collect the boldest claims made. Conduct a quick class survey to find the most outrageous property investment claim.

3 Work with a partner. Decide on the meaning of the idioms below taken from the newspaper article about Felicia.

> have your head screwed on   put all your eggs in one basket
> go pear-shaped   the other side of the coin

Do you have any of these idioms in your first language?

Vocabulary

4 Match the investment jargon on the left with the simpler explanations on the right.

1	boost income streams	a)	charge a lot of money
2	adopt a defensive investment stance	b)	protection against the rises and falls of the market
3	a buffer against market volatility	c)	behaving in an individual manner
4	a diversified portfolio	d)	increase revenues
5	going against the herd instinct	e)	an investment that can't go wrong
6	a lack of transparency	f)	find ways of decreasing risk
7	command a premium price	g)	no ability to see what is really going on
8	a sure-fire investment	h)	a range of investments in different assets

Listening

5 2:25 Listen to Tommaso Mancini, an investment product salesman, speaking at an investment fair. Which of the expressions from Exercise 4 does he use?

6 2:25 Listen again and note down the investment advice he offers on the topics below.

- Planning for retirement
- Currencies
- Property

7 Work with a partner. Which pieces of advice do you agree with?

Speaking

8 Work with a partner. Your aim is to establish your partner's investment profile, preferences and possible plans for the next few years. Think about attitude to risk, favoured geographical areas, expectations of future wealth and types of investment (e.g. financial instruments, property, stocks and shares, exotic investments).

Writing

9 Write a short summary of your partner's investment profile.

7 | Investment

Did you know?

There are many ways of adding emphasis in English. These include changing word order, putting important information at the front of the sentence, adding extra words, and emphasizing by pronunciation and word stress.

▶ Grammar and practice pages 134–135

7.3 Grammar   Inversion and emphasis

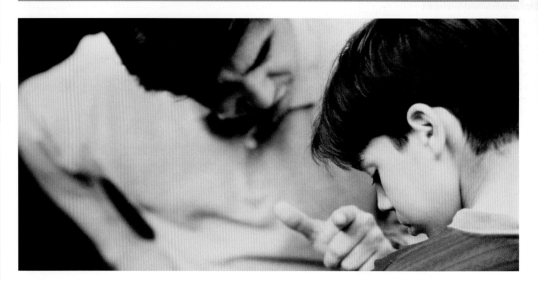

Sentence stress

1 Work with a partner. Discuss how stressing different words in the sentence below changes the overall message. Take turns to say the rest of the sentences aloud emphasizing different words to transmit a particular message. Your partner has to say what the message is.

*I asked **you** to prepare a short presentation about this year's product range.*
*I asked you to prepare a **short** presentation about this year's product range.*
*I asked you to prepare a short presentation about **this** year's product range.*

1 The sales team didn't know it would sell so well in Japan.
2 We don't think that he is ready for promotion yet.
3 The Board said they might consider adopting the revised proposal.
4 Are both the new managers coming with me on Friday?

Inverted conditionals

2 Complete each inverted conditional sentence using *should, had* or *were.*

1 _____ the conditions not be met by the end of May, the submission will be rejected.
2 The United States would seek adoption of a resolution that could be enforced by sanctions _____ they to fail to comply with it.
3 _____ any country withdraw from an agreement consisting of at least three countries, then all the remaining signatories will respond with sanctions.
4 _____ the organization done that, at least they would have entered the debate prepared for what was to follow.
5 _____ it not for historical reasons, we would use the term 'protectionism' rather than 'strategic defence'.
6 The subgroup will consider whether there was material within the representation which, _____ it been made available to the team beforehand, would have altered their bargaining position.

Emphatic structures

3 The following sentences all contain mistakes. Rewrite each to make them correct.

1 Who we made Chief Researcher was Alice Clay.
   The person we made Chief Researcher was Alice Clay.
2 What do I want to focus on today is the importance of evaluating risk.
3 It is short-termism why many investors fail.
4 Scarcely she had made her investment when the global markets crashed.
5 Such a charismatic person was he that he inspired absolute loyalty in his team.
6 May have you the best of luck when you're out there – you'll need it!
7 Only by focusing closely on risk he was able to avoid huge losses.
8 Were the markets really take off, we'll be set to make major gains.
9 Not only you failed to make any gains, but you also lost nearly all our money.

Internet research

Search for the keywords *intellectual investment* to find an example of an organization that have made an investment in this area. Present your findings to the class.

Reformulating for emphasis

4 Rewrite the sentences to make them more emphatic. Use each of the given phrases at the beginning.

1 This bank was actually founded in Edinburgh.
(The place ... / Edinburgh ... / Where ...)
The place where this bank was actually founded is Edinburgh.
Edinburgh is the place where this bank was actually founded.
Where this bank was actually founded is Edinburgh.
2 We need action rather than words.
(Words ... / Action ... / What ...)
3 I'm here today because I want to discuss my promotion prospects.
(The reason why ... / What I ... / My promotion prospects ...)
4 The most important market for raw commodities is undoubtedly China.
(No market ... / Without doubt ... / China is ...)
5 Your attention to detail impresses me more than any other quality.
(What ... / The quality ... / I am more ...)
6 First of all, I want you only to listen.
(All ... / The only ... / Just listen – that's ...)

Emphatic words

5 Complete the Managing Director's speech below using the words in the box to add emphasis. Two of the words are not needed.

absolutely do indeed only rather regrettably scarcely such utter whatsover

I am (1) _____ delighted to be able to report to you today that our flagship investment fund has been a very great success (2) _____. There is little doubt in my mind that this is down to the (3) _____ brilliance of the Strategy Director, Ms Catherine King, who has been (4) _____ an outstanding leader. I have no doubt (5) _____ that the fund will go from strength to strength. (6) _____, though, I (7) _____ have one (8) _____ sad announcement to make. Her deputy, John Seal, has received an offer from another company and will be leaving us next month.

Listening

6 🔊 2:26 Listen to the presentation on investment for business students given by a university professor, and complete the following notes.

1 Main area: _____
2 Particular area of focus: _____
3 Rationale for talk: _____
4 Key perspective: _____
5 Alternative perspective mentioned: _____
6 The most important type of investment: _____
7 Starting point: _____
8 Example idea: _____
9 Examples of people you need: _____
10 Investors want to see: _____

7 🔊 2:26 Listen again and note down as many emphatic structures as you can.

What I particularly want to talk about today is ...

Negotiation

8 Work in three small groups. You work for a company that manages investment portfolios. You are looking to enter into an alliance with another group in order to diversify your client offer.

Group A turn to page 118. Group B turn to page 117. Group C turn to page 120.

9 Form new groups of three. Use emphatic language to persuade the others that your group would make the best partner.

10 Work in your original groups. Report which of the other two organizations you think would make the best ally. Reach a group decision.

Glossary   PAGE 157

bootstrap
intellectual
    investment
strategic defence

7 | Investment

7.4 Management skills　Decision-making

Discussion

1 In small groups, discuss the questions.

1 Which of the methods in the box do you use to make decisions? For what kind of decisions?

> tossing a coin　gut feeling　sticking a pin in a list　seat of the pants
> paired comparisons　drawing straws　reading cards or tea leaves　grid analysis
> talking to a friend/family member/colleague

2 How did you choose your phone, computer or mp3 player? Try to define the steps in the decision-making process.
3 Compare your findings. What features do they have in common?

Grid analysis

2 Grid analysis is a useful decision-making tool, especially in meetings when there are several good alternatives available and multiple criteria to consider.

Match the descriptions a)–h) with steps 1–8 in the decision-making process.

1 define the objective	4 quantify the options	7 monitor performance
2 identify the options	5 weight the criteria	8 take remedial action
3 define criteria	6 make the decision	

a) Evaluating performance of the option you have chosen will be easier if you have well-defined criteria. Plot quantifiable measures on a graph over the evaluation period.
b) Prepare a grid with the options as rows and the criteria as columns. Grade each option from 1 (poor) to 5 (excellent) for each of your criteria.
c) List the conditions that the ideal solution would fulfil, and all the selection criteria that they imply. Making criteria as quantifiable as possible will facilitate the decision-making process.
d) Grid analysis does not guarantee good decisions, but is less subjective than a seat of the pants judgement. Make a decision without unnecessary debate. It is easier for a group to accept a controversial decision when all the factors have been visibly quantified and taken into account.
e) Check that your goal is SMART (Specific, Measurable, Achievable, Realistic, Time-bound).
f) This step may not be necessary if the optimal choice was made. If adjustment is needed, once again, quantifiable measures will help to see exactly where action is required.
g) Unsatisfactory decisions are often the result of not considering enough options. Discussing possible options with other people and keeping an open mind at this stage will help to avoid this risk.
h) Work out the relative importance of the criteria in your decision, and give each a weighting: the higher the weighting, the more important the criterion. On your grid, multiply the score for each option by the weighting, and add up the totals.

3 Match the sample grids for a new factory site with the appropriate steps in Exercise 2.

A

	Cost	Communications	Climate	Workforce	Total
Lille	4	2	1	5	12
Nice	1	2	2	4	9
Lyon	3	4	4	2	13
Nantes	2	3	4	3	12

B

	Cost	Communications	Climate	Workforce	Total
Weighting	*x3*	*x4*	*x2*	*x5*	
Lille	12	8	2	25	47
Nice	3	8	4	20	35
Lyon	9	16	8	10	43
Nantes	6	12	8	15	41

Internet
research

Work with a partner to find out about two decision-making tools developed by Edward de Bono.
Student A should search for the keywords *Six Thinking Hats*.
Student B should search for the keywords *Plus Minus Interesting*.
Explain to each other how to use the tools.

Listening

4 🔊 2:27–2:30 **Listen to four extracts from a meeting about the factory sites in Exercise 3 and answer the questions.**

1 Which step in the decision-making process is being discussed in each extract?
2 Which sites do Claire and Bernard prefer?
3 Do they accept the final choice?

5 🔊 2:27–2:30 **Listen again and put the words in these expressions in the right order.**

1 conditions find ideal need satisfy solution the to to we What would?
2 a and between characteristics desirable distinction draw essential need requirements to We.
3 Can more quantify specifically that we?
4 a all can consider draw Let's list options; our up we?
5 are avenues cover Does everything, explore or other should that there we?
6 a cost five of on one put scale to Where would you?
7 a as as Cost critical give I'd isn't it nearly only workforce; three.
8 can It Nice out rule seem that we would.
9 Do for go Lille we?
10 is it Lille then.

Vocabulary

6 **Complete the expressions from Exercise 4, and find four pairs which have a similar meaning.**

1 out of the _____
2 a make or _____ factor
3 it stands to _____
4 out of the _____
5 the be all and _____ all
6 the _____ speak for themselves
7 it's pretty black and _____
8 it's an open and shut _____

7 **Work with a partner. Suggest more appropriate business language for the meeting below.**

A: ~~Listen up you guys!~~ *Gentlemen, may I have your attention?*
We gotta pick a city for the conference. Gimme your possibles.
B: Chicago, Palermo, Tokyo.
A: That's it?
C: Moscow?
A: OK, how do we pick the best?
B: Decide what you wanna have and what you gotta have.
C: Well, you gotta have cooperation.
A: You wanna put a number on that?

Later ...
A: OK, now casinos; out of five?
B: Five.
C: Nah, clubs before casinos. Three, max.
A: So! Palermo is a no. Tokyo? Moscow? No. So I guess it's Chicago. OK?
B: Yeah. No place like home, eh, boss?

Discussion

8 **Work in small groups. You are managers of *Animal Health*, a veterinary practice catering for domestic and farm animals in Sweden. Your team of vets cover long distances by road to reach their patients in rural and sometimes remote areas. Company cars are an essential tool, an advertisement for your service and also an important perk of the job: good vets are difficult to recruit, and they appreciate being allowed to use them as a family car for weekends and holidays.**

You are meeting to decide which model to choose for your new fleet of cars – a saloon, sports model, station wagon, 4WD SUV, minivan or perhaps another type?

Consider your options and criteria, and use a grid analysis to reach a decision.

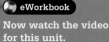
eWorkbook

Now watch the video for this unit.

7 | Investment

- ▶ metaphors, useful finance-related expressions
- ▶ financial report structure
- ▶ writing a financial report

7.5 Writing Financial reporting

Discussion

1 Discuss the questions with a partner.

1 Financial reports often use colourful metaphors. Which of the images below is evoked in the following phrases?

> sports water weather war health

a) Tech. stocks are fighting a losing battle.
b) The firm is in good shape.
c) The company has gone under.
d) A spokesperson gave a ballpark figure for projected losses.
e) The organization should be able to ride out the storm.

2 Explain in your own words what each metaphor means (in the context of the phrase).
3 Why do you think these images are used?
4 Can you think of any other common metaphors using these images?

Model

2 Read the share reports below and answer the questions.

1 What industry does each report belong to?
2 What has affected the share price in the past?
3 What might affect it in the future?

HTTP://ONLINESHAREREPORTS.COM

HOME ● **REPORTS** ● SHARES ● CURRENCY ● COMMODITIES ● FUNDS ● HELP

Confident construction company a wise buy

As the credit crunch bites, outsourcing companies are becoming increasingly attractive: businesses that are feeling the pinch can save costs by letting others take on non-core activities.

Judging by Carillion's trading statement yesterday, the theory seems to be sound. The company expects to deliver double-digit earnings per share growth in the next fiscal year. The group's order book stands at £20bn, compared with £15.8bn last year, with the stock closing up 4% last night.

Business is booming in the Middle East, where the group has a hearty construction division, and the integration of McAlpine, which it bought in February, will help to save costs. The group is expected to post a share price of 410p within the year.

Carillion is a compelling investment opportunity: the chance to buy a company that presently trades well below its peers should not be readily passed up. Buy.

One to watch: Share price 121.5p (+3p)

Relatively new to the market, Zenith is described as a specialist tour company. The bulk of its customers are empty-nesters, where Zenith has carved out a niche for itself.

The first figures published since Zenith's acquisition of Intrip20 in August comfortably beat expectations, with pre-tax profits for the year to 31 October rising to £502,000 from £61,000 in the previous year.

Intrip is New Zealand's largest online travel retailer; the linkup between the two clearly makes strategic sense. Zenith is now in a position to offer its specialist holidays to Intrip's sizeable clientele. The forthcoming launch of holiday websites in the UK is expected to further boost the customer base.

The shares look cheap now, but they'll need to demonstrate more solid progress before any serious re-rating is likely. Analysts are fairly confident they will rise further, driving pre-tax profits up to £3.5m by the end of the year. Well worth keeping.

Analysis

3 Number the four sections in the order they appear in the reports above.

☐ outlook   ☐ recommendation   ☐ news/context   ☐ performance

4 Which section in a financial report (see Exercise 3) do these phrases come from?

1 Investors should take advantage of the recent rally to bite the bullet and sell.
2 The branch is currently generating strong sales and heading back to profit.
3 The stock is worth tucking away; sit tight and look forward to future gains.
4 As a result of soaring oil prices, pre-tax profits look set to hit the £3m mark.
5 Profits are forecast to rise by 4% to 21.6% next year.
6 With recovery back on track, shares are now trading back at levels last seen 12 months ago.

Internet research

Search for the keywords *sports and military metaphors in business* and compile a list of your favourite, or least favourite metaphors. Hold a class debate to decide whether using these metaphors in business is a good or bad thing; do they reflect a macho society which excludes women?

Language focus

5 Match the words and phrases on the left from the reports with the correct meaning on the right.

1	the credit crunch bites	a)	very attractive; not to be missed
2	feel the pinch	b)	developed a specialist area of the market
3	sound	c)	did much better than everyone thought
4	double-digit earnings per share growth	d)	choose not to make use of a chance/opportunity
5	trades well below its peers	e)	sudden reduction in available loans takes effect
6	pass up	f)	notice the higher costs
7	compelling	g)	increase the 'list' of customers
8	carved a niche for itself	h)	reliable
9	comfortably beat expectations	i)	sells for much less than comparable companies
10	boost the customer base	j)	an increase in dividend of at least 10%

6 Put each group of words in **bold** in the correct order, then order. Put the four paragraphs a)–d) in order to make a short financial report.

a) The firm **base boost customer its looks set to** and its revenues by finally **long-awaited the biting on bullet takeover the** of Telyzone, the once troubled alarm specialist **back heading is now profit to that**.

b) **below Currently its peers trading well**, Bigbox Cellphone represents a **be compelling investment not opportunity passed should that up**. Well worth a punt.

c) **year the last pinch feeling After**, first quarter pre-tax profits £3m **beating mark, comfortably the expectations hit**.

d) Having **a carved communications for in itself mobile niche**, Bigbox Cellphone **alarm currently is generating in sales strong the** and surveillance systems market.

Output

7 🔊 2:31 Listen to a stock market report about the fortunes of a production company and make notes in the table.

SourceMedia

Glossary PAGE 158

ballpark figure
bite the bullet
credit crunch
punt
sit tight
tuck away

News context	Performance	Outlook

8 Write a short financial report on SourceMedia.

7.5 Writing

7.6 Case study | Lesage Automobile

Discussion

1 Work in small groups. The automobile business is a good example of a market where many customers feel oversold, i.e. in addition to meeting their basic needs, the product has features that they do not really need or want.

Some manufacturers have begun to respond by offering 'no-frills' products, like Renault's Logan.

Brainstorm examples of existing or possible no-frills products in other markets. Which ones would you (not) be prepared to buy?

Reading

Glossary	PAGE 158

clamour
no-frills
oversell

2 Read the article below and answer the questions.

1 Why was Renault Chairman Louis Schweitzer surprised?
2 What is the Logan's appeal to western European consumers?
3 How is Renault able to sell at half the cost of its main competitors?
4 How should Renault's competitors react?

Got 5,000 Euros? Need A New Car?

Drivers across Europe are clamoring for Renault's ultracheap, no-frills Logan

A strange thing happened when French auto maker Renault rolled out the no-frills Logan, a midsize sedan designed to sell for as little as $6,000 in emerging markets like Poland. Western buyers clamored for the car. So Renault began delivering the roomy, unpretentious five-seater to France, Germany and Spain. The pricier West European version includes a passenger-side airbag and a three-year warranty but still sells for a base price of $9,300 – about half that of the Ford Focus ($17,250) and the Volkswagen Golf ($18,264).

Building cheap cars for the West wasn't what Chairman Louis Schweitzer had in mind when he spent $592 million in 1999 to acquire and retool ailing Romanian auto maker Dacia. He aimed to produce a low-cost vehicle targeted at developing countries, home to 80% of consumers who have never owned a car. But he may well have stumbled onto a rich vein of demand in the West for utilitarian cars, part of the discount mania that has spread across Europe. No matter where the Logan sells, Renault has engineered a small miracle by making a car that is modern but stripped of costly design elements and superfluous technology. Deutsche Bank pegs production costs for the Logan at $1,089 per car, less than half the $2,468 estimate for an equivalent Western auto.

'The concept was simple,' says Kenneth Melville, the Scot who headed the Logan design team. 'Reliable engineering without a lot of electronics, cheap to build and easy to maintain and repair.' To keep costs low, Renault adapted the platform used for its other small cars – the Clio, the Modus and the Nissan Micra. Melville's team then slashed the number of components by more than 50%. The simple design means assembly at the Romanian plant is done almost entirely without robots. That lets Renault capitalize on the country's low labor costs: gross pay for a Dacia line worker is $324 per month. Now, Renault is ramping up production of the Logan from Russia to Morocco. 'The investment in manufacturing is relatively low, so you can have factories that don't have to produce huge volumes to finance themselves,' says Christoph Stürmer, Senior Analyst at researcher Global Insight in Frankfurt.

Other companies are working on cheap cars too. Volkswagen is considering building a $3,650 car for China, and in India, Tata Motors is offering its Nano for $2,500. But for now, the Logan is the one turning heads.

Internet research

Search for the keywords *no-frills chic* to find examples of how low-cost goods and services companies are investing in style to add value without increasing cost. Discuss how this formula could be applied to other products.

Listening

3 ⏺ 2:32 Lesage Automobile is a small independent car manufacturer. After several years of good results, the company is looking to invest to accelerate growth. Listen to two board members discussing their options, and answer the questions.

1 Who is Amelia?
2 Which options do a) Mikhail and b) Jack favour?
3 What are they drinking, and why?

4 ⏺ 2:32 Listen again and complete options 1–8 in the first column of the grid below.

	a)	b)	c)	d)	e)	f)	g) other …	h) other …
1 refuse to _____ – invest in _____								
2 produce a _____ in _____								
3 build own model in _____								
4 _____ cheapest existing model _____								
5 joint venture with _____ using old-generation _____								
6 import and _____ cheap cars from _____								
7 target traditional markets in _____								
8 target _____ markets in _____								
9 other …								
10 other …								

Reading

5 Read Amelia's note below. Find and enter six criteria a)–f) in the first row of the grid above.

Jack,

Here are my ideas so far on the criteria for the no-frills project. Obviously, we need to think about the political implications of relocating part of our production – I want to find out about possible incentives for investment in eastern Europe or Russia. Another area to think about is how a no-frills project affects our corporate image? We need to evaluate the risk, especially now that the Greens are becoming politically and economically more influential.

The analysts say that potential profitability is similar for all projects, so we don't need to worry about ROI at this stage; but we do have to consider how attractive each option is for the low-end customer. And we mustn't forget after-sales, which could be tricky with some of our options.

It's vital to predict how the unions will react. Staff morale is very important. Re: finance – can we use liquidity or debt? The family would prefer to avoid diluting our equity if possible.

What else do we need to take into account, and what are the priorities? Let me know what you think.

Amelia

Discussion

6 Work in small groups. Consider the options and the criteria in the grid above: delete, modify or add other ideas as you feel appropriate. Then quantify the options, weight the criteria and decide what to recommend to the Board of Lesage.

Student A turn to page 115.
Student B turn to page 116.
Student C turn to page 118.
Students D and E turn to page 121.

8 | Free trade

▶ 'hot' and 'cold' cultures

▶ arguments for and against free trade

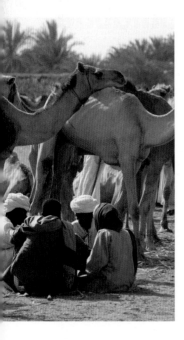

Glossary   PAGE 158

archipelago
commensurately
DRM
dub
funky
hothouse
hurdle
lint

Internet research

Search for the keywords *free trade agreements pros and cons*. Compile a list of arguments for and against free trade.

8.1 About business   Free trade

Discussion

1 Why would governments want to do the following? Think of as many reasons as possible.

1 Require foreign products to pass strict tests before allowing imports.
2 Limit imports of foreign cars to an annual quota.
3 Refuse imports of cheap copies from Asia.
4 Refuse to trade with a particular country.

Reading for gist

2 Read *The price of being a fortress* and choose the best summary.

1 In an increasingly networked world, protecting the individual's right to privacy and defending intellectual property against international piracy are essential in order to preserve a nation's culture, traditions and capacity for technological innovation.
2 Regulating the flow of technology and ideas from other countries by policing virtual borders in order to improve internal security has a potentially disastrous effect on a country's economy, potential for innovation and even human rights.
3 Free trade and exchange of ideas allows individual nations to build on distributed culture, but unless there is regulation, foreign protocols become mandatory, and eventually threaten the country's sense of cultural identity and ability to govern itself.

3 Sort the words and phrases in the box below into 'hot cultures' and 'cold cultures'.

> borderless economies   digital islands   incompatibility   'How did they do this?'
> free flow of data   slower adoption of new products   universal protocols
> security through authentication   Bhutan   global archipelago   'How can we do this?'
> sophisticated consumers

Reading for detail

4 Read the article again and answer the questions.

1 How is the flow of technology different in hot and cold cultures?
2 In what way is the technology gap cumulative?
3 How is consumer behaviour different in hot and cold cultures?
4 How does not accepting universal digital communication protocols slow economic growth?
5 Why do digital islands find it necessary to identify data and users?
6 Why is David Holtzman concerned about America's future?

5 Explain the significance of the following words and phrases.

1 *cultural lint* (lines 1–2)
2 *hothouses* (line 3)
3 *communicable diseases* (line 6)
4 *Bhutan* (line 12)
5 *global archipelago* (line 16)
6 *Fortress America* (line 26)
7 *a coral reef* (line 28)
8 *at a crossroads* (line 70)

Listening

6 🔊 2:33 Listen to two students, Bradley and Rose, talking about free trade. According to Bradley, which of the problems below are due to free trade?

> unemployment   high prices   capital outflow   dumping   pollution
> exploitation of children   toxic products   terrorism   foreign intervention

Debate

7 In small groups, discuss the questions below.

1 Which arguments presented by David Holtzman and Bradley do you agree or disagree with?
2 Does your country have a 'hot' or a 'cold' culture? Why?
3 Is it possible for trade to be completely free? In your opinion, what are the minimum restrictions and the essential freedoms?

THE PRICE OF BEING A **FORTRESS**

No nation is an island – if it cares about its technological future.

BY DAVID H. HOLTZMAN

The great ports of the world always pick up a little cultural lint from the outside world. Some treat their trade zones like hothouses, cultivating a funky mix of the exotic and the indigenous that sinks its roots back into the culture at large.
5 Others treat them like quarantine zones, confining new thoughts, ideas, and technologies as if they were communicable diseases.

Social anthropologist Claude Lévi-Strauss dubbed societies open to trade 'hot cultures' – they warm quickly to the new, and assimilate change. By contrast, 'cold cultures' are insular,
10 expending a great deal of energy to maintain central control.

Both, of course, are connected in an increasingly networked world – today there are as few Bhutans as truly borderless economies. The question is how. Countries on the hot side of the spectrum maintain their own sense of cultural identity and self-
15 governance while gaining the benefits of the larger distributed culture. They are part of the global archipelago, taking fullest advantage of the network effect that comes from collaboration. Nations that put up too many regulatory boundaries – cultural or technological – run the risk of going cold. They become semi-
20 isolated digital islands, losing the economic and intellectual advantages that come from free trade and access to the technology that drives it.

This loss is cumulative, potentially creating an irrevocable, long-term gap. And that gap has as much to do with the free
25 flow of technology within societies as between them. Ironically, Fortress America, despite its status as a great trading power, runs the risk of becoming such an island.

Technology innovation builds in layers; like a coral reef, the dead act as the foundation for the living, a conceptual structure
30 for future innovation. Citizens of archipelago nations grow up with a far larger conceptual structure. They have a global sense of what's technologically feasible – reducing engineering problems from 'How can we do this?' to 'How did they do this?' – and therefore waste less time getting things done. Digital
35 islanders, on the other hand, are cut off from outside innovation; forced to invent from scratch using local materials, even their most 'modern' technology might seem at home on a desert island.

Greater exposure also gives archipelagos more sophisticated consumers. In digital islands, as the gap widens in consumer
40 education, adoption of new products slows commensurately. Slower adoption rates imply less early-stage revenue, which means less investment capital available for new projects. And there's the slower time to market due to regulatory hurdles.

The technology at the foundation of the archipelago
45 accumulates in another pragmatic sense. New digital communication protocols, capabilities and conventions start out as optional but soon become expected and ultimately mandatory. Try setting your browser to refuse all cookies and you'll quickly notice you can't use online shopping carts anymore. If you live in
50 a country where digital rights management systems are required

in order to listen to mp3s, then you won't be able to use devices from Japan or Europe that don't have them. As the consequences of these decisions build up, digital island consumer markets will not be large enough to justify the additional parallel development
55 cost and they will cease being primary consumer markets for new products.

Often in the name of self-defence, digital islands try to fully regulate the flow of content through their virtual boundaries in the same way that they police physical goods – by interdiction.
60 This means imposing physical checkpoints that can be seized if necessary, and forcing all incoming and outgoing information to pass through them – just like the customs zone in an airport. Think of the domain name system, or DRM-regulated music. Law enforcement and customs agents of these nations need to be
65 able to examine all digital content, therefore they have to outlaw strong encryption. And they must legislate absolute and unique authentication of every person, machine and network – because the lawyers need someone to serve papers on, otherwise how can they enforce their rules?
70 Our country is at a crossroads. There are those on the left who want to regulate privacy and identity information, and those on the right who want to control intellectual property. Whichever side prevails, either may ultimately lead to the same endgame – an America technologically isolated from the free flow of the
75 digital archipelago. Imagine how we're going to feel when the rest of the world sees us as desert islanders building a television set from coconuts. Technological simplicity is a high price to pay for 'security'.

'Imagine how we're going to feel when the rest of the world sees us as desert islanders building a television set from coconuts.'

8 | Free trade

8.2 Vocabulary   Forming new words

Reading for gist

1 Read the text about new words and answer the questions.

1 What is the purpose of the article?
2 List the ten ways of creating new words mentioned by the writer, plus one example for each.

Free.trade
in words

COUNTRIES may struggle with fair and free trade, but languages have no such problems, at least when it comes to English: it endlessly imports and exports words. Not only does it take in words from other languages, but its users regularly create new words. You can too. Want to talk about the major emerging economies of Brazil, Russia, India and China? Go for an acronym: *BRIC*. Or just get a letter, *e* for electronic will do, and attach it up: *e-commerce, e-business, e-tailing*.

Need to describe the new concept of moving your production or service abroad – off your own shores? Put the old word and affix together to build a new word: *offshore*. Feel like extending this? How about *offshore* as a verb and *offshoring* as a noun? And an adjective? That'll be *offshorable*. This process can open the floodgates – look out for *onshoring, farshoring, nearshoring*, even *rightshoring*. Just don't ask me what they mean.

Blends are another favourite. Grab zeitgeist words like *global* and start playing. *Globalize* and *globalization* are old hat now, but what about blending in parts of other words: *global* and *local* – *glocalize* will serve, not forgetting *glocalization*. Hate globalization? Reach for Greek: *globaphobic*. Need a noun? Raid an obvious suffix and you've got *glocality*.

Talking of raiding, grab words from other contexts. Feeling dramatic? Don't just start your meeting, *kick it off*. Too spiritual for sport? Be a business *guru*. Love brevity? Go for short and *max out* your credit card. Like phrasal verbs? 'Nounize' them: you used to *stop over*, now you have a *stopover*. Poetic and love rhymes? Bricks and mortar is so last millennium, now it's all *clicks and mortar*. Like metaphors? We've had *glass ceiling*, what about older employees, prejudice and the *silver ceiling*? Or combine two words in a novel combination: *swarm businesses*.

Who's to say these words will still be around in 10 or 20 years? That's not the point. Language is about the here and now. Words are the lifeblood of English. Create them, use them, free trade them. And that's a verb.

Vocabulary

2 Work with a partner. Put the words and phrases from the box below into each of the categories mentioned by the writer according to how you think they are formed.

> B2B   Coca-colonization   al desko   bookmarked   dotcom   NAFTA   e-signature
> goldilocks economy   blog   downsize   dollarize   presenteeism   agflation
> angel investor   infonomics   tiger economy   marketing crusade   ASEAN   get rich click
> cappuccino economy   googled   brandalism

What do you think are the meanings of the words and phrases?

Blends

3 Look at the list of words below. Can you work out the meanings and which two words were blended together to make them?

1 Oxbridge
2 wikinomics
3 flexicurity
4 genericide
5 stagflation
6 philanthopreneur

Combining words

4 Work with a partner. Complete the sentences below using a word from the left and a word from the right.

> career   corporate   future
> spin   venture   virtuous

> anorexia   catalyst   coach
> cycle   journalism   proof

1 What really made it happen for my new company was my _____ – they gave us access to the kind of capital that I just couldn't get my hands on.
2 We've got to be careful and avoid _____, or we'll end up cutting too many jobs and never get back into shape when the economy picks up.
3 We've had falling production costs, leading to higher sales and greater profits – if only we could have such a _____ every year!
4 Our aim this time is to come up with something _____. I don't want our next product to date like the last one did.
5 I don't believe a word of that article. It's just _____. They've bought everything the politicians have said.
6 Not sure of your professional direction? Get the guidance you need with a _____ and go from strength to strength at work!

Creating new words

5 Try to create new words to express the meanings given.

You want a word which expresses **shopping** via **television** or over the **telephone**: *teleshopping*.

1 the theory that **women** are the main contributors to **economic** growth
2 **technology** which is **clean**
3 an online record of someone's **life**, using a **stream** of virtual material such as blogs and video clips
4 a way of **recycling** materials to create something new and more **upmarket** and valuable than what you started with
5 getting the **size** of a company's workforce **right**
6 a **heterosexual** male living in a **metropolitan** environment who spends a lot of time and effort on his appearance
7 like **CEO**s, these job titles all contain 'chief' and any other function, from academic to zoom
8 an economic **effect** like that of **Wal-Mart**, whether (depending on your perspective) keeping wages low or keeping inflation low

Internet research

Search for the keywords *new words* to find examples that have entered the language recently. Note down your ten favourites and try to work out where they came from.

8 | Free trade

▶ most common phrasal verbs

▶ focus on frequent particles

Did you know?

The ten phrasal verbs with the most combinations and meanings are: *come, go, put, get, take, turn, run, bring, look, cut.* The most common particles are: *around, away, back, down, in, into, off, on, out, over, through, up.*

▶ Grammar and practice pages 136–137

8.3 Grammar   Phrasal and prepositional verbs

Focus on frequent verbs

1 Read the *Did you know?* information about phrasal verbs. Then, with a partner, play phrasal verbs tennis. Student A 'serves' by saying a preposition from the list in the *Did you know?* box. Student B 'returns' by saying a short sentence using this preposition plus an appropriate verb from the list. Student B then says another preposition from the list which Student A 'returns' with another correct verb/preposition combination, etc. Score a point each time your opponent answers incorrectly. If your partner can't find a verb/preposition combination, you must be able to give one or they score two points.

Student A: *Off.*
Student B: *We'll have to put off our meeting until next week. Over.*

2 Choose the correct verb from the box to fill in the spaces in the text. Remember to use the correct verb form.

> bring   come   cut   get   go   look   put   run   take   turn

Free trade has long been a controversial issue. You might have to (1) _____ back to Genghis Khan to see where free trade really began: in the wake of his conquests trade (2) _____ off between Europe and Asia in the thirteenth century when precious fabrics, stones and perfumes were transported along the Silk Road. Half a millennium later, you would have to (3) _____ to the eighteenth century economists such as the Scot Adam Smith, who (4) _____ forward the view that it was free trade which (5) _____ about an increase in wealth for those nations involved. However, advocates of free trade have often struggled to (6) _____ their message across in the face of strong opposition and widespread protectionism. After the Second World War, a group of nations (7) _____ up with an international organization in the form of the General Agreement on Tariffs and Trade (GATT), which aimed to (8) _____ down on tariffs and protectionist practices in general. Although this organization (9) _____ into a number of difficulties during its lifetime, it was widely seen as successful. In 1995 the World Trade Organization (WTO) grew out of it: this organization aims to (10) _____ for new ways to promote free trade.

3 Explain each phrasal verb above in your own words, and suggest possible collocations.

4 Which one of the four particles cannot be used with each verb?

1	come	about / behind / forward / through
2	go	from / together / under / with
3	put	aside / back / for / through
4	get	across / against / ahead / at
5	take	above / from / in / to
6	turn	back / down / on / under
7	run	by / down / above / up
8	bring	forward / in / into / past
9	look	ahead / into / through / without
10	cut	about / back / into / out

Focus on frequent particles

5 Complete the sentences about free trade and development with the particles in the box.

Internet research

Search for the keywords *GATT and WTO* to find out the history of world trade talks since the Second World War. Write down the main dates and historical milestones so that you can tell a partner.

against away (x2) behind down for off on (x3) round to (x2) up (x3) with (x4)

1 It is our policy to do _____ protective tariffs and other trade barriers.
2 How can they get _____ protectionist policies when the President is advocate of free trade?
3 We need to face _____ the fact that, in the short term, small economies do not always benefit from lowering their trade barriers.
4 Playing your opponents _____ each other is not the best way to try to negotiate long-standing agreements.
5 Less developed countries find it difficult to stand _____ their rights in trade negotiations with superpowers.
6 Once countries fall _____ their national debt repayments, their debt increases even more.
7 It is difficult to persuade less developed countries to give _____ the idea that protectionism is in their best interest.
8 The government needs to cut _____ its spending in order to decrease the national debt.
9 The two men didn't get _____ each other, mainly due to their opposing views on free trade.
10 Some former opponents of free trade have come _____ the idea once they have understood the benefits.

Listening

6 🔊 2:34 Listen to the sales and marketing team of a European biotech company discussing their strategy in the Asian market. As you listen, complete the notes summarizing the discussion with the phrasal verbs in the box in the correct form.

branch out break into call off come up with crack on eat into give up kick off soldier on weigh up

Summary of discussion

Dave suggested that the meeting should (1) _____ with a review of the new trading laws. Jin disagreed, saying that this would (2) _____ the time available. He proposed instead to immediately (3) _____ with formulating a strategy for growth in Asia. Sara expressed doubt as to whether the time was right to try to (4) _____ new markets, particularly to (5) _____ into completely new territory such as Asia. Jin reminded the group of the opportunities in Asia and the urgency of (6) _____ a strategy for faster growth. Dave was sceptical and questioned the wisdom of (7) _____ plans for Europe where they had established market share. He proposed they should (8) _____ carefully the possible advantages and disadvantages before going ahead. Jin denied that he had ever proposed (9) _____ the European campaign. He said that the company should (10) _____ with the slow business of growing European market share, whilst simultaneously developing their activities in Asia.

7 🔊 2:34 Match the phrasal verbs used in the meeting with more formal and neutral synonyms below. Some of the synonyms match with more than one phrasal verb. In such cases, note the differences in meaning they indicate.

1 begin _____
2 enter _____
3 abandon _____
4 continue (briskly) _____
5 diversify _____
6 continue (slowly) _____
7 erode _____
8 consider _____
9 cancel _____
10 produce _____

Speaking

8 Work with a partner. Make ten quiz questions using the phrasal verbs from Exercises 5 and 6. Make sentences with these verbs and then blank out the verbs for your partner to complete.

8 | Free trade

8.4 Management skills   Leading the team

Discussion

1 **Work with a partner and discuss the questions.**

1   What groups or teams are you a member of? Think about work, study, sports, clubs and associations and hobbies.
2   What are the strengths and weaknesses of the leaders or managers of those teams?
3   List the qualities of the ideal team leader.

Glossary   PAGE 158

in/out of the loop

Reading

2 **Read the information about the roles we take on when working in teams or groups and answer the questions, if possible with someone who is in the same team as you.**

Research conducted by Dr Meredith Belbin defined nine essential roles in an optimal, balanced team. One of the key jobs of a team leader is to ensure that each role is represented. Obviously, in a small team, members need to play more than one role.

Action-Orientated Roles	Shaper	drives the team to overcome obstacles and perform
	Implementer	puts ideas into action
	Completer-Finisher	ensures thorough, timely completion
People-Orientated Roles	Coordinator	acts as a chairperson
	Teamworker	encourages cooperation
	Resource Investigator	explores outside opportunities
Thought-Orientated Roles	Plant	presents new ideas and approaches
	Monitor-Evaluator	analyses the options
	Specialist	provides specialized skills

1   Which person's job includes the following responsibilities?
   a) bring specific experience, knowledge or ability to the team
   b) develop the team's contacts with other people and organizations
   c) clarify goals, lead meetings, delegate tasks
   d) motivate the team and encourage them to work harder
   e) weigh up alternatives and avoid taking unnecessary risks
   f) build morale and defuse conflict
   g) get things done in a practical and concrete way
   h) make sure quality standards and deadlines are respected
   i) come up with innovative solutions to difficult problems
2   Who plays these roles in your teams?
3   Which role(s) do you enjoy or dislike playing? Why?
4   How do you think team leaders can ensure that all the roles are represented in a team?

Listening

3 🔊 2:35–2:40 Listen to six extracts where a manager is getting people to do things, and match them with the function and team role concerned.

coaching a completer-finisher ☐   giving constructive criticism to a plant ☐
taking on a specialist ☐   delegating to a shaper ☐
empowering a resource investigator ☐   motivating a monitor-evaluator ☐

4 🔊 2:35–2:40 Listen again and complete the key requests.

1 I think you should _____ _____ and _____ _____ _____ those contacts, don't you?
2 Just _____ _____ _____ _____ _____ on what you decide, would you?
3 I wonder if you could get Jack and Ella to do something _____ _____ _____ _____ for China?
4 This time round, I'd like you to _____ _____ _____ the whole logistics side of things.
5 You've made _____ _____ in the last six months, so let's just _____ _____ _____ _____ _____, all right?
6 Don't you think that _____ _____ _____ _____ foreign exchange is really Phil's baby?
7 Perhaps we should just _____ _____ _____ _____ _____ _____, OK?
8 If you were able to _____ _____ _____, I'd really appreciate being able to call on your skills.

5 Where would you put each request in Exercise 4 on the scale below?

◀━━━▶

delegating/observing   participating/supporting   selling/coaching   telling/directing

Roleplay

6 Work in small groups. You work for Mile High, a new airline which targets a niche market of 18- to 35-year-old flyers with its slogan, 'the party plane'. The company's current priority is to take market share in the English-speaking world. You are going to have meetings on the three agendas below. After each meeting, discuss which team role(s) each person played: team members should give the leader feedback using the checklist on page 121.

Student A turn to page 117.   Student C turn to page 119.
Student B turn to page 115.   Students D and E turn to page 120.

Internet research

Search for the keywords *meeting behaviour cartoons* and *boss cartoons* to find illustrations of undesirable behaviour in meetings and from leaders. Compare your findings and discuss ways of dealing with such behaviour.

eWorkbook

Now watch the video for this unit.

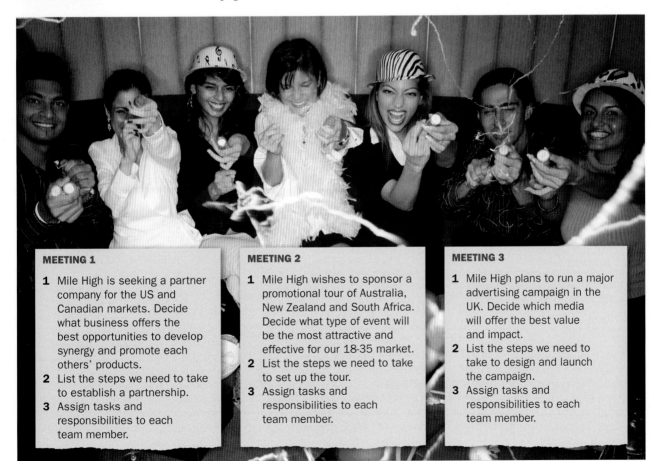

MEETING 1

1 Mile High is seeking a partner company for the US and Canadian markets. Decide what business offers the best opportunities to develop synergy and promote each others' products.
2 List the steps we need to take to establish a partnership.
3 Assign tasks and responsibilities to each team member.

MEETING 2

1 Mile High wishes to sponsor a promotional tour of Australia, New Zealand and South Africa. Decide what type of event will be the most attractive and effective for our 18-35 market.
2 List the steps we need to take to set up the tour.
3 Assign tasks and responsibilities to each team member.

MEETING 3

1 Mile High plans to run a major advertising campaign in the UK. Decide which media will offer the best value and impact.
2 List the steps we need to take to design and launch the campaign.
3 Assign tasks and responsibilities to each team member.

- appropriate style
- adverb and adjective collocations
- writing an email in appropriate style

8.5 Writing   Style

Discussion

1 **When a company exhibits at a trade show, there are many steps to take and people to contact. Decide on the most likely chronological order for the stages below.**

☐ evaluate results   ☐ follow up contacts   ☐ invite customers to dinner
☐ invite prospects to the show   ☐ order booth and furniture
☐ organize end-of-show dinner   ☐ register for show   ☐ thank guest speaker

Model

2 **Read the five email extracts relating to a big food and beverages trade show in Moscow. Choose the best date, greeting and salutation/sign-off for each.**

1 April	19 April	25 April	2 May	3 May

Alexsandr,	Hi Volodya,	Dear Ilia Mikhailovich,	Dear Ms Kramer,	Dear Customer,

Best wishes,	Sincerely,	Best regards,	Sincerely yours,	Good luck,
Ana Khouri	Sonia Tremain	Pete Welsh	Ana Khouri	Pete
PR Officer, BBD	Trade Show Manager, BBD	Sales Manager, BBD	PR Officer, BBD	

✉ | ⬇ INBOX | REPLY ⬅ | FORWARD ➡

❶ Subject: End-of-show speech   Date: _____

_____

On behalf of Tania Alms and the Board of BBD, I would like to thank you for the thoroughly entertaining speech you gave at our end-of-show dinner. Both the style and the substance of your talk were outstanding, and your ideas certainly sparked a lively debate among all of those in attendance. Thank you once again for taking time out from your busy schedule to ensure an enlightening and memorable evening for our customers.

_____

✉ | ⬇ INBOX | REPLY ⬅ | FORWARD ➡

❷ Subject: Delivery of booth   Date: _____

_____

This is to confirm our telephone conversation of a few minutes ago. The booth we ordered for FoodFest Moscow has still not been delivered to Crocus Expo, despite your logistics people's assurances that it would be there two days ago. The only way we can now be ready in time is by pulling an all-nighter – hardly the best preparation for a show! Letting us down like this is totally unacceptable. Unless you can offer significant compensation for the inconvenience caused, we will have no option but to make alternative arrangements in future.

_____

✉ | ⬇ INBOX | REPLY ⬅ | FORWARD ➡

❸ Subject: Trade show   Date: _____

_____

As you know, BBD will be exhibiting at FoodFest Moscow from 26 to 28 April; we hope you will honour us with a visit to our booth (E24). To mark BBD's 50th anniversary, Tania Alms, President and CEO, requests the pleasure of your company at an end-of-show dinner to be held at 8.30pm on the 28th at Noah's Ark restaurant, 9 M. Ivanovsky Lane, with special guest speaker Professor Ilia Mikhailovich Volyov. Please confirm your attendance by reply.

_____

✉ | ⬇ INBOX | REPLY ⬅ | FORWARD ➡

❹ Subject: BBD technical data sheet
Date: _____

_____

I want to thank you for stopping by our booth at FoodFest Moscow last week. Since there were so many attendees at the show, I wanted to make sure that all of your questions about our bottling equipment were answered.
As you may already know, BBD is famous for its radically innovative solutions. At the show you may have seen our latest wrap-around labeller; in order to refresh your memory, I've attached a technical data sheet.
If you would like further information please feel free to give me a call. I look forward to seeing you at the Americas Food & Beverage Show in September.

_____

✉ | ⬇ INBOX | REPLY ⬅ | FORWARD ➡

❺ Subject: Trade show staff
Date: _____

_____

You have been hand-picked to staff our booth at the upcoming FoodFest Moscow because you have exactly the skills and knowledge we need. Not only do you know all about our products, our competitors and our customers; what's more, you're friendly, you're good with people, and you're not afraid to strike up a conversation. A trade show is a unique opportunity to reach more prospects face to face in a couple of days than we could ever see in a month of field selling, so I'd just like to remind you that …

_____

Analysis

3 Read the extracts again and answer the questions.

1 Which email is aggressive, motivating, commercial, cordial, formal?
2 Which email associates two pairs of ideas for more impact? What are they?
3 Which email associates two groups of three ideas for more impact? What are they?
4 Which email uses two adverbs to emphasize the writer's attitude? What are they?
5 Which email uses two polite formulae to flatter the receiver?

Language focus

4 Pairing, (facts and figures) tripling, (signed, sealed and delivered), repetition (better products, better prices and better service) and alliteration (product, price, place, promotion) are frequently used to increase impact. Choose the correct word from the box to complete each example.

> customers   enchanted   looking   process   sales
> second   sell   shareholders   unacceptable   unimaginative

1 It's unfair, it's unprofessional and it's _____.
2 The new CEO will be welcomed by staff and _____ alike.
3 Substantial improvements have been made in both product and _____.
4 Trade shows are all about first impressions, no _____ chances, and the third degree.
5 Cutting corners doesn't win prizes, it doesn't win friends, and it certainly doesn't win _____.
6 The exhibition was as uninspiring as it was _____.
7 A good salesman is not only good-hearted and good-humoured, he's good-_____ too.
8 Follow this simple advice and you'll get more leads, more appointments, and above all, more _____!
9 Visitors come to the show hoping to be wooed, seduced and _____ by new products.
10 We take a no-frills approach; pile 'em high and _____ 'em cheap.

5 Adverb and adjective collocations give a text more colour. Choose the adverb which is commonly used to intensify each group of adjectives below.

> highly   radically   thoroughly   totally

1 unacceptable, irresistible, honest, inappropriate
2 entertaining, miserable, inadequate, unreasonable
3 recommended, controversial, effective, qualified
4 innovative, different, simple, altered

> deeply   perfectly   utterly   widely

5 disappointing, concerned, honoured, disturbed
6 available, praised, accepted, used
7 valid, happy, timed, executed
8 disastrous, boring, petrified, charming

6 Choose an appropriate adverb and adjective collocation from Exercise 5 to replace the more tentative synonyms in *italics* in the report below.

Although the substance of Dr Clavain's presentation was (1) *quite acceptable*, unfortunately the style was (2) *not very suitable* for this audience. As a result, many people found the session (3) *somewhat uninteresting* and left the room well before the end. Whilst Dr Clavain is a (4) *well trained* physician whose views are (5) *not usually contested*, it would seem that a (6) *slightly modified* approach is needed. Regrettably, a majority of researchers possess (7) *less than perfect* presentation skills and it should come as no surprise that many conference speeches are (8) *not as good as expected* for the audience and the organizers alike.

Output

7 Write two or more of the following messages using appropriate style and collocations.

1 An email thanking a consultant for a team-building session run at your institution or company.
2 A complaint to a hotel after a disappointing conference weekend.
3 An invitation to an awards ceremony to be held at your institution or company.
4 A follow-up message to a visitor to your institution or company's open day.
5 A motivational message to members of your team before an important event.

Internet research

Search for the keywords *adverb and adjective collocations* to find more typical combinations. Google the adverbs you find, in inverted commas and with an asterisk (e.g. *"painfully *"*), to discover which adjectives they collocate with. Compare their popularity on googlefight.com (e.g. *painfully shy* versus *painfully aware*).

Glossary   PAGE 158

alliteration
all-nighter
booth
woo

8.5 Writing

▶ duopolies and oligopolies

▶ market potential

▶ negotiating future strategy

8.6 Case study   The cartel

Discussion

1 Work in small groups. VISA and Mastercard®, Coca-Cola® and Pepsi, and Airbus and Boeing are well-known examples of duopolies – two companies sharing dominant control of a market.

Brainstorm the advantages and disadvantages of a duopoly or oligopoly for companies and consumers.

Reading

2 Read the article below and answer the questions.

1   Who are the 'holo pioneers', and why are they 'going head to head'?
2   What is the significance of the phrase 'there can be only one'?
3   How do supply and demand affect past, present and future prices and sales?
4   Why is the duopoly expected to continue?
5   What winning strategy does the article suggest?

HOLO PIONEERS GO HEAD TO HEAD

The race for market share is on in the lucrative new hologram video market. Like VHS and Betamax, and the Compact Disc, Compact Cassette and vinyl record before them, the UK's Holoplay PLC and America's ThreeD-Vision Inc. must slug it out in the marketplace, knowing that format wars are fought to the death. With very similar but incompatible technologies on offer, consumers must choose their champion: history has shown that there can be only one.

Both companies rolled out holo-players six months ago in the US and Europe. After a slow start, sales are now picking up steam, with each company dominant in its domestic market. As greater production capacity comes on stream, analysts predict the current $3,000 plus price tags will start to fall. However, with apparently watertight patents making me-too products risky, at least until a winning format emerges, it seems unlikely that other manufacturers will rush to join the fray.

With the rest of the world eagerly awaiting the chance to buy a holo-player, especially the huge Asian markets, the stakes are high: whichever player is prepared to slash its margins first could take the lion's share of a global market slated to hit 200m units per annum five years from now.

Listening

3 🔊 2:41 Listen to a conversation between two Holoplay employees, Toby and Jasmin, and mark the statements *T* (true), *F* (false) or *D* (it depends).

1   Jasmin has time to spare because her boss is on holiday. ☐
2   Staff have been warned not to discuss the confidential meeting. ☐
3   Holoplay and ThreeD-Vision are meeting to set up an illegal organization. ☐
4   Jasmin expects the companies will fix the same price for all markets. ☐
5   Toby assumes the companies will agree not to compete in the same countries. ☐
6   Jasmin says supply will soon outstrip demand. ☐
7   Jasmin thinks Toby is right to stand up for free trade. ☐

Glossary	PAGE 159

duopoly
oligopoly

Discussion

4 In small groups, look at the charts below and discuss the questions.

1 Which markets have the best potential for Holoplay and ThreeD-Vision?
2 What strategies might they consider to avoid a format or price war?

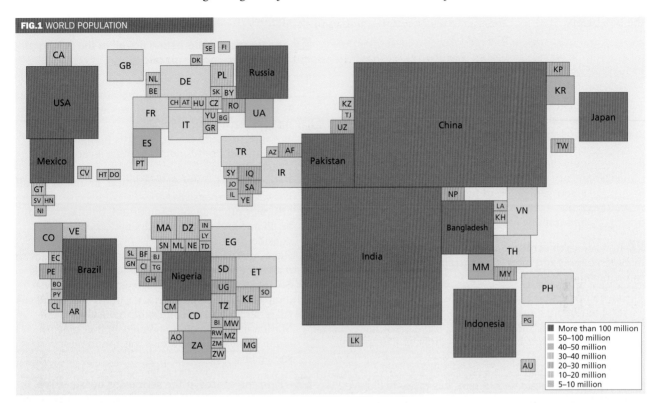

FIG.1 WORLD POPULATION

Legend:
- More than 100 million
- 50–100 million
- 40–50 million
- 30–40 million
- 20–30 million
- 10–20 million
- 5–10 million

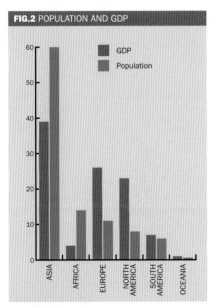

FIG.2 POPULATION AND GDP

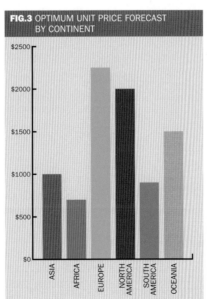

FIG.3 OPTIMUM UNIT PRICE FORECAST BY CONTINENT

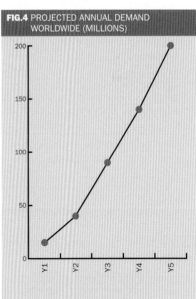

FIG.4 PROJECTED ANNUAL DEMAND WORLDWIDE (MILLIONS)

Negotiation

5 In teams, meet to negotiate the agenda opposite.

Team A are from ThreeD-Vision Inc.
Turn to page 121.
Team B are from Holoplay PLC.
Turn to page 119.

AGENDA

1 Recommended retail price
2 Production levels
3 Commercial policy and territories
4 Cost-cutting through shared purchasing and distribution networks
5 Profit-sharing
6 AOB

Review 7

1 Complete the extract from a company mission statement by filling in the spaces with the words from the box below.

> assisting   creating   investing   limiting
> maximizing   promoting

1 _____ financial returns and shareholder value within a socially responsible framework
2 _____ good practice and sustainable policies
3 _____ environmental damage and excessive waste
4 _____ only in enterprises which promote sustainable development
5 _____ a new generation of funds which put progress before profit
6 _____ and training entrepreneurs in developing regions

2 Rewrite each sentence beginning with the word in *italics*, expressing more emphasis but keeping the same meaning.

1 If a counter-bid is launched we are going to have to raise our offer.
   Should _____.
2 In the next session I would like to draw up a long-term investment plan.
   What _____.
3 If someone had told us that ours was the only bid, we could have offered less.
   Had _____.
4 The sealed bids must not be opened for any reason before the closing date.
   Under _____.
5 We might be able to increase our bid if we were in a stronger position financially.
   Were _____.
6 Maurice D'Arby is the candidate we have appointed.
   The _____.
7 Sandra Notham is the Sales Executive who has performed better than any other.
   No _____.
8 Lack of professional discipline is the issue that most concerns me.
   The _____.

3 Fill in the missing letters to complete the investment terms.

1 something expensive: a pr_m__ _m pr_ _ _ _d pr_ _ _c_
2 preferring safer choices: _ _sk-a_ _ _ _s_
3 rely on a single investment: _u_ a_ _ y_ _ _ _ _g_ _ i_ o_ _ b_s_e_
4 strong, low-risk firms: _lu_ c_ _ _ _ c_m_ _ _ _ _ _s
5 wide range of investments: _iv_ _s_ _ _ _d _ _r_f_l_ _
6 increase income: b_ _s_ r_ _ _ _ _u_s
7 share price fluctuations: _ _ _k_t _o_a_ _l_ _ _
8 acting as a group: th_ _e_ _ i_s_ _ _ _c_

9 insufficient clarity: _ _ck _f t_ _ _ _p_r_ _ _y
10 property: _ _i_k_ _n_ m_ _ _a_

4 The words in **bold** below are all in the wrong places. Put them in the correct places.

1 No, we can't consider Maxine Slade for the post – she's out of the **reason** because of her other commitments.
2 Is cost important? I can't believe you're asking – it's a make or break **equation**.
3 It stands to **white** that whoever is prepared to pay a deposit up front is demonstrating a certain level of commitment.
4 Relocation is not the right solution, it's out of the **all** as it's way too expensive.
5 OK, nice office décor is important, but it's not the be all and end **factor** – there's new equipment to consider first.
6 Right, that's clear then: a net profit up 22% in adverse market conditions – the figures speak for **running**.
7 So Tulay's the better candidate and Joe's not even interested in the job, I guess it's pretty black and **case**.
8 All in all it's an open and shut **themselves** – only Marina had access to the money at that time, she was alone in the building, and it was found on her – she's guilty.

5 Fill in the spaces in the sentences below using an appropriate word from the box. Remember to put it in the correct form.

> beat   boost   carve   forecast   generate
> step   trade   underpin

1 Bespoke Artworks have been _____ a niche as a provider of works of art to satisfy the most demanding clients' requirements.
2 Planet Zero are _____ up the pace in their quest to acquire high-quality outlets in key cities for their tried and tested café-bar format.
3 With consumer interest in the sector rising fast, Just Earth Organics look set to _____ healthy profits in the foreseeable future.
4 Recent growth in the sector is _____ by solid consumer demand.
5 Drilling Solutions are _____ a 20% rise in pre-tax profits on the back of rising industry costs.
6 Unveiling like-for-like sales figures up 6%, Michael Thorn announced that Food Star's performance had 'comfortably' _____ market expectations.
7 Following a third profit warning in as many months, Q&J shares were _____ at 70% below their peak yesterday.
8 With their acquisition of rival mortgage provider Southern Marsh, Town and Country Bank have significantly _____ their client base in the south.

Review 8

Free trade

1 The words in **bold** in the following text are all in the wrong places. Put them in the correct places.

Greater liberalization of the world's markets would result in a reduction in global poverty, a top official has said. Trade commissioner Douglas McAvic argued that the best way of increasing the incomes of the world's poorest 20% would be for countries to unilaterally abolish 'market-distorting' (1) **goods** to trade. The latest (2) **protectionism** of talks promises to be every bit as acrimonious as the last, with free marketeers such as Mr McAvic pitted against those in favour of greater (3) **reform** for 'strategic' national industries. With continuing increases in both the quantities and value of (4) **barriers** being traded internationally, both camps, however, do agree on the need for (5) **progress**. Where they differ is on exactly which type of reform. Only time will tell whether some (6) **agreement** will be made, or whether the talks end up going the way of the previous round – without any formal (7) **round** being reached.

2 Choose the right phrasal verb from the box to replace the words in *italics*.

> branch out   call off   come up with   get through
> go in   soldier on   take in   weigh up

1   Given the current economic situation, it is vital that we *diversify* into new markets and seek out new investment opportunities.
2   Provided we can *survive* the current downturn I have no doubt that we can significantly grow our market share.
3   An immediate raise, new responsibilities and the possibility of promotion next year – wow, that's a lot for me to *absorb* right now.
4   OK, listen up you guys, now I want you to follow this three-stage plan: *enter* big, *assess* the opportunities and risks, and *produce* that killer business plan.
5   It's true we've had a few setbacks recently, but I think if we *continue* with our present strategy, we'll eventually start to see the returns.
6   We had to *cancel* the meeting because most people couldn't make it.

3 Fill in the missing letters to complete the key words in the text below.

A great team needs a great range of different types of players to fulfill different roles. You might have some great ideas, but what you really need is an (1) i_ _l_ _ _ _ _ _ _r to actually put people's ideas into action. If your team is too inward-looking, a resource (2) i_ _ _ _ _ _ _g_ _ _ _r could work wonders in exploring outside opportunities. All of us need (3) _m_ _w_ _ _n_, to make sure we have the confidence to work to our full potential. Not that we should do everything ourselves – it's great to (4) d_ _ _ _ _ _ _! And what about someone to pull it all together and act as a chairperson? That'll be a (5) c_o_ _ _ _ _t_ _. A final word: who steps in to (6) c_ _ _h the boss? Everyone else in the team, of course.

4 In each group of five, match each example of the new word in **bold** in sentences 1–10 with its type of formation a)–j).

1   Airports and other transport hubs are now targeting **transumers** – the big-spenders who are just passing through. ☐
2   Remember the **NIMBY** – Not In My Back Yard? Now it's the **BANANA** – Build Absolutely Nothing Anywhere Near Anyone – and put a stop to all new development. ☐
3   In the old days a **crusade** was religious persuasion, now it's all about marketing persuasion. ☐
4   Wired up? Fully **gadgeted**? Now you can **office** to your heart's content, globally, 24/7. ☐
5   If the name Spiro Jonas sounds familiar it's because the former sports **celeb** has now reinvented himself as one of the most sought-after business **celebs**. ☐
6   It used to be Marxism-Leninism, now it's more like **Market Leninism**. ☐
7   Unattached? Need a companion for that corporate event? Get some **arm candy** with that attractive young person you need. ☐
8   Watch out for those clever email scams, and don't open any **Trojan horse** attachments. ☐
9   **Outsourcing** is so last millennium – go for **crowdsourcing** and get the work done almost for free. ☐
10 Too many chiefs? From **CAO** (Chief Accounting Officer) to **CZO** (Chief Zoom Officer – yes, really) you can lump together all those **C-titles** you hate into the **CXO** category. ☐

a) acronyms
b) change the part of speech
c) shortened words
d) blends
e) raid words from other contexts

f) combine old words and affixes to create new words
g) attaching letter
h) rhymes
i) combine two words in a novel combination
j) metaphors

5 Choose the correct adverb from the box to complete the sentences.

> deeply   perfectly   radically   totally   utterly   widely

1   His behaviour was not only _____ inappropriate for the occasion, it was embarrassing!
2   I found it _____ disturbing and upsetting that the company reacted in this way.
3   It's true that she missed the meeting, but she had a _____ valid excuse for it.
4   Introducing such a _____ different approach might be more difficult than you think.
5   Unfortunately, at the time of writing, the new model is not yet _____ available.
6   It turned out to be an _____ disastrous idea: the company was bankrupt within a year.

Additional material

1.6 Case study The glass ceiling
Discussion (page 21, Exercise 7)
Student A

Argue the case for doing the MBA and whatever else it takes to change attitudes at SEVS and get to the top. Too many women give in too easily and never fulfil their potential: Gemma shouldn't waste her talent.

2.2 Vocabulary Corporate social responsibility
Discussion and presentation (page 25, Exercise 7)
Group A

> **INTERNET**
>
> # Tablets for Schools
>
> ### How it works
> The Adlam's Tablets for Schools project allows UK schools to exchange vouchers from purchases at Adlam's supermarkets for tablet PCs and other IT equipment. Simply fill in your order form on our website.
>
> ### How to take part
> UK schools for children of all ages are eligible to take part in the project. Orders for equipment must be received by Thursday 14th December. Any vouchers received after this date will be banked for use in the following year. The final date for banking vouchers is Friday 30th December. No further vouchers can be accepted after this date.
>
> ### Collecting vouchers
> One voucher is given for every £20 spent in Adlam's stores and petrol stations in a single transaction. For every functioning mobile phone your school collects, you will receive 20 vouchers, and five for a non-functioning phone. For every recyclable inkjet cartridge your school collects, you will receive ten vouchers.
>
> For all information about mobile phone recycling, please visit the mobile phone recycling website. Customers donate their vouchers to schools, who can exchange the vouchers for free tablet PCs.

2.4 Management skills Time management
Discussion (page 28, Exercise 3)
Student A

Monday sees us switching into high gear after the weekend: doctors warn we are 33% more likely to have a heart attack on a Monday. Given that people are more demanding and aggressive, this is a day for delegating, setting goals, following your boss's instructions and avoiding conflict.
Tuesday is the peak day for work output and efficiency for many people, and therefore one of the best days to have meetings. However, a new study suggests that productivity is curbed mid-afternoon when it's peak time for online job-hunting.
Wednesday is transition day between hardball, demanding behaviour and a more amenable disposition, but the focus is still on getting things done. This is the best day for creative thinking, strategy and brainstorming.

4.4 Management skills Assertiveness
Roleplay (page 55, Exercise 7)
Student A
Situation 1

You are a union representative at a telecoms company. Your members are network technicians who currently work two shifts, one week early, from 6am to 2pm, and the other week late, from 2pm to 10pm. You have just heard rumours that, because of increased demand, management are now planning to open a third, night shift, from 10pm to 6am. You are furious, firstly because you have not been consulted, and secondly because working nights would be impossible for many of your members, especially the women. You feel that management are trying to exploit your members; you go to the HR Manager's office to find out if the rumours are true.

Situation 2

You are the head of the accounts department of a large company. You know that some of your staff are unhappy with their working conditions, and with the Office Manager, Mr Jamal. Some of their complaints are justified, but generally conditions are better than in most departments, and Mr Jamal is the most efficient Office Manager you have ever had. You would like to make improvements, but in return you need to obtain productivity gains: at the moment too many working days are lost with people calling in sick. You have agreed to meet one of the accountants who seems to be an unofficial staff representative: you expect a difficult meeting, and you will need to be assertive in finding solutions to satisfy everybody.

5.6 Case study **Presnya Taxi**

Reading (page 73, Exercise 5)

Student A

go upmarket, e.g. limos, business only or ladies only cars?

could we use direct mail?

change name, logo, etc. to something more in line with target customer profile?

make clearer, more targeted promise to customers – what?

think laterally, e.g. taxi motorbikes, equipped with comfortable passenger seat, protective clothing and helmet, radio telephone, etc. – radical solution to traffic, comfort and image problems?

Can we find a partner business to share resources and costs?, e.g. hotel/restaurant chain, airline, railway, B²B, football club, other?

Should we have a website?

3.6 Case study **WEF Audio**

Simulation (page 47, Exercise 6)

Group A

You are in favour of introducing a Just-In-Time system. In your view, outsourcing and relocation are much too risky. An on-demand supply chain would mean that no jobs would be lost, and there would be little need for new investment. Franz Theiner is now almost 80, and his judgement is unreliable. He should be encouraged to enjoy his retirement, and to leave the management of the company to Karl Hoffmann, who has a business school education that Eva Theiner does not have.

1.6 Case study **The glass ceiling**

Discussion (page 21, Exercise 7)

Student C

Play the devil's advocate: disagree with everything the others say; challenge them to really convince you they are right.

8.4 Management skills Leading the team

Roleplay (page 107, Exercise 6)

Student B
Meeting 1
Your opinion is that a supermarket chain would be Mile High's best partner in North America. You feel strongly that you need a partner which can offer a wide range of products and services to associate with your flights. Make sure that your talents are recognized and that you are assigned the most interesting tasks.

Meeting 2
You are the team leader for this meeting. Your opinion is that a mobile drive-in cinema would be an exciting and innovative way to promote Mile High in Australia, New Zealand and South Africa. You feel strongly that you need an event which is associated with one of your airline's customer benefits – the latest and best in-flight movies from around the world.

Meeting 3
Your opinion is that the press is the most effective media to advertise Mile High in the UK. You feel strongly that with a total circulation of 12 million the press represents the best value for money. Make sure that your talents are recognized and that you are assigned the most interesting tasks.

7.6 Case study **Lesage Automobile**

Discussion (page 99, Exercise 6)

Student A
You are sceptical about the real potential of a no-frills product, and sensitive to the risks involved in locating production outside western Europe. You are cautious and resist any major investment in what you see as a passing fad.

5.3 Grammar **Prepositions**

Speaking (page 67, Exercise 7)

Student A
Your job as Regional Marketing Negotiator (North America) is now under threat because of the failure of the North American marketing operation. The strategy document proved ineffective, the software was full of bugs and didn't work properly, the hardware failed in the heat of California, and you felt there was a lack of support from Dimitri Karras in Head Office. During the meeting you need to defend yourself and explain why you think you have been let down by Dimitri Karras. Write the following complex prepositions on pieces of paper. Each time you use one, put the piece of paper on the table. The first person to use all their prepositions wins.

> in the light of   in comparison with   with a view to
> in line with   on account of

2.2 Vocabulary Corporate social responsibility
Discussion and presentation (page 25, Exercise 7)
Group B

INTERNET

The Hovey International Prize for Sustainability

The Hovey International Prize for Sustainability is a £1 million prize awarded to organizations demonstrating a comprehensive approach to economic, environmental and/or social sustainability.

Previous winners include community projects for water and sanitation, agriculture and conservation, child health, local employment and renewable energy.

The Hovey Foundation was established in 1986 by George Hovey, founder and president of Hovey Mining Corp. The award is one of the world's most significant, privately funded prizes. One prize is awarded annually. Additionally, grants valued at £20,000 are awarded to the remaining nine shortlisted organizations, with the specific intention of investing in certifiable training and capacity building for the organization.

To ensure the credibility and integrity of the Prize, The Hovey Foundation has formed a partnership with the European Sustainability Council (ESC) to develop, facilitate and manage the programme.

Prize and grant recipients are selected by an independent, high-level international panel of key opinion leaders, who consider both past performance as well as evaluating how organizations will continue to contribute to and impact on sustainability through their ongoing activities.

The inaugural prize was awarded in 2009.
www.georgehoveyfoundation.com

2.4 Management skills Time management
Discussion (page 28, Exercise 3)
Student B
Thursday and Friday find us most open to negotiation and compromise. These could be the best days to ask people to do things: because we want to finish work before the week is out, we are more likely to agree. These just might be the best days to ask for a pay rise – certainly much better than a Monday.
Friday is the day when experiments show workers take more risks, have more accidents, and are more likely to make riskier decisions. It's a good day to confront colleagues with a grievance – or even to make them redundant – because they can come to terms with what you've said over the weekend.
The weekend and holidays frequently see workers who manage high stress through the week succumbing to headaches, fatigue and colds. It may be more tempting to head for the pub after a stressful week, but apparently exercising on a Friday night can help reduce the risk of weekend illness.

3.6 Case study WEF Audio
Simulation (page 47, Exercise 6)
Group B
You are in favour of outsourcing production of the new products: perhaps even the traditional products and the company's administrative processes too. In your view, Just-In-Time or relocation will never enable the company to reduce salaries and costs enough to be competitive with the Chinese. It may be possible for the new provider to lift out some jobs in order to limit the impact on the workforce. Eva is now the majority shareholder of the company, and she should be as objective as possible in making the best decisions for the business, irrespective of her own, her father's and her husband's preferences.

4.4 Management skills Assertiveness
Roleplay (page 55, Exercise 7)
Student B
Situation 1
You are an HR Manager at a telecoms company. Until now your network technicians have worked two shifts, one week early, from 6am to 2pm, and the other week late, from 2pm to 10pm. Because of increased demand, management are now planning to open a third, night shift, from 10pm to 6am. You will be hiring new staff, but you will need some of the experienced technicians to agree to work the night shift. Unfortunately, the plans for a third shift have been leaked before you are ready to talk to the unions. You expect a lot of resistance to the change, but you hope to be able to persuade the union that the new system is in everybody's interest.

Situation 2
You work in the accounts department of a large company. You and your colleagues are very unhappy with your working conditions: the open-plan office is freezing in the winter and stifling in the summer, and noisy all year round; the furniture is old and uncomfortable. The Office Manager, Mr Jamal, is a former sergeant major who thinks he is still in the army and treats staff like children. You have asked to meet the head of department to try to obtain some concessions. In the past, you have tried a diplomatic approach, but nothing has changed: now you feel that only an aggressive, direct approach will get results.

7.6 Case study Lesage Automobile
Discussion (page 99, Exercise 6)
Student B
You are convinced that a no-frills project is essential to Lesage's future. This is a great opportunity for the company to grow, and you are in favour of bold action which will result in a really competitive project. Resist any half-measures; ideally you would like to make a big impact by marketing an even cheaper car than the Logan.

1.6 Case study The glass ceiling
Discussion (page 21, Exercise 7)
Student B
Argue the case for putting her husband and daughter first. No job can ever provide the same satisfaction as bringing up children. Gemma doesn't seem to have the maturity or the patience to be a marketing manager: she should choose quality of life over status and money.

5.6 Case study **Presnya Taxi**
Reading (page 73, Exercise 5)
Student B

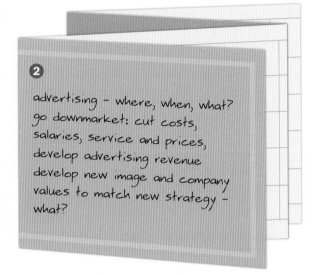

1

make current, 'we do better' strategy more visible – how?
organize events – what?
Can we use the Internet to enhance customer service/experience, perhaps with partners?
what about sponsoring a basketball team?

2

advertising – where, when, what?
go downmarket: cut costs, salaries, service and prices,
develop advertising revenue
develop new image and company values to match new strategy – what?

8.4 Management skills **Leading the team**
Roleplay (page 107, Exercise 6)
Student A
Meeting 1
You are the team leader for this meeting. Your opinion is that a national or international bank would be Mile High's best partner in North America. You feel strongly that you need a partner with a long-term personal relationship with its customers.
Meeting 2
Your opinion is that an extreme sports event would be an exciting and innovative way to promote Mile High in Australia, New Zealand and South Africa. You feel strongly that you need an event which will differentiate the airline from the usual boring promotional parties. Make sure that your talents are recognized and that you are assigned the most interesting tasks.
Meeting 3
Your opinion is that TV is the most effective media to advertise Mile High in the UK. You feel strongly that you need a campaign which will grab customers' attention, and as they say, a picture paints a thousand words. Make sure that your talents are recognized and that you are assigned the most interesting tasks.

7.3 Grammar **Inversion and emphasis**
Negotiation (page 93, Exercise 8)
Group B
You manage a medium-sized investment portfolio in stocks and shares. You want to grow your business and attract a significant body of new clients in a different investment area. By far the quickest and most effective way of doing this is to enter into an alliance with an investment management company which specializes in a different area. You have narrowed the field down to two companies: A, which specializes in real estate, and C, which deals in commodities. In the current investment climate, you have good reason to believe that each of these groups also wants to diversify and form an alliance. Antitrust laws forbid alliances between more than two groups.
Use the information below to prepare your arguments to persuade the other two groups that you are the best company to form an alliance with.

Consider:
- how long the company has been established
- its corporate structure and ownership
- how large its client base is
- where in the world the company mainly operates
- any strategic plans for the future regarding geographical expansion; number of employees
- recent operating profits
- proportion of the company's budget spent on research.

3.5 Writing **Emails**
Output (page 45, Exercise 7)
Student A
Situation 1
1 You design and market smartphones in Europe. Student B assembles your product in China. You have been experiencing regular delays in delivery of your new model, which is in great demand. Customers are frustrated when they have to wait more than two weeks for delivery. Write an email to Student B asking for an explanation and a promise of improvement.
2 You have received an email from Student B concerning their price. Write an appropriate reply.
3 You have received a second email from Student B in reply to your email about delivery times. Write an appropriate answer.

Situation 2
1 You supply electrical sub-components from your factory in eastern Europe for your customer, Student B, a Japanese car manufacturer. Your last two invoices have not been paid; write an email to Student B asking for an explanation and quick settlement.
2 You have received an email from Student B concerning a quality problem. Write an appropriate reply.
3 You have received a second email from Student B in reply to your email about your invoices. Write an appropriate answer.

6.1 About business Crisis management
Discussion (page 74, Exercise 1)

1c Tylenol, a Johnson & Johnson® company, was praised for recalling 31 million bottles when this happened in 1982. After falling to 8%, the product subsequently recovered its 35% market share when it was relaunched in a tamper-proof package.

2c Wendy's™ restaurants lost millions of dollars in sales and had to make redundancies when a woman claimed she had found a finger in her chilli in 2005. The company contested the woman's story, and she was eventually sentenced to nine years in prison for filing a fraudulent insurance claim.

3b In 2007, CBS cancelled a show and terminated a contract worth $40 million with Don Imus, a TV and radio talk show host who had made racist remarks about a female basketball team.

4b Eric Dezenhall, the co-author of *Damage Control*, says that his company refuses this type of PR contract.

3.6 Case study WEF Audio
Simulation (page 47, Exercise 6)
Group C

You are in favour of relocating the company's production unit to North Africa, eastern Europe or even Asia. In your view, quality is still your key USP, so although cutting costs is critical if the company is to survive, it is essential to retain control over production, and to keep the company's competitive advantages secret. Relocating key production staff (including Karl Hoffmann) to the new site would guarantee quality whilst cutting costs. You feel strongly that as General Manager, Eva should be allowed to run the company in the way she wishes, without interference from her husband or her father.

1.6 Case study The glass ceiling
Discussion (page 21, Exercise 7)
Student D

Argue the case for taking up the headhunter's offer and moving to Sweden. Gemma's career prospects will be infinitely better in a country which takes equal opportunities seriously.

7.6 Case study Lesage Automobile
Discussion (page 99, Exercise 6)
Student C

You are not against a no-frills project, provided that the workforce in the French factories is protected. Resist any proposals which could mean that jobs might be lost in the short, medium or long term.

7.3 Grammar Inversion and emphasis
Negotiation (page 93, Exercise 8)
Group A

You manage a medium-sized investment portfolio in real estate. You want to grow your business and attract a significant body of new clients in a different investment area. By far the quickest and most effective way of doing this is to enter into an alliance with an investment management company which specializes in a different area. You have narrowed the field down to two companies: B, which specializes in stocks and shares, and C, which deals in commodities. In the current investment climate, you have good reason to believe that each of these groups also wants to diversify and form an alliance. Antitrust laws forbid alliances between more than two groups.

Use the information below to prepare your arguments to persuade the other two groups that you are the best company to form an alliance with.

Consider:
- how long the company has been established
- its corporate structure and ownership
- how large its client base is
- where in the world the company mainly operates
- any strategic plans for the future regarding geographical expansion; number of employees
- recent operating profits
- proportion of the company's budget spent on research.

3.5 Writing Emails
Output (page 45, Exercise 7)
Student B
Situation 1

1. You assemble smartphones in China for your European customer, Student A. You have recently had to agree to salary increases for your workers to avoid a strike. This will mean a 4% increase in the price you invoice Student A. Write an email explaining the situation.
2. You have received an email from Student A concerning delivery times. Write an appropriate reply.
3. You have received a second email from Student A in reply to your email about the price increase. Write an appropriate answer.

Situation 2

1. You manufacture cars in Japan. Student A provides electrical sub-components from their factory in eastern Europe. You have identified a quality problem in the latest batch you have received. Write an email to Student A asking for an explanation and compensation for the inconvenience you have suffered.
2. You have received an email from Student A concerning invoices. Write an appropriate reply.
3. You have received a second email from Student A in reply to your email about the quality problem. Write an appropriate answer.

2.2 Vocabulary Corporate social responsibility

Discussion and presentation (page 25, Exercise 7)

Group C

> **INTERNET**
>
> ### The Yaxley Pharma Nursing Excellence scheme
>
> In June 2010 the first graduates of Yaxley Pharma's Nursing Excellence scheme returned home to seven East African countries to take up nursing positions in local health centres. Under the scheme, Yaxley sponsors female students from rural areas to take nursing degrees in the United Kingdom. So far Yaxley has donated in excess of £1.5 million to train some 120 nurses. The programme is run in partnership with The Manchester College of Nursing, the Department of Health and the Hospitals Association of East Africa. After completing their training, the newly-qualified nurses put their skills to work in their local communities for a minimum of three years.

5.3 Grammar Prepositions

Speaking (page 67, Exercise 7)

Student C

You are the Managing Director of Rainbow Software Solutions and you want to get to the bottom of why the attempt to break into the North American market was such a terrible failure. You have great faith in the cloud-based communications software that Rainbow has developed and you pushed for it to be rolled out early because you wanted to be first in the market with such an innovative product. You are reluctant to believe that a few minor technical problems could have caused the problem and you suspect that the failure is entirely due to an incompetent sales and marketing team, particularly Dimitri Karras, the Marketing Director. Write the following complex prepositions on pieces of paper. Each time you use one, put the piece of paper on the table. The first person to use all their prepositions wins.

> in the wake of   in comparison with   in accordance with
> on account of   in the light of

8.4 Management skills Leading the team

Roleplay (page 107, Exercise 6)

Student C
Meeting 1
Your opinion is that the post office would be Mile High's best partner in North America. You feel strongly that you need a partner which will bring respectability to your flights – the company's image is currently too risqué. Make sure that your talents are recognized and that you are assigned the most interesting tasks.

Meeting 2
Your opinion is that a rock concert tour would be an exciting and innovative way to promote Mile High in Australia, New Zealand and South Africa. You feel strongly that you need an event which will attract your core customer base and reinforce the 'party plane' image. Make sure that your talents are recognized and that you are assigned the most interesting tasks.

Meeting 3
You are the team leader for this meeting. Your opinion is that direct mail is the most cost-effective way to advertise Mile High in the UK. You feel strongly that you need a campaign which is as well-targeted as possible on your 18-35 customer base.

8.6 Case study The cartel

Negotiation (page 111, Exercise 5)

Team B
Holoplay PLC
You are meeting representatives of ThreeD-Vision Inc. to negotiate the terms of an agreement which will protect your mutual interests. Depending on the outcome of your negotiations, the result may be anything from a vague gentlemen's agreement to a fully-fledged cartel.
Your holo-player costs you $650 per unit to produce. At the moment your market share is 70% in Europe and 30% in the US.
Your projected annual production capacity is as follows: (million units)

Y1	Y2	Y3	Y4	Y5
5	20	40	70	100

Your corporate objectives are to:
1 maintain market share and margin in Europe
2 improve market share in the US
3 keep prices as high as possible and move into other markets gradually.
Your competitive advantage: although your holo-player is a little more expensive to produce than ThreeD-Vision's, you believe your quality is better: tests show that at the same price, 75% of customers will choose your product.

1.6 Case study The glass ceiling

Discussion (page 21, Exercise 7)

Student E
Argue the case for accepting the status quo and trying to find a compromise. Gemma should not have to decide between her family and her career: millions of women manage to reconcile the two, so why not her?

3.2 Vocabulary **Logistics**
Discussion (page 38, Exercise 1)

1c) according to a study by the Cardiff Business School

2a)

3c) according to an advertisement for shipping company P&O

4c)

5c) according to industry analysts and academics

8.4 Management skills **Leading the team**
Roleplay (page 107, Exercise 6)

Students D and E
Meeting 1
Express your own opinions and feelings on who would be Mile High's best partner in North America. Make sure that your talents are recognized and that you are assigned the most interesting tasks.
Meeting 2
Express your own opinions and feelings on the most exciting and innovative way to promote Mile High in Australia, New Zealand and South Africa. Make sure that your talents are recognized and that you are assigned the most interesting tasks.
Meeting 3
Express your own opinions and feelings on the most effective media to advertise Mile High in the UK. Make sure that your talents are recognized and that you are assigned the most interesting tasks.

5.3 Grammar **Prepositions**
Speaking (page 67, Exercise 7)

Student B
You are the Marketing Director, Dimitri Karras and you are in a difficult position because of the failure of the North American marketing operation. The Production Department insisted on launching the software before it had been tested properly so it turned out there were bugs in it and no one had calculated that the heat of California would cause the software to malfunction. On top of this, the Regional Marketing Negotiator totally lacked the vision to develop a coherent marketing strategy or to come up with any ideas for addressing the problems. During the meeting you need to defend yourself and explain why you think you have been let down by the Production Department. Write the following complex prepositions on pieces of paper. Each time you use one, put the piece of paper on the table. The first person to use all their prepositions wins.

| owing to | with a view to | in line with | as a result of |
| prior to |

7.3 Grammar **Inversion and emphasis**
Negotiation (page 93, Exercise 8)

Group C
You manage a medium-sized investment portfolio in commodities. You want to grow your business and attract a significant body of new clients in a different investment area. By far the quickest and most effective way of doing this is to enter into an alliance with an investment management company which specializes in a different area. You have narrowed the field down to two companies: A, which deals in real estate, and B, which specializes in stocks and shares. In the current investment climate, you have good reason to believe that each of these groups also wants to diversify and form an alliance. Antitrust laws forbid alliances between more than two groups.
Use the information below to prepare your arguments to persuade the other two groups that you are the best company to form an alliance with.

Consider:
- how long the company has been established
- its corporate structure and ownership
- how large its client base is
- where in the world the company mainly operates
- any strategic plans for the future regarding geographical expansion; number of employees
- recent operating profits
- proportion of the company's budget spent on research.

2.2 Vocabulary **Corporate social responsibility**
Discussion (page 24, Exercise 2)

1 The business of business should not be about money, it should be about responsibility. It should be about public good, not private greed.
ANITA RODDICK, FOUNDER OF THE BODY SHOP

2 CSR has built-in incentives for hypocrisy because when businesses face a conflict between making money and social responsibility, making money tends to prevail.
GEORGE SOROS, ENTREPRENEUR AND PHILANTHROPIST

3 Ethics is the new competitive environment.
PETER ROBINSON, CEO MOUNTAIN EQUIPMENT CO-OP

4 People are going to want, and be able, to find out about the citizenship of a brand, whether it is doing the right things socially, economically and environmentally.
MIKE CLASPER, PRESIDENT OF BUSINESS DEVELOPMENT, PROCTOR AND GAMBLE (EUROPE)

5 There is one and only one social responsibility of business – to use its resources and engage in activities designed to increase its profits so long as it stays within the rules of the game ...
MILTON FRIEDMAN, ECONOMIST

7.6 Case study Lesage Automobile
Discussion (page 99, Exercise 6)
Students D and E

You have an open mind about the advantages and disadvantages of a no-frills product. Treat each proposal on its merits, and try to be as objective as possible about the pros and cons.

3.6 Case study WEF Audio
Simulation (page 47, Exercise 6)
Group D

You are in favour of preserving the status quo. The company is fundamentally healthy and profitable: sales are increasing, and costs will fall now that the new product development stage is finished. In your view, making any major changes would be dangerous and unfair to the people who have worked for WEF all their lives. The company has always had good relations with the unions, and these should not be jeopardized. Although Franz Theiner is now almost 80, he is still President of the company: as the founder his belief in quality should be respected. The company should make no changes to the successful strategies he has developed over the last 50 years, and the personal problems of the next generation should not have an impact on business decisions.

8.6 Case study The cartel
Negotiation (page 111, Exercise 5)
Team A

ThreeD-Vision Inc.

You are meeting representatives of Holoplay PLC to negotiate the terms of an agreement which will protect your mutual interests. Depending on the outcome of your negotiations, the result may be anything from a vague gentlemen's agreement to a fully-fledged cartel.

Your holo-player costs you $500 per unit to produce. At the moment your market share is 70% in the US and 30% in Europe.

Your projected annual production capacity is as follows: (million units)

Y1	Y2	Y3	Y4	Y5
8	25	60	100	150

Your corporate objectives are to:
1 maintain market share and margin in the US
2 improve market share in Europe
3 build market share as quickly as possible in Asia and other markets.

Your competitive advantage: although Holoplay's product has slightly better quality levels than your holo-player, you can produce larger volumes more cheaply; you expect to reduce your costs per unit to $400 when you reach annual production of 60 million units.

8.4 Management skills Leading the team
Roleplay (page 107, Exercise 6)

Leadership
checklist

During the meeting, did the team leader:

- [ ] share information and feelings freely?
- [ ] show interest in others' ideas and feelings?
- [ ] prioritize tasks and manage time efficiently?
- [ ] delegate or assign tasks sensitively?
- [ ] allow initiative?
- [ ] communicate goals and priorities?
- [ ] identify problems and obstacles, and develop strategies to deal with them?
- [ ] foster enthusiasm for the project?
- [ ] deal with disagreement or conflict assertively?
- [ ] employ appropriate management style(s)?
- [ ] use active listening techniques?
- [ ] display body language consistent with their message?
- [ ] use sound bites and rhetorical techniques to highlight key points?
- [ ] adopt a logical and systematic approach to decision-making?
- [ ] obtain a consensus for decisions taken?
- [ ] ensure that all team roles were represented?

Grammar and practice

1 Personal development

Tense and aspect

Tense is how verb forms are related to time. In English we can choose present or past.

Aspect refers to how we see things: perfect (completed or finished) or continuous (in progress). As English has no future tense, lots of other forms are used instead (see module 2.3).

Present tense	
+ nothing (i.e. simple)	*I live*
+ perfect aspect	*I have lived*
+ continuous aspect	*I am living*
+ perfect and continuous aspects	*I have been living*

Past tense	
+ nothing (i.e. simple)	*I lived*
+ perfect aspect	*I had lived*
+ continuous aspect	*I was living*
+ perfect and continuous aspects	*I had been living*

Conversations and narratives use the widest range of tenses and aspects. Academic writing has fewer verbs with an aspect and the continuous is particularly unusual. Over 90% of verbs in academic texts are in the present or past simple.

1 Fill in the spaces in the text below with an appropriate verb from the box. Do not change the verb form.

> be   don't envisage   has suggested   intend   'm   put
> smarten up   to build   to take   to watch
> 've been learning   've learned

Over the next two years my plan is (1) _____ on what I have achieved recently and make myself more employable. First, I (2) _____ to focus on brushing up my academic writing skills in English. That will (3) _____ a good start. I (4) _____ English for about six years now, but it's only recently that I (5) _____ how to write an academic essay in English. I (6) _____ any particular obstacles as far as my work is concerned, but I do need (7) _____ the initiative more. My line manager (8) _____ that I (9) _____ my appearance a bit. I guess he has a point. I should also consistently (10) _____ work first – after all I (11) _____ not a student anymore! It would be disastrous for my colleagues (12) _____ me throw away everything I've worked for so far. In short my new motto is: focus, plan, act!

Some structures are normally followed by the past tense, even though the actual time being referred to is the present. These include: *it's (about/high) time, I wish, I'd rather* and unreal (hypothetical) *if*.

In the structure *have something (done)* we use the past participle. Informally we can say *get something done*.

2 Complete the sentences by putting the verb in brackets into the most appropriate tense and aspect.

1   It's time I _____ (look) again at my training priorities.
2   Commodity prices _____ (not rise) this fast since 2008.
3   I wish I _____ (have) more time to finish the job properly.
4   Our sales figures _____ (get) worse by the day – something must be done about it.
5   I had the document _____ (draw up) by the new legal firm – they did a great job.
6   How long _____ (be) you here for – is it next Tuesday you fly back?
7   It _____ (be) when I was flying to Shanghai that the idea came to me.
8   That must be the tenth time you _____ (ask) me that question.
9   I need a reply. Tell Francesca I _____ (wait) for her to get back to me.
10   _____ (you/write) many applications yet?
11   This time I really _____ (need) you to deliver the goods and come up with something brilliant.
12   I'd rather you _____ (not advertise) that position just yet – we haven't definitely got funding for it.
13   You look like you _____ (run) through the rain – why are you all wet?
14   You _____ (look) a lot more up for it these days – I guess your holiday did you the world of good.

The present continuous

This may refer to the immediate present, but it often refers to around now, whether the weeks, months or years (or longer) around now. In all cases the present continuous refers to events which are unfinished.

3 Read the sentences below and decide whether the present continuous in each one is most likely to refer to: right now (*RN*), around now (*AN*), the longer term (*LT*) or the future (*F*).

1   The polar ice caps are melting. ☐
2   I'm seeing Diego then – how about 11.30? ☐
3   The local currency is still slipping against the euro. ☐
4   He's becoming more and more forgetful. ☐
5   Ahmad's just finishing it off – I'll get it to you very soon. ☐
6   I'm working on my dissertation so I won't be able to see you for a while. ☐
7   Sea levels are rising and some low-lying coastal settlements are being threatened. ☐
8   She's having a baby. ☐
9   Are you laughing at me? ☐
10   They're building a new multimedia centre when the old library gets knocked down. ☐

Conditionals

If sentences can be quite complicated. The *if* clause is typically first, but the order of the clauses can be reversed for a change in emphasis. The descriptions below are based around time and reality:

Timeless, universal, always true – 'zero' conditional (*if* + subject + present tense, subject + present tense): *If interest rates go up, the cost of borrowing normally increases*.

Future time, quite likely – First conditional (*if* + subject + present tense, subject + modal): *If she does well in the interview, she will/should/may get the job.* [paraphrase: 'on condition that she performs well in the interview, the chances of getting the job are reasonably good']

Future time, unlikely – Second conditional (*if* + subject + past tense, subject + *would*): *If she got the job I'd be amazed.* [paraphrase: 'it's possible, but I really don't think it's at all likely that she'll get the job']

Present time, unreal – Second conditional (*if* + subject + past tense, subject + *would*): *If we had the resources we would be able to help you.* [paraphrase: 'we don't have the resources so it's not possible to help you']

Past time, unreal – Third conditional (*if* + subject + past perfect, subject + *would have* past participle): *If I'd realized what a cowboy outfit this company was I would never have taken the job.* [paraphrase: 'this company is a cowboy outfit, but when I took the job I didn't realize this, so now I'm upset about it']

Past unreal event affecting real present time – mixed third and second conditional (*if* + subject + past perfect, subject + modal + infinitive): *If I had passed the exam I might/would be in a better job now.* [paraphrase: 'I failed the exam which means I'm now in a worse job']

Present unreal event, past real event – mixed second and third conditional (*if* + subject + past tense, subject + *would have* past participle): *If the company operated there, they would have been badly affected by last week's currency crash.* [paraphrase: 'the company doesn't operate there, so they haven't been affected by last week's currency crash']

4 Choose the most appropriate tense to complete the following sentences.

1 I'd be surprised if he _____ (reach) his sales targets this year.
2 If you _____ (ask) me there's no chance it'll happen.
3 If you _____ (pass) by the office on your way out, could you tell Arne I'll be down in a minute?
4 People who complain are generally happier if you _____ (sit down) and spend a bit of time listening to them.
5 If only I _____ (know) about her problems I wouldn't have dismissed her so quickly.
6 The report would be finished by now – if you _____ (leave) me in peace and _____ (give) me enough time to get on with it.

7 If only I _____ (listen) to your advice, I wouldn't be in this mess now.
8 Be thankful we're not in real estate – if we _____ (be) in the business of selling houses we _____ (hit) really badly by the recent property crash.
9 There's no way the sales results would be so bad if we _____ (be) part of the team from the beginning.
10 In my view, she would never have got so far if it _____ (be) for her family connections.

Active and passive voice

Active: *They are constructing a new retail outlet.*
Passive: *A new retail outlet is being constructed.*

To form the passive voice use *be* as an auxiliary verb and keep the same tense and aspect, in this example the present continuous. The passive is used: to focus on one topic, *Oil is produced ... Oil is refined ... Then it is transported ...*; to make a text more formal or objective; when we do not know or want to avoid saying who did something, *Mistakes have regrettably been made*, or it is unnecessary, *The equipment should then be disconnected*.

The passive voice is more common in academic writing than other kinds of text, accounting for about 20% of verbs, but it is quite rare in conversation – just 2% of verbs.

5 Read the following text and decide whether the active or passive forms are the most appropriate.

Employees and motivation

In recent years (1) *a great deal of research has been done / they have done a great deal of research* into motivation in the workplace. Yet misconceptions (2) *are persisted / persist*. Not only (3) *do many employees believe / is it believed by many employees* that money is the main source of motivation, but also that motivation must come from outside. This external, or extrinsic, motivation might be in the form of rewards for (4) *the achievement of a specific degree of success by employees / employees who have achieved a specific degree of success*. While (5) *such rewards may be wanted by employees / employees may want such rewards*, they might not be aware that a different kind of motivation is equally powerful. (6) *Intrinsic motivation plays a major role / A major role is played by intrinsic motivation* in getting workers on task and on the road to success. This kind of motivation comes from within and (7) *external rewards do not affect it / is not affected by external rewards*. Finally, employees (8) *can help themselves / can be helped by* individually drawing up a personalized plan involving self-motivational techniques.

The future in English

Not only *will*, the most neutral modal, but all the other modals are used to talk about the future. Other ways include *ought to, going to*, the present tense for timetabled events and the present continuous for arrangements.

There are also many longer forms popular in journalistic writing which can include one or more of the following: a modal verb, state verb and finally the main verb:

may	be	about to	finish
might	appear	bound to	
must	look	likely to	
could	seem	unlikely to	
can		sure to	
shall		set to	
should		certain to	
ought to		due to	
will		poised to	
would		destined to	
		on the point of	
		on the verge of	finishing
		on the brink of	

1 Read the newspaper article and fill in the spaces with the missing future forms from the box.

> are expected to focus mainly on   can tackle
> could significantly worsen   is likely to seek
> is set to ask for   leaves   'll see   meet   move
> should have   take   would be lost

US President Doug Winehouse and John Diaz (1) _____ today in London for formal talks on a wide range of issues. They (2) _____ the current financial crisis and the next round of trade talks. The British Prime Minister (3) _____ concessions on certain UK exports to the United States, while Mr Winehouse (4) _____ reassurances on sustaining current troop levels from his UK counterpart. Although there is less than a year before President Winehouse (5) _____ office, Mr Diaz hopes that they (6) _____ a wide range of important issues before his actual departure. Diaz feels that without action now the world trade and security prospects (7) _____ and the chances of making a positive impact (8) _____. 'As we (9) _____ towards greater economic integration over the coming months, and provided we (10) _____ action soon, the situation (11) _____ every chance of success,' said Mr Diaz yesterday. We (12) _____.

2 Choose the most appropriate future form for each sentence.

1 The report _____ ready for you by the end of the week – I've already written most of it.
   a) will have been   b) is   c) should be

2 What do you think about the latest proposals? Do you think they _____?
   a) 're likely to work   b) must work   c) 're sure to work

3 My meeting is supposed to be at two, but it _____ late – it always does.
   a) 's going to start   b) 's bound to start   c) should start

4 Following the recent adverse trading conditions, a series of profit warnings _____.
   a) are on the brink of being made
   b) look likely to be made   c) can be made

5 And with an insurmountable lead and just one game to go Marina Splendova _____ the women's final!
   a) will win   b) is winning   c) is on the verge of winning

6 Why not take my laptop – I _____ it until tomorrow.
   a) won't be needing   b) am not needing
   c) don't seem to need

Verb patterns in advice structures

A major area in which we refer to the future is to express functions such as offering advice, suggestions and recommendations. The most common tense for these is the present. The *-ing* form (gerund), *would* (as we're giving advice which is not yet real) or the imperative form are also used.

3 Match a beginning on the left with an ending on the right to make advice structures.

1 My view is that you should
2 I would recommend that
3 I'd advise
4 You want
5 If I were you
6 It's high time you
7 Go
8 It looks as if you

a) putting strategy before image.
b) are going to have to allow your workforce to settle down before the next big change.
c) I'd come up with a new mission statement.
d) for it!
e) give your staff a raise.
f) to get your sales staff working better as a team.
g) concentrated on finding out how people see the company.
h) you listen to your boss a bit more.

Modal verbs

Verbs comprise about one in six words in texts, and one in every ten verbs is a modal. In order of frequency the core modals are: *will, would, can, could, may, should, must, might* and *shall*.

Modal verbs are used to express both personal meanings and more impersonal, logical meanings; their major functions are to express stance (see 6.3), which is personal, and impersonal notions such as possibility and prohibition. Modal verbs are not associated with things that actually exist; they are used for things which are possible, likely, necessary, uncertain, habitual or expected.

4 <u>Underline</u> the modal verb in each sentence which does not fit the meaning given in brackets.

1 I *must / will / shall* be out of the office on Friday – it's the first day of my holiday. (future, certain)
2 It *oughtn't to / won't / shouldn't* be a problem to meet the deadline. (future, probable)
3 We *might / should / may / could* all end up in jail if we go ahead with this. (future, possible)
4 Unless they get the order authorized in time it *can't / shouldn't / won't* be delivered. (future, impossible)
5 They *will / should / must / may* win the contract. (future, predicting)
6 *Need / Must / Shall* we register in advance or can we just turn up on the day? (future, obligation)
7 For health and safety reasons you *can't / ought not to / may not / must not* go into that part of the building. (prohibition)
8 What I think we *should / may / ought to* do now is consult our lawyer. (recommendation)
9 *Shall / Can / May / Might / Could* I take next Tuesday off? (permission)
10 You *might / could / may* wish to work a little on your grammatical accuracy. (advising)

Tentative and speculative language

When speaking or writing, users of English often use language which is to some degree indirect, cautious or softened. This language is either fairly personal, **You might want to consider that**, or more impersonal, **It seems likely to fail**. Such language allows room for manoeuvre by avoiding very definite statements. It also means the speaker can avoid offence and sound more polite.

Modal verbs and semi-modals, certain adverbials including prepositional phrases, e.g. **in a way**, noun phrases, e.g. **There is little doubt that**, and the passive voice, e.g. **It is widely claimed that**, can all be used to make language sound more tentative. The future forms above can be used to produce speculative language. Modal verbs cannot be used with tenses (present and past) as they are an alternative to tenses.
They can be used with an aspect and can be made passive. The **perfect** (modal + **have** + past participle) is used mainly to speculate in past time, e.g. **She might have miscalculated.** and the **continuous** (modal + **be** + present participle) in present time: **They could be developing the same idea even as we speak.**

5 Rewrite each sentence using the phrase in brackets, using a more tentative style but keeping a similar meaning.

1 If you ask me, the whole plan is bound to fail.
   (little doubt) _____
2 Most people believe that the causes of inflation are rising commodity prices, but it's not that simple.
   (widely believed) _____
3 In my view, we need our customers to love us more.
   (would argue) _____

4 How about talking to him about it?
   (to consider) _____
5 She probably got the sums wrong.
   (may well) _____
6 They're working on it now, almost certainly.
   (be working) _____
7 There's no way he'll ever convince the CEO to change our logo.
   (highly unlikely) _____
8 The outcome will be negative.
   (no real possibility) _____

6 Two sentences in each group of three are close in meaning. Choose the one which is different, and identify why.

1 a) There is widespread agreement that the two treaties are in fact somewhat similar.
   b) It seems to me that certain similarities do exist between the two treaties.
   c) In some respects the two treaties are actually rather similar, in my view.
2 a) The new restaurant format ought to result in increased per-customer spend.
   b) Per-customer spend could increase on account of the new restaurant format.
   c) Customers should soon be spending more, given the new restaurant format.
3 a) There is little possibility that agreement will be reached by the Friday deadline.
   b) The chances of reaching agreement by the Friday deadline are quite significant.
   c) Agreement is unlikely to be reached by the Friday deadline.
4 a) The latest sales figures would suggest a consumer downturn despite other evidence to the contrary.
   b) Certain evidence may suggest otherwise, but a consumer downturn seems likely given the latest sales figures.
   c) A consumer downturn could be a possibility, in line with convincing evidence to suggest this.
5 a) A major shift in consumer behaviour towards more 'sustainable shopping' could happen soon.
   b) We are on the verge of a major shift in consumer behaviour towards more 'sustainable shopping'.
   c) Consumer behaviour is about to shift significantly towards more 'sustainable shopping'.
6 a) It seems doubtful whether we can make any price increases stick in the current economic climate.
   b) In the current economic climate price increases would seem to be an attractive option for us.
   c) If we put up prices in the current economic climate we would probably have to lower them again quite soon.
7 a) You may wish to consider improving your current punctuality record.
   b) Your current punctuality record would seem to be one area on which you could focus.
   c) You must take steps to substantially improve your current punctuality record.

Nouns modifying nouns

> We can use one or more nouns to modify the head noun:
> **business + activity = business activity**
> **information + resources = information resources**
> The head noun is normally the final noun, and this is the noun which can be replaced with a pronoun:
> **information resources = they/them**
> These structures can become longer noun phrases if more detail needs to be added.

1 Complete the noun phrases in the text using appropriate words or phrases from the box.

> allocation   allocation issues   business   cost reduction
> costs   information resources   optimization model
> problem

Given the significant competitive pressures on (1) our operating _____, our priority must now be both to cut down on what we spend and make better use of what we have. In other words, we must focus on (2) effective resource _____. This involves allocating the four resource inputs of (3) any _____ activity, regardless of the particular type of business. These include (4) physical, human, financial and _____. As a company, (5) our main resource _____ are concerned with flexibility and scarcity. To tackle what is essentially (6) a resource allocation _____ we need an effective solution. In order to make the best use of the resources available it is likely that this solution will take the form of a (7) carefully-formulated _____: such models typically aim both to use resources better and reduce overall costs. Finally, after formulation of (8) our _____ strategy, we need to have robust systems in place to ensure its effective implementation.

Longer noun phrases

> In order to 'pack in' information, long noun phrases can be built up by adding words before the head noun, and/or after it. For example, the noun **climate** can become the head of a long noun phrase:
> **a difficult investment climate characterized by over-regulation**
> Noun phrases often begin with a determiner, after which adjectives and/or nouns can be added, then the head noun, possibly followed by a prepositional phrase or a relative clause. Relative clauses are often used when giving definitions.
> These long phrases are used in many kinds of writing, particularly academic writing. They can function as the subject, object or complement in a sentence. Noun phrases are also the most frequent type of structure to follow prepositions.

2 Each sentence in the text below contains a longer noun phrase in *italics* which has been mixed up. Put the words into the correct order.

1 In a world in which consumers expect goods to be ever-present on the shelves, *chain effective management supply* of the full range of goods available is more critical than ever.
   In a world in which consumers expect goods to be ever-present on the shelves, <u>effective supply chain management</u> of the full range of goods available is more critical than ever.

2 If the shelf is empty, the consumer will most likely give up and buy nothing, or buy *rival a product* from another retail outlet, in which case the customer may be lost forever.

3 Yet how can today's logistics operators assure *supply success chain* within ever-tighter financial constraints?

4 While the difficulties involved are considerable, the rewards for *innovative which successfully are solutions most the implemented* can be exceptional.

5 Some companies have gone for *from shelf approach the back an called innovative*, which involves putting first whatever the consumer wants, whatever the difficulties involved.

6 In this way, shelves are always, it is hoped, abundantly stocked, but the downside is that costs rise – to constantly focus on the 'shelf', the supply chain has to be more flexible and fast-acting, which necessitates *operating an rise costs unavoidable in* and a fall in company profits.

7 One consideration which cannot be ignored is packaging – by putting the consumer first, companies have to supply their goods in *of ever-increasing size formats range an*.

8 Consider the cost implications of supplying *sold different of or at all the rice tea variations store size your local*.

9 These sell quickly to their target consumers, but the more products *variation principle size applied of this is to* the more costs escalate – and this means not just production costs but those of supplying the goods.

10 *the container approach the adopted massive industry alternative by shipping* is to standardize supply systems, times and sizes.

11 However, just as this is undoubtedly cheaper, today's consumers are not content with a one-size-fits-all approach, which brings us back to our starting point: distribution of a large and growing range of goods is *issues challenging chain managers one of facing the most supply* today.

Relative clauses

Relative clauses are a common form of postmodification, and directly follow a head noun, expanding the meaning and specifying the reference of the head noun. These clauses contain the main elements of a clause (verb, subject, etc.) and are introduced by a relative pronoun or relative adverb. Relative pronouns are *which, that, who, whom, whose* and relative adverbs include *where, when* and *why*.

Defining relative clauses
These postmodify a noun phrase, giving more information about it.
We interviewed students who had scored over 70% in our test. (All the students we interviewed had scored over 70%.)
The relative pronoun can be omitted if it is the object, but not if it is the subject of the relative clause.
Did you do the homework (which) I gave you? [object]
A noun phrase is a type of phrase which has a noun as head. [subject]

Non-defining relative clauses
These add rather than restrict, giving non-essential, extra information following a noun phrase. There is a comma before them, and the whole relative clause can be missed out.
Buy it at the college shop, which has loads of stationery.

3 Tick (✓) all the possible correct endings for the noun phrases in the sentences below.

1 This is definitely the strategy
    that we should adopt. ☐
    which is the most viable. ☐
    what I feel is the right one. ☐
    whose purpose is to win hearts and minds. ☐
    I've decided on. ☐
2 Patricia Di Fabia is the person
    which we should hire. ☐
    that would be best for the job. ☐
    I believe would be an outstanding leader. ☐
    whom could be the right choice. ☐
    who I think is the strongest candidate for the post. ☐
3 We need to construct our flagship depot in a place
    we feel to be at the heart of the manufacturing region. ☐
    is situated in a central location. ☐
    where transport links are optimally sited. ☐
    that has the strongest transport links. ☐
4 Ray Lewis is an investor
    whose vision is aligned to ours. ☐
    that never lets us down. ☐
    I have always admired. ☐
    which needs treating with circumspection. ☐
    who builds long-term relations with companies. ☐
5 That is the main reason
    I won't be able to meet the deadline. ☐
    why she failed to inform you. ☐
    which I was given. ☐
    that we unfortunately can't help you. ☐

Noun clauses

Noun clauses can be introduced by:
the subordinator *that*: *That study independent of the teacher is necessary for success is obvious.*
a *wh*- word: *Where you go is entirely up to you.*

Noun clauses can function as subject, object, complement or adverbial in a clause. Their structure is similar to noun phrases.

4 Fill in the spaces in the noun clauses using words from the box.

how	that	what	where	who	why

1 _____ is of paramount importance is not _____ you come from but _____ you want to work here.
2 _____ you want to transport the goods halfway around the world when you could make them locally is impossible for me to understand.
3 We need to know not just _____ you've decided but _____ you arrived at your decision.
4 _____ no one realized it was the start of a long bull run explains why so little investment took place.
5 _____ said what when is of no concern to me; all I need to know is precisely _____ course of action you've agreed on.

5 In each group of five, match the sentence beginnings with the appropriate endings to complete the definitions.

1 An excuse is the reason ☐
2 A logistics manager is a senior employee ☐
3 Today's younger consumer is typically someone ☐
4 The 'sell-by date' is the date by ☐
5 An instruction manual is a booklet ☐

6 A non-negotiable deadline is the day by ☐
7 A distribution centre is a place ☐
8 'Keiretsu' is a Japanese term ☐
9 Industrial effluent is a substance ☐
10 A global citizen is a person ☐

a) who is keen to purchase the latest technology.
b) which tells you how to operate something.
c) who oversees all the transportation and delivery systems.
d) why people fail to do something.
e) which a product must be consumed.
f) where goods are sorted and redirected before being transported on.
g) which you have to get something done, come what may.
h) that comprises potentially hazardous liquid waste from a factory.
i) which refers to the system of companies with closely connected shareholdings and business relationships.
j) who has a positive outlook on the world and strives to tackle issues such as inequality.

Coordinators

Coordinators join equal units by linking them together. They mainly join clause + clause *I identified the problem and I sorted it out*, but they also join phrase + phrase *a difficult choice but the right one*, and word + word *black or white*.

There are very few coordinators in English. The most important and frequent coordinators are: *and, but, or*. Other words which can be used as coordinators are: *so, for, nor, yet, and so, either, neither.*

To join two or more similar or equal items: *and*
To join two or more contrasting items: *but*
To join two or more alternative items in a positive sentence: *either, or*
To join two or more alternative items in a negative sentence: *neither, nor*
To join purpose or consequence: *so*
To express reason: *for*

1 Match each sentence 1–6 with a sentence a)–f) using a coordinator from the box to make compound sentences. Make any other minor changes as necessary.

and but nor or so yet

1 We must not give in to workplace bullying. _____ ☐
2 You can claim for meals when you're away. _____ ☐
3 Their population consumes above-average levels of fat in their diet. _____ ☐
4 Workplace fatigue can have a negative impact on productivity. _____ ☐
5 I want you to study hard. _____ ☐
6 You can sort the conflict out directly with Clive. _____ ☐

a) I want you to pass your MBA.
b) We shouldn't allow any kind of offensive language among staff.
c) Their longevity is one of the highest in the world.
d) We can bring in an impartial arbitrator.
e) Make sure you don't spend too much on fine wines!
f) We should all limit the number of hours we work.

Subordinators

Subordinators are words which join units that are not equal in status, and they develop rather than link. Subordinators are normally the first word in the clause and are dependent on main clauses to make sentences.

Subordinators express more meanings than coordinators and there are about 60, although only a third of these are used frequently. Some subordinators have two or three meanings (*as* and *since* are both used for reason and time) and some meanings are expressed by several different subordinators (concession can be expressed by *although, even though, though* and *while*).

2 Fill in the spaces in the second sentence of each pair below with a subordinator from the box to express the same cause and effect meaning as the first sentence.

because in case in order to so that whenever while

1 US unemployment rose yesterday, helping fuel a dramatic increase in the price of oil.
   Yesterday the price of oil went up dramatically partly _____ US unemployment rose.
2 Some traders thought oil prices would fall. However, they rose.
   _____ some traders had expected oil prices to fall, they did in fact rise.
3 Short sales trading involves selling a commodity and then making a profit by buying it back more cheaply.
   Short sales traders sell a commodity _____ buy it back later more cheaply, thereby making a profit.
4 There are systems in place to suspend dealings on any company share price falling by more than 30% in one session.
   _____ a company's shares fall by more than 30% in one session, all dealings on the shares are suspended.
5 Wall Street banks borrowed heavily yesterday to cover their rising debt obligations.
   Wall Street banks borrowed heavily yesterday _____ they could cover their rising debt obligations.
6 Economic conditions could get worse, so it is a good idea for consumers to tighten their belts.
   Consumers are advised to tighten their belts _____ economic conditions worsen.

Meanings of subordinators

There are lots of subordinators in English, many with similar meanings. We use them to express over a dozen meanings, mostly connected with relationships between two entities:
purpose: *to, so that*
reason: *as, because*
concession: *although, whereas*
time: *when, while*
place: *where, everywhere*
manner: *as, as though*
condition: *if, provided (that)*
result: *so, so that*
exception: *excepting that, but that*
similarity: *as, like*
comparison: *as if, as though*
contrast: *while, whereas*
preference: *rather than, sooner than*

3 In each of the following sentences, <u>underline</u> the subordinator that is incorrect.

1 Calm down! You look *as if / like / so that* you're about to have a heart attack!
2 You can borrow it *unless / as long as / provided* you give it back.
3 *As / Since / While* you actually know her well, perhaps you're the best person to tell her.
4 You can be working on the drafts *whenever / while / when* I'm dealing with the enquiries.
5 *Supposing / Granted / If* they cancel – what do we do then?
6 We had better leave by 6am, *in order to / except to / so as to* avoid the early morning traffic.

4 Two of the three sentences in each group below are correct and essentially mean the same. Identify the one different or incorrect sentence in each group.

1 a) Once we get all the statements we can investigate the allegations.
  b) Until we get all the statements we can investigate the allegations.
  c) As soon as we get all the statements we can investigate the allegations.
2 a) Given that we now have all the necessary information we can make a decision.
  b) As we now have all the necessary information we can make a decision.
  c) While we now have all the necessary information we can make a decision.
3 a) Do it wherever you want.
  b) Do it anywhere you want.
  c) Do it everywhere you want.
4 a) By all means take a break, in case you get back here by four.
  b) By all means take a break, providing you get back here by four.
  c) By all means take a break, as long as you get back here by four.
5 a) Tell me when she arrives.
  b) Tell me the minute she arrives.
  c) Tell me now she arrives.
6 a) Until you can guarantee the product works, the deal's off.
  b) Provided you can guarantee the product works, the deal's off.
  c) Unless you can guarantee the product works, the deal's off.
7 a) Just as I'm officially on holiday next week you can contact me on my mobile if necessary.
  b) Although I'm officially on holiday next week you can contact me on my mobile if necessary.
  c) While I'm officially on holiday next week you can contact me on my mobile if necessary.
8 a) He interviewed pretty well, except that he got one or two facts wrong.
  b) He interviewed pretty well, such that he got one or two facts wrong.
  c) He interviewed pretty well, save that he got one or two facts wrong.
9 a) I'm against appointing him though his attitude just isn't right.
  b) I'm against appointing him because his attitude just isn't right.
  c) I'm against appointing him since his attitude just isn't right.
10 a) Don't give up – even if they put pressure on you to.
  b) Don't give up – even when they put pressure on you to.
  c) Don't give up – even though they may put pressure on you to.

About prepositions

The most common prepositions consist of one word, but there are also many complex prepositions consisting of two, three and four words. Prepositions of three and four words have a common short preposition at each end, e.g. *in, at, to, for, with*, and a word which carries more meaning in the middle, e.g. *connection, account, respect*. Prepositions are much more frequent than other grammatical words in academic writing, accounting for about 15% of all words.

Although prepositions are usually followed by a noun phrase, they can also be followed by other structures: *I am not interested in that job* [noun phrase] / *in learning Chinese* [-ing form] / *in what you are telling me* [wh-clause]; *The new Financial Director will be appointed from outside the company* [prepositional phrase].

1 Fill in the spaces in the sentences with an appropriate preposition. Do not use any preposition more than once.

1   I feel we should compensate him _____ the extra expenses he has incurred.
2   He may be creative, but he's terrified _____ making mistakes.
3   The company name has been misspelled _____ the whole document!
4   This form should not have been completed _____ pencil – it doesn't show up on the photocopy.
5   Your new credit card should be signed immediately _____ receipt.
6   Clearly the deal had been executed _____ due care and attention being paid to the unintended consequences.
7   You have _____ Friday to come up with a better proposal.
8   We can report that the stolen prints have now been recovered _____ the police _____ a rogue dealer and restored _____ their rightful owners.
9   Should the equipment in any way be damaged _____ shipping, please contact the manufacturer, not your local retailer, at once.
10 The matter needs to be looked into _____ too long.

2 Make complex prepositions by putting the words from the box into the appropriate structures below.

accordance	form	behalf	case	exchange
course	common	line	light	face	connection
region	account	compliance	keeping	return
wake	regard	conjunction	contact	reference
respect

in _____ for	
in the _____ of	
with _____ to	
in _____ with	
on _____ of	

3 Now fill in the spaces in the sentences below with an appropriate preposition from Exercise 2.

1   I propose that we re-examine our procedures _____ recent developments.
2   _____ our CEO, who is unfortunately unable to be with us today, I would like to apologize for any misunderstandings regarding our recent press statement.
3   _____ your advertisement in *BizPosts* of 12 July, I would like to request further information on post SMO2.
4   All proceedings have been conducted _____ national and international laws.
5   Our latest quarterly earnings are _____ market expectations.
6   Insurance stocks have been hit hard _____ recent natural disasters and terrorist attacks.
7   Our total losses were _____ $10m.
8   We managed to succeed _____ strong opposition.

4 The words in **bold** are in the wrong places. Put them in the correct place.

1   As usual it's **subject to** me to make the travel arrangements – but I'll make sure somebody else does it next time!
2   Our products must be presented in the same way in every retail outlet, **as for** their location.
3   **Irrespective of** a problem with our supplier, we are unable to offer our full range of goods at present.
4   Once your salary hits £40,000 it will be **together with** the higher rate of tax.
5   **Such as** expectations, Mr Malbec has been appointed team leader.
6   What we need is a TV campaign **down to** an Internet advertising push, to maximize our customer reach.
7   How about a brand new style for our outlets, **owing to** funky and contemporary, or maybe just comfortable and homely?
8   **Contrary to** our next steps, we can focus on these in tomorrow's meeting.

5 Underline the main preposition in the prepositional phrases 1–8 and match these with the appropriate category a)–h) according to their structure.

1   from outside the company ☐
2   to the intended recipient ☐
3   by then ☐
4   just before the final whistle ☐
5   except to escape in emergencies ☐
6   in the light of what you just said ☐
7   for better or for worse ☐
8   in playing the saxophone ☐

a)   prepositional phrase + noun phrase
b)   prepositional phrase + *-ing* form
c)   prepositional phrase + *wh-* clause
d)   prepositional phrase + prepositional phrase
e)   prepositional phrase + *to* infinitive
f)   prepositional phrase + adverb
g)   prepositional phrase + adjective
h)   adverb + prepositional phrase + *(any complement)*

Prepositions at ends of sentences and clauses

There are a number of common reasons for ending a sentence or clause with a preposition, including **wh-**questions and clauses, passives, infinitives, relative clauses and exclamations. The following examples illustrate how natural it is to end a sentence or clause with a preposition:

What's the weather like?
So that's what she was referring to!
That university's very hard to get into.

In these cases, a preposition becomes separated from the rest of its phrase, sometimes known as the complement of a preposition. In the examples above, the complements are **what, that** and **that university** respectively.

6 Fill in the spaces in the sentences below using the words from the box.

about	after (x2)	at	by	in	on	with

1 He's very difficult to work _____.
2 What are you looking _____?
3 The subject I want to talk to you _____ today is …
4 What I would like to focus _____ this morning is …
5 What a terrible situation she's ended up _____!
6 I know his work is being looked _____ by a temp while he's away. What I want to know is, who's the temp being looked _____ _____?

7 Now match the sentences in Exercise 6 with the following structures which can have prepositions at the end.

Wh- Questions
Passive Forms
Relative Clauses
Exclamations
Wh- Clauses
To- Clauses

Formal prepositions

8 Make the text slightly more formal by substituting the language in *italics* with words from the box below.

akin to	amid	barring	considering
notwithstanding	pending	regarding	versus

(1) *Unless there are any* accidents, the Social Advancement Party (SAP) look set to win this week's election in a landmark victory. (2) *Taking into account* their recent buoyancy in the opinion polls and the moribund state of the opposition, SAP are clearly staking their claim to the history books by coming from almost nowhere to win an outright majority. Celebrations, premature perhaps, have already been taking place (3) *in the middle of* feelings of optimism and above all the need for change. Some have billed the contest a classic fight of the establishment (4) *against* the people. (5) *Until we know* the final outcome, though, all predictions remain speculation, warns the SAP leader, Mr Max Fiorini. Yet the battle is arguably (6) *like* one of those sports events where the result is a foregone conclusion: (7) *despite* a stated intention to 'fight to the death', the opposition has scarcely managed to muster much popular support. Now (8) *about* the next five years, who's for a spot of prediction …?

Perspective adverbials

We can comment on something from many perspectives. For example, we can add a perspective adverbial containing our required perspective to a sentence. These allow us to offer a clear context and framework for what we are saying.

From a financial/ethical/practical/social/personal/medical perspective, the mission has been quite a success.

Because these adverbials are used to contextualize, they are most likely to come at the beginning where they sound more natural:

From a financial perspective the mission has been quite a success.
The mission has, from a financial perspective, been quite a success.
The mission has been quite a success from a financial perspective.

As with other adverbials, we can put them at the beginning of the sentence, in the middle or at the end. There are many other perspectives, including politics, the environment, science, ethics, etc.

1 Complete the sentences with an appropriate perspective adverbial based on the phrases in brackets.

cultural	ethics	finance	historical	personal	
technologically					

1 The whole project has been a disaster – we've lost about $60,000 so far.
(in terms) _____

2 We will need to make sure there is no conflict of interest.
(are concerned) _____

3 From the company's point of view the plan looks great, but I would question it – it means I've got more responsibility but no extra money.
(from a) _____

4 The harbour bridge is an amazing feat of engineering, but they certainly broke the bank in building it.
(speaking) _____

5 We would be the first company ever to have such a far-reaching policy in place.
(to put) _____

6 It's a risky proposition – just look at all the differences in behaviour, appearance, values, you name it.
(if we) _____

Stance expressions

The main way to add an opinion, attitude or evaluation to a text is through a stance adverbial. Stance adverbials can be prepositional phrases, adverbs or clauses beginning with subordinators such as *if* and *because*. The information added is essentially subjective, and can add information on areas such as knowledge, reality, truth, certainty or style: *without doubt, arguably, as Smith argues ...* Any of these adverbials can be added to a sentence.

Instead of adverbials such as *undoubtedly*, there are other ways of expressing stance: *There is little doubt that ...; Few doubts remain concerning ...; It is doubtful that ...; I would doubt that ...* These structures are part of the sentence structure and, unlike adverbials, cannot simply be added or removed.

2 Match the stance expressions in 1–6 with the correct ending a)–f).

1 I don't believe
2 Worries persist
3 It is regrettable that
4 There is no real doubt in my mind
5 As my boss says,
6 She is, without question,

a) over the possible loopholes in the latest contract.
b) there is much chance of a reconciliation between the two parties.
c) the best candidate for the job.
d) that we made the right decision.
e) this would never have happened if the risks had been properly assessed beforehand.
f) details of the deal were prematurely leaked to the press.

Position of adverbials

There are three main positions for adverbials in English: at the beginning, middle and end of a sentence.

Adverbials which link and frame the text (*consequently, later, perhaps, therefore, finally*) typically appear at the beginning.

Stance adverbials and adverbs of frequency, manner and certainty (*probably, undoubtedly, slowly, generally, definitely, usually*) most frequently come in the middle of a sentence, usually before the main verb. Stance adverbials can also come at the beginning of a sentence, or, as an 'afterthought', at the end.

Circumstance adverbials are those which tell us where, when, how (long/much) or why something happened. Adverbial clauses beginning with subordinators (*because, although* – see 4.3) tend to come at the end of a sentence, except for those with *if*, which usually come at the beginning.

3 Put the stance adverbial in *italics* in a more appropriate place in the following sentences.

1 Please note that the latest 100 transactions can *only* be displayed or printed.
2 It is a high-risk course of action *admittedly*.
3 Nothing *hopefully* should go too badly wrong.
4 The target consumers are not going to pay that sort of money for our software *definitely*.
5 The files containing personal data *regrettably* have been temporarily mislaid.
6 It is the best decision for maximum growth *without doubt*.
7 You have tried hard *certainly*. But *actually* you haven't achieved a satisfactory level of success.
8 They should never have allowed it *to my mind*.
9 It won't *in my view* work.
10 They've got the legal side *apparently* all taken care of.
11 It's *in actual fact* a pretty good plan.
12 *Definitely* I'll back you up should you need me to.

Stance and formality

There can be differences in formality between different forms. For example, *if I am quite honest* sounds more formal than *honestly*. Often there are several expressions with similar meanings, ranging from fairly informal to formal: *in other words/if I might put this another way*.

Structures which are more objective also tend to sound more formal; *It is widely thought/There is some confusion ...*, *Confusion exists ...*

4 Underline the stance adverbial with the most appropriate level of formality for each sentence of an internal written report.

1 *Considering the issues involved / All in all / When all is said and done* I believe that our approach to risk is sound.
2 *Honestly / In my view / If you ask me*, I am not entirely in agreement with your suggestion.
3 *Anyway / Incidentally / By the way*, this underlines the need for staff training at the earliest opportunity.
4 We need to focus more on 'soft' communication strategies *like / such as / e.g.* non-verbal messages.
5 Our core clients should *maybe / perhaps / likely* agree to the new terms.

Reformulating

5 Change the type of adverbial in each of the sentences beginning with the words given, keeping the same meaning.

1 If this document falls into the wrong hands, make sure you inform the Finance Director *immediately / the minute ... / as soon as ... / without ...*
2 I believe that our approach to risk is sound. *overall / on ... / all ...*
3 *In other words ... / To put ... / If I may ...*, risk is where just about anything can happen and we don't have much idea even what all the eventualities are.

4 *Also ... / In ... / What is ...*, our fall-back position is looking pretty weak.
5 *Honestly ... / In all ... / To be perfectly ...*, I don't actually agree with what you are suggesting.

Adverbials as discourse markers

Text is held together, or made cohesive, through the use of discourse markers, most of which are adverbials. These may reflect the writer's stance, or may simply link the text together. Linking adverbials can be used to express one of the following functions:

Adding: *in the first instance, secondly*
Summarizing: *in short, on balance*
Rephrasing or exemplifying: *for example, to put this another way*
Inferencing or showing result: *as a result, in consequence*
Contrasting or conceding: *by comparison, however*
Making transitions: *in the following section, incidentally*

6 Make the introductory text on risk management cohesive by identifying which adverbial in *italics* cannot be used to fill each gap.

(1) *Essentially / Definitely / Basically*, the management of risk involves assessing just about every conceivable eventuality, whether unpredictable actions by employees such as gambling with company funds, or even acts of God. (2) *Nevertheless / However / Thus*, acts of God are not normally seen as predictable in the way that human acts are. What the risk assessor has to do is (3) *overall / firstly / initially* work out what the possible risks might involve, and (4) *then / so / next*, and this is the most important part, come up with contingency plans to deal with them. This is (5) *certainly / totally / undoubtedly* not an easy job. The task itself involves risk: risk, for example, that something vital has been forgotten or that the contingency plans are not (6) *actually / indeed / basically* workable. (7) *Next / So / Therefore* every effort has to be made to carry out these risk assessments and insure against them or have a contingency budget for them. Whenever disaster does strike, I agree (8) *ultimately / entirely / completely* that dealing with it is another matter altogether!

Emphasis adverbs and adverbials

Certain adverbs can be used to add something either to a particular phrase in a sentence or to the whole sentence. When the adverbs add something to, or 'modify' a particular phrase, they nearly always come just before the phrase.

She's managing **extremely effectively** [adverb modifying adverb]

That's **absolutely fascinating** [adverb modifying adjective]

It was **quite a surprise** [adverb modifying noun phrase]

rather to my annoyance [adverb modifying prepositional phrase]

Almost half *failed* [adverb modifying determiner]

Alternatively, when the adverbs add something to the whole clause or sentence, they are being used as adverbials. Along with subject, verb, object and complement, adverbials are clause elements. Unlike the other clause elements adverbials are mobile and can often be put in different places in the clause or sentence.

1 Put the emphasis adverb in brackets into the most appropriate place in the sentence.

1 I have no complaints with their service. (whatsoever)
2 I am appalled that they should let you down in this manner. (utterly)
3 You have made an extremely useful contribution. (indeed)
4 Had I known about his directorship at the time, I would have trusted him. (scarcely)
5 We were more impressed with their level of service than their reasonable fee. (even)
6 This project is more challenging than the previous one. (rather)
7 The share price ended up doubling, to my surprise. (somewhat)
8 Merely tracking the all-share index is an unacceptable policy, given their high management fees. (absolutely)

2 Complete each sentence by putting the words in brackets in the correct order.

1 (why the I oppose reason) his approach is that he concentrates on tiny details rather than the broader picture.
2 (is it not his but punctuality) his aggression that is the real problem.
3 (stake is what at is) nothing less than the company's future well-being.
4 (tactics would to by only resorting underhand we) be able to win – and we're not going to stoop that low.
5 (no you under should put circumstances) more than 10% of your assets into that fund.
6 (would changes I be would where make) in the areas of responsibility and accountability.
7 (I witnessed rarely have) such firmness in the teeth of such opposition.
8 (approach would the how problem I is) irrelevant – it's your department and your responsibility.

9 (not they respond should), we do have a secret Plan B.
10 (on what we the focus need product is to), not the process itself.

3 Cross out the extra word in each of the following sentences.

1 Mr Fortinbras was the person to whom I appointed Chief Investment Strategist.
2 Not only by shedding 5% of the workforce was the company able to get through the recession.
3 Had you to put that question to me last week we might have avoided this mess.
4 What do I aim to do by Thursday is complete my final report.
5 It is commodities what I particularly want you to focus your attention on in the coming months.
6 Under no circumstances should you to borrow to invest.

Inversion and fronting

Subject and verb can be inverted in certain situations:

• with the modals **had, should, were** when they are used in conditional sentences. In these cases *if* is omitted: **Had I known, I wouldn't have done it.** (= *If I had known …*)
• after certain prepositional phrases, particularly those indicating place or negative structures: **In the town where I was born lived a man who made a billion.**
• after negative structures such as **hardly, scarcely, never, on no account, no sooner.** With these structures the auxiliary verb follows directly after: **No sooner had she finished/did she finish/was the job finished, she was told it wasn't actually necessary.**

For emphasis and more dramatic effect, sentences can start with the complement of verbs such as *be, seem, appear, look*: **Even more alarming is the lack of transparency.** These sentences can easily be 'reversed' for a more conventional order: **The lack of transparency is even more alarming.** The sentences often begin with *wh-* clauses for even more emphasis: **What is even more alarming is the lack of transparency.**

4 Rewrite the following sentences to make them more emphatic, using a range of structures.

1 The dip in consumer confidence is also clearly significant.
2 If you ever need any further assistance, please do not hesitate to contact us.
3 I will never again go to so much trouble for so little gain.
4 He failed to turn up on time. He didn't apologize either.
5 The inflationary risk appears to be far more serious.
6 If I had caught my flight I would not have missed the meeting.
7 You cannot claim expenses without a receipt at any time.
8 If a solution were found, we would implement it.

5 Match the first parts of the sentences 1–6 with the right endings a)–f).

1 It is hard to overestimate ☐
2 Above all what is needed ☐
3 What resulted in fact ☐
4 Nearly half of these workers ☐
5 Around the middle of next year ☐
6 In no way ☐

a) have had no training whatsoever.
b) is a root-and-branch reorganization of our whole auditing systems.
c) we should be seeing a measurable improvement.
d) can Moira be blamed – she was on leave at the time.
e) was a system that neither offered value for money nor worked.
f) how far people's mindsets will have to change to meet the challenge.

Characteristics of formal language

While most spoken language tends to be fairly informal, presentations can be a little more formal, with academic and report writing the most formal and impersonal.

In more formal writing contractions are avoided, so **don't** is written as **do not**.

There are various other informal expressions which have more formal equivalents: **not any/not much/not many → no/little/few**, etc. **/ and so on, and so on and so forth → and other/and further examples**. Also, there might be fewer abbreviations in more formal writing: **e.g. rice, potatoes, etc. → for example rice, potatoes and other carbohydrates**.

Finally, with a few exceptions adverbs 'stranded' at the ends of sentences are best repositioned just before the main verb: **They have achieved success quickly → They have quickly achieved success.** This is particularly the case when the adverb applies to the whole clause.

6 Say whether each sentence is appropriate (*A*) or inappropriate (*I*) for the given context.

1 Mother to child: So great is my love for you that I propose to buy you an ice cream. ☐
2 Email to friend: Scarcely had I arrived at work this morning when I was asked to participate in a meeting. ☐
3 News report: Such was the strength of negative sentiment that at one point the Dow Jones was down 5%. ☐
4 Central bank communiqué: Far more serious is the threat of inflation to the economy as a whole. ☐
5 Notice on park railings: Under no circumstances may bicycles be chained to these railings. ☐
6 Boss to employee: Not only did you submit the report late, you also cut and pasted most of it from the last one. ☐

7 Visiting colleague to foreign headquarters: Were you to allow me to have a hot drink, might I request a black coffee? _____
8 After-dinner speech at a black-tie company dinner: Unaccustomed as I am to speaking to such a distinguished audience, may I just say what a pleasure it has been to have worked on the Go-For-Excellence project. _____

7 Read the following formal internal memorandum from a marketing manager to the CEO and choose the most appropriate form to reach the right level of formality.

(1) *In recent years / For quite some time now* the company has demonstrated its determination to succeed in some of the most challenging markets in the world. (2) *Not only have we / We have definitely* been successful, (3) *and also / but also* we have been seen to be successful by our customers and competitors alike. However, (4) *what we now need is / we now need* a completely new strategy. (5) *Mainly / Most of all*, significant new investment is required. Our continuing sales growth would be in jeopardy (6) *if we don't do this / were such investment not to be implemented*. In my view, the person (7) *to manage / who should manage* such a project is the Head of Marketing. I am happy to go on record as saying that under no circumstances (8) *I should agree / should I agree* to the current Deputy Marketing Manager being considered for such a role. The postholder would (9) *legitimately be accountable for all aspects of the new strategy / be accountable for all aspects of the new strategy legitimately*. (10) *Last but not least / Lastly*, the importance of appointing the right person for this critical post (11) *can scarcely be / scarcely can be* overstated.

Background to phrasal and prepositional verbs

There are over 12,000 idioms in English, and about half of these are phrasal verbs and prepositional verbs. Phrasal and prepositional verbs mostly have a more formal synonym *look into/investigate*. Most texts in English contain a considerable number of phrasal and prepositional verbs. These are sometimes called multi-word verbs.

The four main types are:

1 phrasal verb (verb + adverb particle) with no object, e.g. *come up*.

2 phrasal verb (verb + adverb particle) with an object. These are separable (the base verb is separated from the particle with the object), e.g. *put it off/put the meeting off*. If the object is longer, or newly mentioned, it often comes after the particle, e.g. *put off the training meeting*. Pronouns always come between verb and particle: *put it off* is correct, but *put off it* is incorrect.

3 prepositional verb (verb + preposition) always with an object. These are inseparable because a preposition normally comes directly before its object and not after it, e.g. *look into the problem/look into it*, but not *look the problem into* or *look it into*.

4 phrasal-prepositional verb (verb + adverb particle + preposition), e.g. *look up to the CEO*. The parts of these verbs cannot be separated by the object, but occasionally it is possible to put an adverbial just before the preposition, e.g. *get on well with*.

Type 3 express a wider range of meanings than type 1 and 2 phrasal verbs. The latter are mostly for physical activities, while prepositional verbs cover both physical activities and many mental activities.

Many phrasal verbs have a one-word synonym. Some, such as *get on with* do not have an obvious one-word synonym and need several words to fully describe the meaning.

1 Fill in the spaces with an appropriate particle to complete the text. Two particles are required in one of the spaces.

Time is running (1) _____ for the global trade talks. If this statement sounds familiar it is because you may have come (2) _____ it before. The latest twist leaves something new for officials to mull (3) _____. Not only have they had to deal (4) _____ ever-increasing demands from the major players, but now they have to face (5) _____ the prospect of new demands from new entrants to the world stage. It turns (6) _____ that no fewer than six countries have now signed (7) _____ to join the WTO. And they are not wasting any time in calling (8) _____ their very own demands to be met. For instance, countries which were formally part of larger republics are asking to be set (9) _____ from their often larger neighbours in a bid for special smaller country status. Officials yesterday were attempting to offer an upbeat assessment, playing (10) _____ differences and 'local disagreements' and focusing instead (11) _____ 'commonalities'. Something else might sound familiar – the sound of bureaucrats papering (12) _____ the cracks and making (13) _____ that most countries have not fallen (14) _____ with their trading partners and everything is fine. Watch this space.

Phrasal verb grammar

Technically speaking, if the particle is an adverb then the verb is a phrasal verb; if it is a preposition then the verb is a prepositional verb – this explains why prepositional verbs cannot be separated, for a preposition comes before (*'pre'*) its complement (*'position'*). Therefore with the prepositional verb *look after*: *look after your own interests* is correct, but *look your own interests after* is incorrect. If a verb has two particles, for a similar reason the first is an adverb and the second a preposition: *do away with* (= eliminate).

The type which we are least likely to notice is type 3, because we might think of it simply as a verb and a preposition, but it is the most frequent type.

2 Put the phrasal and prepositional verbs in brackets in the correct place in the sentence and in the correct form. Separate the parts of the verbs where necessary.

1 Most of the time I pretty well my boss. (get on with)
2 Give us a break and stop how hot it is in here, will you? (go on about)
3 About the conference next week, could you just the refreshment arrangements with the caterer? (firm up)
4 Demand should really in the months ahead. (take off)
5 Your brainstorming session won't work – it. (call off)
6 I suggest we that staff away-day we've been talking about until things have settled down a bit. (put off)
7 OK, now small groups and three innovations we can all. (get into / come up with / buy into)
8 I know we've a lot of problems recently, but we do need to all this us and. (come up against / put behind / move forward)
9 Now everyone – it's time we all our checks and balances and just trusted each other to just the job. (do away with / get on with / come on)
10 I've just the perfect idea – your language skills, then we can our translator. (think of / work on / do away with)
11 The procedure, exactly what we have to do, and then they won't have any more reason to it wasn't clear. (lay down / spell out / make out)
12 Stressed? Can't it? Madeleine and she'll it all for you. (deal with / talk to / sort out)

Phrasal verbs with two particles

A relatively small number of phrasal verbs have two particles. The middle word of the three (the adverb particle) often has a literal meaning: *walk away with* and *walk away from* both have a sense of movement away, not towards. The most common prepositions at the end of the verbs are: *for, on, to, with*. The prepositions in the verbs generally carry less meaning than the adverb particles.

3 Fill in each space with two particles from the box. Each particle can be used more than once.

against	away	behind	down	for	off	on
round	to	up	with			

1 You'll have to cut _____ snacking if you're serious about losing weight.
2 I guess we need to face _____ the fact that we're not market leader anymore.
3 Since I've been ill I've really fallen _____ my work.
4 We no longer need it – let's do _____ it!
5 Don't be pessimistic – she'll come _____ my way of thinking soon enough.
6 He's missed two weeks now, after coming _____ a mystery virus.
7 Anyway, this headhunter came _____ me at the trade fair and made me an offer I can't refuse.
8 The contract comes _____ review next year, and I say we should bid for it.
9 Don't let him play you both _____ each other.
10 You've got to stand _____ yourself – no one else will – it's a bullfight out there.

Presentations

Prepositional verbs, such as *look into*, are quite frequent in academic writing. In presentational and many spoken texts, both prepositional and particularly phrasal verbs are typical.

Phrasal verbs are part of less formal language and are often associated with other style changes:
*Just **put forward** any new strategy ideas to Marketing as and when you **come up with** them.*
*Any new strategy ideas should be **proposed** formally to the Marketing division as they are **developed**.*

4 Rewrite the following sentences by changing the verbs in *italics* into more appropriate, less formal, phrasal verbs.

1 You know, I reckon we ought to *diversify* whatever areas which are going to *rise* the fastest.
2 Not now, that discussion would *erode* our valuable time – we've got a lot of items to *finish* this afternoon.
3 So many issues *arose* from that session – there's just too much for me to *absorb* right now.
4 First, *assess* the issues, then *formulate* your plan.
5 Don't *surrender* – *persevere* until the job's done.
6 Time to *abandon* Plan A and *commence* with Plan B.

Phrasal verb particles

Each of the 12 most common particles (*around, away, back, down, in, into, off, on, out, over, through, up*) can have several meanings, but often there is one overall essential meaning.

Focus on *out*

5 Match the different uses of *out* with a meaning a)–e).

1 The results don't look so bad once we strip out the effects of inflation. ☐
2 It's an ongoing question as to how long they can stay out of the euro. ☐
3 Alex dropped out of his MBA after flunking his first essay. ☐
4 I don't think we can keep them out much longer, as they fulfil all the criteria. ☐
5 In my view, it's time we branched out into more exotic products and locations. ☐

a) leaving
b) removing
c) preventing
d) outside, not inside
e) moving outwards

Focus on *off*

6 Match the different uses of *off* with a meaning a)–f).

1 That's fine, just drop me off here and I can walk the rest. ☐
2 Time to head off. We should just make it. ☐
3 His comments sparked off negative sentiment and a round of selling. ☐
4 Why don't we round off the meal with a toast to our director and founder? ☐
5 It's non-core – we should sell that division off. ☐
6 Close off that whole area – we don't want anyone unauthorized getting in. ☐

a) leaving
b) removing
c) starting
d) stopping, finishing
e) preventing, keeping away
f) getting out

Recordings

Business fundamentals
Business and investment cycles

 1:01

Over time, economies tend to grow – the average annual growth rate for the UK since 1830, for example, has been just under 2%, enough to allow major changes in standards of living. However, growth is not steady; periods of below-average growth, or contraction, are followed by periods of above-average growth, or expansion.

On the chart, you can see that the first cycle starts here, in the boom phase: as growth increases, so does inflation and central banks raise interest rates in order to control it. When borrowing money to invest becomes too expensive, economic activity peaks and then slows down, sometimes abruptly; this second phase is called a slump, which is then followed by a period of recession. In recession, central banks lower interest rates to encourage spending. Eventually, the economy picks up and we move into the fourth stage, recovery – and then back to a boom. As you can see on the chart, one cycle follows another, punctuated by ups and downs called peaks and troughs, but providing a long-term trend of growth.

Variations in the business cycle are caused by many different factors; overproduction, overexpansion of credit, speculative bubbles, and shocks like wars, political upheavals, and so on. Economists disagree about the length of the business cycle, or indeed whether the cycle is inevitable, but it still provides a useful model to explain how business works.

 1:02

The investment cycle can be divided into four phases. The first phase is Accumulation. When prices have bottomed out, 'value investors' will buy, principally in the technology and industrial sectors, despite the ongoing bear market. In this phase, initial hope develops into relief, and eventually, as prices begin to rise, optimism.

In the second phase, Mark-Up, optimism overcomes the fear of losing money and the market becomes bullish, as investors go through excitement, thrill and finally euphoria, buying household products, food and services.

Of course, wise investors know that the bull market will not last forever, and in the third phase, Distribution, they become more cautious and sell shares to buy utilities and bonds. Anxiety sets in, and as prices drop the mood turns to denial, fear and depression when investors realize it is too late to sell for a profit.

In the final phase, Mark-Down, investors who cannot afford to wait for a recovery start to panic. In the end, many will capitulate and take losses in desperation. Value investors who sold earlier at a profit now have the chance to buy cyclicals at low prices and enjoy the next mark-up.

Recruitment

 1:03

Good afternoon everyone and thank you for inviting me to speak to you today. I'd like to start with a short presentation of our recruitment process. After that, I'll be happy to take any questions and to discuss how we can help with your particular recruitment needs. Is everyone happy with that?

All right, then. The first step in the recruitment process is what we call set-up. We work closely with the line manager to develop a very clear definition of who you would like to hire. As you are well aware, interviewing 'maybes' is time-consuming and inefficient, so we make sure we eliminate borderline profiles immediately.

The next step is sourcing. As this slide shows, it's incredibly important. If you don't start with a strong pool of candidates, your recruitment will almost certainly fail. So, to reach the widest range of candidates possible, we use both traditional methods – basically contacting potential candidates by phone – and new online search and social networking techniques. When we identify strong potential candidates, we generate excitement and energy around our clients' opportunities. We've found that energetic candidates keep the process moving more efficiently, and more quickly.

We continue this approach at the next stage, which is screening. Here, we set up informal discussions by telephone to get to know the candidates better. As you can see, effective screening involves not only screening candidates *out* of the process, but also attracting the strong candidates *in*. It's a subtle skill that can really make a big difference to the time it takes to fill a position.

Now, moving on to the interview stage, this is obviously an incredibly important piece of the puzzle. It's the stage where, of course, our recruiters have to hand over to the hiring manager. But we believe it's crucial to keep the energy flowing. So after screening, *we* set up the appointments for you, and we put special effort into making sure these interviews happen just as quickly as possible.

Next we come to feedback. Have a look at this next slide which shows some examples. By collecting feedback from hiring managers, we can help them in several ways. If necessary, we can make process adjustments to prevent good candidates from getting screened out. And often, we can help hiring managers become better interviewers by giving them training and advice. The more closely we work with hiring managers, the faster and smoother the process becomes.

So, the next stage is to make the best candidate an offer, and as you can see on the slide, we target an offer acceptance rate of 95%. A successful candidate who refuses an offer represents a huge waste of time and investment. Successful recruitment means understanding a shifting mix of facts, opinions and emotions, and we do our very best to manage that process flawlessly and make the right offer to the right candidate.

So, that brings us to the final step, which is much more than simply making sure the new employee shows up for orientation. After offer acceptance, we stay in regular contact with the new employee, right up to the first day of work. That way we can help you start building a long and productive relationship between your new employee and the company.

1 Personal development
1.1 About business Developing your career

 1:04–1:06

1
I think the key to surviving at work is the same as it's always been. Bosses have huge egos, and you have to feed those egos if you want to be effective. You have to scratch a few backs, and laugh at your manager's jokes even if they're not funny.

But seriously, though, there's a right and a wrong way to befriend your manager – well, think of him, or her, as a person rather than as a figure in authority. Remember, they want to get on with the people they work with as much as you do. Show them you're a good guy on a personal level, not just professionally. Managers promote people they know and like, so developing a friendship with yours is a smart career move.

Bringing up office politics and client complaints will only remind them that they're your manager. But talk about more personal stuff, you know, like their favourite team or holiday destination, and you're speaking to a friend. Direct the conversation to things that feel natural. After all, this is how friends interact.

2
When the time comes for a promotion in your office, your manager will be thinking about all the great times when his or her team worked together successfully. You need to get more of your manager's mind share, and occupy it more often. So, for example, sending regular updates – even if there's nothing much to say – keeps you on your manager's mind as somebody who is getting the work done. If you've been part of successful projects, opt for others that you know you'll succeed in. This'll help build your manager's confidence in you, and that will help you become the person your boss will turn to when more important projects come up.

3
Whatever your job, the desire to give it your all and get to the top is incredibly strong and often results in other aspects of your life suffering.

Some jobs require open lines of communication via smartphones and so on, but try to turn them off when you're not at work. Being keen isn't a sign of determination, but a lack of focus on your personal affairs. If you really have to work at home, find a place where you can't be disturbed, and put a time limit on your work.

At times, workloads become unbearable, and however sympathetic your manager might be, he or she'll try to get you to do as much as is humanly possible. But the keyword here is humanly. There are limits to how much we can accomplish. So sometimes, it is OK to say no and turn down assignments. It doesn't mean you've failed, but that you're in control and you know your limitations.

1.2 Vocabulary **Behavioural competencies and setting goals**

 1:07

Jill: OK, Tony, let's move on. Have a look at the list of behavioural competencies. Which do you think you've demonstrated over the last few months?

Tony: Well, this is the first time that I've had to coordinate a group of people. I've done a lot of work with my team over the last six months. This has all been quite new for me and it's been challenging but also really rewarding.

J: What aspects have you found particularly useful, or satisfying?

T: Well, organizing the promotional campaign for the European tour for the Bosnian group was a lot of fun. It was tough, but I felt we achieved a lot given that it was all quite last minute, and the musicians weren't easy, as you know.

J: Yes, OK. I think you had a lot of support from your colleagues on that, didn't you?

T: Yes, the team were great, working all hours, especially Hannah, who's so new to the job. I think she really rose to the challenge of dealing with the press.

J: That was good. She's doing well. How did you make sure she was given all the support she needed?

T: Well, we had regular update meetings every week so that she could tell me about any problems or concerns she had. I also always made sure that I was available for her when she needed me; she found it really difficult in the beginning to assert herself and not let the journalists get the upper hand. She would often come to me and we would work together on what she was going to say to them.

J: Yes, that seems to have been a strategy that worked. Was there anything that you don't think you handled particularly well with regards to the Bosnian project?

T: In the beginning, as I said, it was all quite last minute – I was always so busy dealing with other stuff, you know, juggling all the other projects, that I found it really hard to plan ahead.

J: Can you think of a specific example?

T: Yes. The one that sticks in my mind the most was when I was trying to arrange the transport for the French leg of their tour. At one point I got so far behind that we almost had to rearrange a couple of their concert dates because I had forgotten to book their accommodation for the next town. Karla had to spend a lot of time on the phone calling hotels so that they had somewhere to stay. I dread to think where they might have ended up staying! It could have been really embarrassing.

J: Yes, I understand, Tony. What do you think would help you in this …?

1.3 Grammar **Tense, aspect and voice**

 1:08

Ed: So, what have you been up to since I last saw you?

Jon: Oh, hasn't anyone told you? I have decided to go for promotion. You know, for the new Area Manager job.

E: Great! What exactly would you be doing in the new job?

J: Well, you need to be quite flexible as there's a lot of travel involved – in fact, the responsibilities cover six different countries.

E: That'll suit you down to the ground – you have always got out and about a lot I seem to remember. By the way, you know Jacob is going for it as well?

J: No, but I'm not threatened – he blew his reputation for competence over that lost documents episode.

E: OK, but what have you been doing to make sure you actually get the job?

J: Well, by the end of the week I will have worked out my interview strategy and there's no question they can ask me I can't answer.

E: Aren't you being a bit overconfident, or should that be arrogant?

J: We'll see. Drinks are on me if I get it.

E: Deal.

1.4 Management skills **Self-awareness and communication**

 1:09

The Johari window© is so called because it was created by Joe and Harry – Joseph Luft and Harry Ingham, back in 1955 in the United States. It's a useful tool for helping people to reach a better understanding of their interpersonal communication and relationships. The window has two columns and two lines: the column on the left contains information which you know, and the column on the right, information which you don't know. Similarly, the top line contains information which other people know, and, as I'm sure you've already guessed, the bottom line has things which others don't know. Has everybody got that? Good.

So, that means that the window has four panes, which each tell us something about ourselves. The pane on the top left is called the Arena. It tells us things about ourselves which are public knowledge; things that you know and that other people know. The pane on the bottom left contains things that you know, but that others don't know. It's called the Façade, because other people's perceptions of you are incomplete if you choose not to share certain information about yourself.

Now you can probably work the last two out for yourselves. The last two panes are called the Blind spot and the Unknown. The Blind spot, as its name suggests, covers the things which other people see, but we ourselves are blind to. Asking other people for feedback can help us reduce our Blind spot. The Unknown, obviously, covers the things nobody knows, your hidden talents and undiscovered potential. The remaining adjectives that neither you nor your partner chose in the previous exercise either do not describe your personality, or perhaps describe traits of your character which nobody has discovered yet.

 1:10–1:14

1
A: OK, shall I have a go at this?
B: Be my guest.

A: Well, I have to confess that I sometimes tend to panic, you know, if it all becomes too much. I get very stressed out.
B: You're kidding! You always seem so cool, calm and collected!

2
A: Would you like to take this one?
B: Sure. But, frankly, I'm more used to success. Hm. How do I cope? I've never really thought about it that much; let me see …

3
A: How motivating is it? I haven't the slightest idea! I've never had enough to tell!
B: Mm. Personally, if I'm totally honest with myself, I'd have to say, *very*.
A: It can't buy you love!
B: No, it can't. But it does make the world go round, doesn't it?

4
A: OK, your turn.
B: I'll pass on this one, if you don't mind.
A: No, of course not. Hm. What don't I like about myself? That's not easy to answer.
B: Let's leave that one, shall we?
A: Yeah, good idea.

5
A: Wow, that's a long way in the future! I honestly haven't got a clue! How about you?
B: I'm not sure. If you really pushed me, I suppose I'd say I hope I'll be working in a large company, a multinational, perhaps somewhere abroad …
A: … and earning megabucks!
B: Am I really so transparent?

1.6 Case study **The glass ceiling**

 1:15

Ruben: So how is Gemma taking it?

Steve: Well, not great. She's pretty angry, to be perfectly honest. I mean, let's face it, what else does she have to do to get the job? If she was a man, we'd be begging her to take it!

R: Steve, you know as well as I do that the boss will never agree to a woman Marketing Manager. You can sing Gemma's praises as much as you like, but you're not going to change his mind.

S: So even if she does the MBA, you reckon it won't make any difference?

R: 'Fraid not; not here, anyway. But between you and me, I wonder if she's really ready.

S: Why not? You said yourself it would give her the marketing know-how she needs.

R: Yeah, it's not that. I just feel she lacks maturity – you know, the way she tends to rush into things. I know you Americans are obsessed with efficiency, but there are limits!

S: That's a little below the belt, isn't it, Ruben? Anyway, she's half Spanish, as you well know! OK, I agree, she's a self-starter, and she's not always very patient. But she's very intuitive: when she knows she's found the right solution, she just goes for it!

R: Intuitive, yes … but not always very logical. I'm not sure how well she really thinks things through. You've got to be able to argue your case on an MBA – it'd certainly take her out of her comfort zone. But at the end of the day, I'm not convinced she has what it takes to fight the system here in Spain. Does she really want her career badly enough to do an MBA? It's going to be tough. I just feel she might be happier if she accepted the situation and made her family her priority, rather than banging her head against a brick wall.

S: Well, I don't know, and I'm not sure she does – although she certainly seems to have plenty of self-belief ... There's only one way to find out, and I for one will be backing her to do the MBA. I think she could surprise us all.

R: Well, I certainly wouldn't stand in her way. If that's what she wants to do, she deserves her chance – even though it may mean we lose her sooner rather than later. But I still think at the end of the day, she'll back down.

S: Hmm.

🔊 **1:16**

Xabi: Hi Gem! What's for dinner?

Gemma: Yes, I did have a good day at work, thank you, what about you?

X: Come on, Gemma, let's not go there, I'm starving, that's all – I didn't have time for lunch.

G: Well, I didn't have time to think about dinner. I've only just finished putting Nina to bed.

X: Well, is there something I can do to help?

G: You can make something if you want. I'm not hungry.

X: You're still upset about not making Marketing Manager, aren't you? Look, if the people at SEVS don't appreciate your talents, why not go somewhere else? I'm making good money now, you could go part-time, maybe do an MBA, or even stop work for a few years. We could move out into the country, you could spend more quality time with Nina ...

G: Spend more quality time in the kitchen, you mean!

X: Gemma, you know that's not what I mean. Look – Nina's four already. Don't you think it's time we started thinking about giving her a little brother or sister?

G: Listen, Xabi, if you think I'm just going to stay at home and cook, clean and make babies, then you'd better think again! I've always wanted a real career, and I'm determined to have one!

X: Yes, but if SEVS won't promote you ...

G: Then I'll go elsewhere! In fact, I've already had an extremely good offer I'm thinking about accepting.

X: You've had another job offer? Well, that's great – but why didn't you tell me?

G: Because I knew you wouldn't like it.

X: Come on, Gemma, I admit I'd rather you spent more time at home, but if you've had a good offer, you know I'd never stand in the way of your career.

G: Really?

X: Really. So what is it?

G: It's Svenska Glastek: they've offered me a job as Marketing Manager in their automobile division; I could really go places with the Swedes, I mean, they practically invented equal opportunities!

X: Svenska Glastek? I didn't know they were in Spain.

G: They aren't. The job's in Stockholm.

X: Stockholm? Now, hold on, Gemma, I can't possibly move to Stockholm ...

G: See, I told you you wouldn't like it!

X: But my home's here in Seville – there's my career to think about, and my family, and my friends ...

G: Well, I've had it up to here with your career, your family and your friends! What about my career? You men are all the same! When are you going to start taking women seriously?

2 Corporate image

2.1 About business Corporate image

🔊 **1:17**

Narrator: Cynics might assume its environmental moves are mere greenwash, but 'they are more than cosmetic,' according to Tim Lang, professor of food policy at City University.

Tim Lang: I was sceptical when McDonald's started altering its menus and playing around with greener options. I thought it was a temporary blip, but they've hardwired it into their system. There is another problem, however – will they be able to maintain this commitment to more sustainable foods? And will they be able to maintain their prices? The fundamentals of the food supply chain are going in an awesome direction – energy, oil, water and food commodity prices are all rising. McDonald's is no longer in denial mode. They are more engaged, but will they be able to engage with these fundamentals? They will not be alone. All big food companies are facing these changes. But as a meat purveyor, McDonald's is going to be very exposed.

N: What seems to have changed, and what is most noticeable among the customers I meet, is an absence of embarrassment or defensiveness about dining under the golden arches. There is an acute awareness of the health perils of junk food and a healthy cynicism about the corporate food industry, but it no longer seems to affect McDonald's sales. Giles Gibbons, Managing Director of Good Business, the corporate responsibility consultancy created by Steve Hilton (the man who rebranded the Conservatives), believes that customers are still not completely convinced by its revamp. McDonald's comes bottom of Good Business's 'concerned consumer index', which suggests that people remain suspicious of its brand.

Giles Gibbons: The business has regenerated itself, but the brand is lagging behind. It's a very long road. You can't win people's trust back overnight. You've got to continue to take leadership decisions that people are delighted and surprised by, and over time that will lead to people feeling more trusting and happy to associate themselves with you.

N: Why McDonald's is thriving despite this enduring cynicism is because people have realized that their concerns about obesity, industrial food production and environmental degradation cannot be the fault of one brand, argues Gibbons. Or, to put it a different way, if all global food corporations are as bad as each other, why worry unduly about McDonald's? 'Companies have responded, but people also understand the issue of obesity better,' says Gibbons. (It's only Prince Charles who makes crotchety statements about banning McDonald's these days.)

GG: The debate is more grown-up at the same time as McDonald's has evolved. The combination of these two factors means that people are less embarrassed to be associated with it.

2.2 Vocabulary Corporate social responsibility

🔊 **1:18–1:23**

1

Eco-efficiency was a phrase coined by the Business Council for Sustainable Development to describe the need for companies to improve their ecological as well as economic performance. Minimizing the company's environmental impact, particularly around highly visible aspects of its operations or in areas where it makes financial savings, is a particularly popular tactic amongst companies whose products are inherently destructive to the environment. For example, an oil company installing solar panels on the roofs of its petrol stations and reducing the carbon emissions of its operations whilst remaining committed to a continual increase in oil and gas production.

2

Donating to charities is a simple and reputation-enhancing way for a company to put a numerical value on its CSR 'commitment'. McDonald's network of Ronald McDonald Houses to 'improve the health and well-being of children', and BP's sponsorship of the National Portrait Award are two high-profile examples. Because it's easy and very PR friendly, corporate giving is more easily dismissed as a PR exercise than other forms of CSR. In an effort to respond to this criticism companies are shifting to making larger donations to a smaller number of charity 'partners' and combining giving with other activities.

3

Cause-related marketing, such as Tesco's highly successful 'computers for schools' promotion, is a partnership between a company and a charity, where the charity's logo is used in a marketing campaign or brand promotion. Companies choose charities which will attract target consumers. The charity gains money and profile, and the company benefits by associating itself with a good cause as well as increasing product sales.

4

The Reebok Human Rights Awards, Nestlé's Social Commitment Prize and the Alcan Prize for Sustainability are high-profile examples of corporate sponsored award schemes. Through award schemes, companies position themselves as experts on an issue and leaders of CSR simply by making a large donation.

5

Corporate codes of conduct are explicit statements of a company's 'values' and standards of corporate behaviour. Codes vary in content and quality from company to company, and cover some or all of the following issues: the treatment of workers, consumer reliability, supply chain management, community impact, environmental impact, human rights commitments, health and safety, transparency and dealings with suppliers, and other issues. Some codes are monitored by external verifiers. In many cases these are large accounting firms such as Ernst & Young or PricewaterhouseCoopers™. This has led to the criticism that monitors will place the aims of the company, and not the environment or society, at the forefront when carrying out their assessment.

6
Many companies develop community projects in the vicinity of their sites, to offset negative impacts or 'give back' to the community and local workforce. Community investment covers a whole range of initiatives including: running health programmes, sponsoring schools, playgrounds or community centres, employee volunteering schemes, or signing a memorandum of understanding with communities affected by a company's impacts. GlaxoSmithKline, the pharmaceutical multinational, for example, supports a wide variety of health and education programmes in areas where it operates, ranging from training midwives in Vietnam to AIDS awareness outreach for Brazilian teenagers.

2.4 Management skills Time management

🔘 1:24–1:28

1
Margarita: Have a seat, Robin.
Robin: Thanks.
M: I know you're busy, so I'll get straight to the point. We're expecting budget cuts, so I'd like you to look into ways of reducing our travel costs. The reason I'm asking you to do it is that you're the person who has to make the most business trips, so you know more about it than anyone else.
R: Well, that's probably true.
M: So, is that something you'd be prepared to take on?

2
R: When do you need my report?
M: Well, the absolute deadline would be the end of the year. But I'd like to move as quickly as possible, really. Think about how much time you'll need, and let me know what you decide. In any case, I suggest you give me an update every two weeks or so, OK?

3
M: That's great, Robin. So, I'll let Kim know you're handling the project, and I'll send out a memo to all the reps asking them to make time to talk to you.
R: Thanks, Margarita. What about the travel bureau, should we tell them?
M: No, I think we should leave them in the dark for the moment, don't you?

4
M: I'd appreciate it if you could treat this as confidential, at least for the time being.
R: Of course. No problem. But, erm, I'm just a little bit concerned about the workload. I'm still trying to clear the backlog from my trip to Brazil!

M: Yes, I realize that, and I certainly don't want to overload you. I thought I'd get Estelle to take over some of your paperwork for a few weeks. How does that sound?

5
M: As a first step, could you get back to me with proposals we can run past Human Resources? If they're happy, you can go ahead and draw up new procedures. Overall, we need to cut the travel budget by at least 15%. Are you comfortable with that?
R: Sure.

2.6 Case study Pixkel Inc.

🔘 1:29

Caitlin: I think everybody knows that Bill wants me to develop a strategy to improve our corporate image, so the main reason I called this meeting was just to try to get a handle on what's happening, and what you feel needs to change, OK? Unfortunately, Bill can't make it – he's busy in the lab.
Ben: Ha! The invisible man strikes again!
Carla: Let's try to be constructive, OK? Maybe I can start. This is Carla, by the way. Don't get me wrong, Caitlin, I think a coherent image strategy is very valuable, but surely our first priority has to be getting everybody pulling in the same direction!
B: Ah, come on, Carla, get real! We're talking cash flow and supply chain here, not one of your touchy-feely, HR team-building programmes!
Cai: Sorry, hang on, is that Ben?
B: Yep.
Cai: Look, Ben, can we come to you next? Let's just let Carla have her say, all right?
B: OK, OK. Just trying to keep the meeting on track.
Cai: Carla?
Car: Thank you, Caitlin. I was just saying you can't have an effective image strategy when everybody is pursuing their own agenda. Right now there's just no team spirit; problems are always someone else's fault. I'm telling you, we can't seem to agree on anything! It's no surprise we can't keep our people – I already had three developers quit this year!
Lena: It might help if conditions were more in line with a high tech image. Those labs are like prison cells!
Car: Lena's absolutely right there, unfortunately – and it doesn't make hiring any easier, I can tell you!
Cai: OK. Thanks, Carla. Ben, let's hear what you have to say now.
B: Well, like I said, our cash flow problems really damaged our profile in the marketplace! We're not paying our suppliers, so they ain't too happy, and our customers know we're cash-starved, so they're literally squeezing us dry!
L: Yeah – and with the Chinese and the Indians slashing prices, it's no picnic! We're still increasing our volumes, but we're being forced to discount more and more.
Cai: This is Lena, right?
L: Yeah, sorry, Caitlin.
Cai: That's OK – Ben?

B: Yeah, Lena's team's having a hard time. I'm trying to take us upmarket, but to do that we need some serious money, and finance just keeps cutting our budget!
Alex: Now hold on a minute, Ben, that's not fair! Costs have to be kept under control!
B: Under control? My marketing budget is down 15% this year! You people in Palo Alto have *no idea* how difficult …
Cai: Hang on, Ben, and um …
A: Alex.
Cai: Alex. Sorry. Look, we're all in the same boat – let's just focus on the problems, OK?
Car: You see what I mean?
Jerry: Can I come in here, Caitlin? Jerry Woo.
Cai: Sure, go ahead, Jerry. You're over in Taiwan right now, is that right?
J: Yeah, I'm with our subcontractors here. I don't know how much you know about our chipsets? Our digital pixel technology provides far better resolution, contrast and colour than standard CCD cameras, so you'd think they'd be easy to sell, right? Unfortunately, Lena's people don't seem to be able to get their act together.
L: Jerry, it's not as simple as that …
J: Just hear me out, OK? It's the same problem with marketing – lots of talk about added value, but in the end we're still discounting! So, I'm working day and night to supply enough product, and taking the blame when we can't deliver, but we're not making any profit! From where I stand, the answer is pretty obvious!
B: I can't believe I'm hearing this!
L: Caitlin, it's Lena again, can I just say something here?
Cai: Just a second. OK, Jerry, I hear what you're saying. Thanks for that.
J: Sure. Just my two cents.
Cai: Now, Lena?
L: Well, it's always easy to blame sales! OK, we have a good product, but it's *completely invisible!* The final customer doesn't have any idea what the chipset does, or who made it – so it's really tough to persuade manufacturers they're getting added value from using *our* technology rather than one of the big names. I'd like a lot more support from marketing – not just on things like the logo, the slogan, colour coding or the website, although they all could use serious updating: no, I'm talking about educating customers to demand high-quality chipsets in their digital cameras. That would really make our lives a heck of a lot easier!
Cai: Yes, I see what you mean, Lena. All right, can I bring Alex in? We haven't heard much from you yet, Alex, what's your take on all this?
A: If you set the cash flow problem aside for a moment, the figures aren't actually that bad. As long as we keep costs under control, which I've more or less managed to do up to now, we have excellent growth and we're still in the black. The real problem is just a general lack of direction. Nobody really knows what our medium- or long-term strategy is supposed to be. I mean, we haven't even got a corporate mission statement, let alone a business plan!
Cai: OK, thanks for that, what I think we need to do is …

1:30–1:37

Alex O'Driscoll: The obvious place to start is with a clear mission statement and a commitment to social responsibility; you know, some high-profile community project to show we can be trusted.

Lena Zimmer: Remember 'Intel Inside'? Nobody had ever heard of Intel, but look at them now! That was a stroke of genius!

Carla Buenaventura: We need to work on the Sales Teams' image and communication skills – customers' judgements are based 72% on appearance, 20% on how you communicate, and only 8% on the actual words you use!

Ben Rainey: We should take a leaf out of Microsoft's® book: they never refer to 'Word' or 'Excel' – it's always 'Microsoft Word' and 'Microsoft Excel'.

Jerry Woo: We should develop a neat logo, a great slogan, and use celebrity endorsements: look what they did for Nike. 'Just do it', the swoosh, and the world-class performers – that's a winning combination!

Alex O'Driscoll: Why not make Bill the next Richard Branson? Everybody knows Virgin because of his publicity stunts, like the hot-air balloon, and they don't cost an arm and a leg either!

Lena Zimmer: T-shirts, baseball caps, polo shirts, staff uniforms ... and maybe change our name? Make Pixkel visible and cool!

Ben Rainey: How about a viral movie to build our brand? Did you ever see that series of short films BMW did with Clive Owen? That was awesome!

3 Supply chain

3.1 About business **Outsourcing**

 1:38

Let me start by asking you a question. In five years' time, how many of you will still be employed by the same company as today? Well, probably not more than half of you. If that idea shocks you, get used to it, because BPO, business process outsourcing, is here to stay. Some of you will still be sitting at the same desk, doing similar work, with the same colleagues – but you'll be consultants working for an outsourcing service provider. That's 'lift-out'!

Take BT, for example, the giant London-based telecommunications company. At one time, BT had an HR staff of some 14,500 employees. Today, only about 500 are left; but another 1,100 have become employees of Accenture HR Services.

So, what happens to staff who are lifted out? Well, the 'bad' news is, their workload usually increases! Outsourcing providers work on the assumption that business processes can be performed more efficiently than they were by the corporation; when you increase efficiency, clearly, you increase the workload.

The *good* news is that the job becomes more interesting. Most people are very attracted by the idea of working for several different clients instead of a single corporation; we find that between 50% and 60% of employees who are outsourced are happier as a result.

The other very significant benefit is that lift-out provides more and much better career opportunities. If you're working in HR in a large industrial corporation, your career choices are pretty limited. HR is seen as a cost, and it's very difficult to move to another department. But in a specialist firm like Accenture, HR is a source of revenue, rather than a cost; so it's perfectly possible to move to marketing, or sales, or even high-level management.

Of course, there is always the risk of the 'knowledge drain' if too many employees refuse the lift-out and prefer to leave the company altogether, taking with them a great deal of valuable knowledge and experience. To minimize that risk, you should provide regular updates on the outsourcing process; you should take every opportunity to explain the benefits for the employee and for the company; and you should have an open door policy to give advice to anyone who needs it.

3.2 Vocabulary **Logistics**

 1:39

In simple, forward logistics, goods, information and financial transactions move from one end of the supply chain to the other. As you can see in the top half of the slide, traditionally raw materials are moved to the manufacturer, where they are transformed into finished goods. These then move forward via warehouses and distribution centres to retail outlets, and then on to the consumer.

The goal of reverse logistics is to maximize the value of all goods which, for one reason or another, are removed from the primary distribution channel. This is achieved by moving them beyond the expected end point of the supply chain. So in the bottom half of the slide, you can see that goods can be moved back from the consumer toward the manufacturer. Products can be repositioned and sold to customers in a different geographical location or in a different retail organization; they can be returned to distribution for salvage or, for example, for donation to charity, or they can go back to the manufacturer to be destroyed or recycled.

🔊 1:40

So how do USF Processors provide added value using reverse logistics? First of all, by using technology, especially scan-based trading, to provide cradle-to-grave control over the supply chain. For instance, by repositioning product between different stores we can minimize and often eliminate stockouts. Another example is date codes: by managing date codes proactively, we can minimize stales; obviously this is particulary important in the grocery business. Also, by managing in-store inventory we can predict unsaleables in sufficient time to be able to reposition them in secondary channels, for example, in thrift stores.

Another very real issue in today's world is the threat of bioterrorism; in the event that a product recall becomes necessary, USF Processors can manage the recall process quickly and efficiently in order to mitigate the manufacturer's liability. Similarly, where product is unsold, efficient handling of returns allows us to minimize cost exposure. And

because we capture and utilize accurate, meaningful and objective data on all these processes, manufacturers and retailers can improve their business relationships and achieve dramatic improvements in contracting.

3.4 Management skills **Managing change**

🔊 1:41

Interviewer: Goran, you specialize in helping companies to manage change; more specifically, in helping retailers move towards an on-demand supply chain. First of all, remind us exactly what an on-demand supply chain is, will you?

Goran: Sure. The on-demand supply chain is top of every retailer's wish list: a way of adjusting all a company's business processes, in real time, to meet customer needs and demand, literally day by day, and even hour by hour.

I: So you provide exactly what your customers want; no less, and no more? No waste, no unnecessary overheads or logistics, no stockouts, no returns: is that really possible?

G: Like I said, it's top of the wish list! But the on-demand model can be created today if businesses are prepared to share the right information at the right time. It's all about working together – what we call CPFR.

I: Which stands for ...?

G: Collaborative planning, forecasting and replenishment. Basically, it's what happens when retailers, manufacturers and logistics partners put their heads together and think outside the box; when they design an ideal system, irrespective of the traditional boundaries between individual businesses.

I: Yes, I can see that. But it seems the change involved in setting up an on-demand supply chain can be difficult to accept – which is where you come in?

G: That's right. One of the first things we do in helping a retailer change to CPFR is to look at a force field analysis. We identify two types of forces: driving forces, which are the forces pushing the company towards change, and restraining forces, which are the factors pushing in the opposite direction, resisting change and trying to maintain the status quo. Very often there's an equilibrium between the driving forces and the restraining forces – so nothing happens. My job is to try to strengthen the driving forces, and weaken the restraining forces.

I: Can you give us some examples of these forces?

G: Well, increasing consumer power is a very strong driving force. If retail companies can't adapt to the global marketplace, they simply won't survive. It's probably the most powerful force for change. Then there's the prospect of significantly better results: if companies can move goods faster and avoid stockouts then obviously results are better. That may not be the strongest driving force, but obviously it's very significant.

I: So what about the restraining forces, what are they, things like inertia?

G: Well, inertia is certainly one of them. It's

easier to do nothing than to change! But that's a relatively weak factor. There are much more powerful restraining factors. For example, a lot of retailers are afraid of giving away their secrets.

I: Really?

G: Oh, yes. Many retailers think they're taking a big risk if they tell supply chain partners how their business works. Actually, they couldn't be further from the truth. When suppliers really understand how the retailer's business works, they're usually delighted to go out of their way to help.

I: I see. And what other restraining factors are there?

G: Well, other issues are not quite as strong as secrecy, but a couple of common ones are related to investment: being afraid of not investing in the right technology, for example, or simply worrying about not getting a good return on investment.

 1:42–1:49

1

OK, Maria. The reason why I want you to hold a brainstorming session is to encourage people to stop burying their heads in the sand. We all need to step back so we can see the big picture and develop a really clear vision of where we want this company to go.

2

At this stage, you should encourage staff to tackle problems themselves. It's them that need to be empowered to make change work. Give them autonomy, and then make sure you catch them doing something right, and congratulate them!

3

Well, Maria, you've done a great job. What's essential now is to re-freeze things, to consolidate the changes so they really stick. We don't want people to dismiss CPFR as just the flavour of the month, do we?

4

Now, the thing that people need to take on board is that this is really urgent. What they don't realize is that if we don't unfreeze the situation fast, your supply chain is going to start falling apart!

5

As the next step, Maria, what you should do is get all the staff on board. It's them that should take ownership of the project, so you need to communicate so well that they really buy into making this thing work.

6

Another thing you have to bear in mind is that if you let up, people can very easily slip back into old habits. So let's build momentum by rolling out the changes in waves, OK?

7

I suggest we hold a team-building day. What's really critical at this early stage is to engage the hearts and minds of the team who are going to guide the project to success.

8

Right now it's getting into the habit of winning that counts most. What would be really good would be to get everyone together every Friday to celebrate each week's progress. Or every two weeks if you want, but what's important is that it's short term.

3.6 Case study **WEF Audio**

 1:50

Bettina: Hi George. This seat free?
George: Uh huh.
B: Thanks. Good Schnitzel?
G: Mm. Excellent. The food's really improved here recently.
B: Yeah – Eva's latest strategy to reduce staff turnover. Doesn't seem to be working, though.
G: No. People here just don't like change, even when it's for the better.
B: Have you seen the latest scorecard?
G: Yes. Not great, is it? Too much competition from China and Hong Kong.
B: Well, I'm not sure that's really the problem. OK, the Chinese are a lot more efficient than we are, but sales are pretty good, and still rising.
G: Hm – for the moment, but I reckon the writing's on the wall. Our core business is stagnant. It's the new products that are boosting revenue; they already account for nearly 40% of turnover. The thing is, they only contribute 10% or 12% of profits. With our traditional methods, we're just not competitive. Our margins are just too small.
B: I'd agree that we've been too focused on product development for the last two years, when we should have been worrying about profitability.
G: That's exactly what I'm saying. Look at inventory – the products are becoming more and more sophisticated, so we're tying up more and more cash in stocking components. Not to mention returns. We've never had that problem with the 'Emotion' speakers. And we need to hire more and more workers, but we can't even keep our skilled people happy because of the extra workload from increased sales! It's a vicious circle!
B: Hm. More water?
G: Please.
B: So what are you saying? We should drop the new products?
G: No, we have to think of the future. But we need to introduce Just-In-Time. Streamline the process, cut production costs, increase productivity and cut delivery times. Today's market wants product on demand. I know Karl would like to try it.
B: Maybe he would, but the old man would never agree to it! Quality is everything for Franz, you'd never persuade him we'd maintain quality levels with Just-In-Time. And what you mustn't forget is that if you don't hold inventory, then your suppliers have to increase theirs, so that's likely to push costs up.
G: Mm. Can you pass the bread, please?
B: There you go. What *I* say is we should outsource all the new products, and just focus on the high-end speakers. Offshore contractors can produce much more cheaply than we can. They'd handle returns too, and we could forget all the staffing headaches.
G: You think Franz would trust them? And what about Karl? The new products are his baby – I can't see him telling a Chinese subcontractor all his secrets! No, it's too risky, it could very quickly damage our

reputation. And apart from anything else, we've already invested a lot in production here in Austria.
B: Hm. I'm not sure that would count for much. You going to eat that dessert?
G: Be my guest, I'm supposed to be on a diet.
B: Waste not, want not, I always say. Mm! So, have you heard the latest rumours about Eva and Karl?
G: What do you mean?
B: Well, you know, their marriage has been on the rocks for a while now, even though Franz is keen to keep them together. I've heard that Eva wants to relocate the new products to North Africa. OK, she'd have to find premises, but apparently you can build a factory really cheaply over there – and, of course, the salaries are far lower than they are here!
G: Well, it might cut costs – but the logistics would be complicated, and the unions would go ballistic! But what's it got to do with Karl and Eva's marriage?
B: Can't you see? Eva doesn't just want to relocate production to North Africa – she wants to relocate Karl!
G: Hm!

4 Managing conflict

4.1 About business **Management style**

 1:51–1:55

1

There are a great many models for describing management style and conflict management, but many of them are based on McGregor's theory x and theory y. Like the horizontal and vertical axes on a graph, McGregor's theory confronts opposing views of human motivation. The theory x manager assumes that people are lazy; they need to be cajoled, threatened or even punished in order to get the work done. The theory y manager, on the other hand, believes that workers can be creative, self-motivated and autonomous; the role of the theory y manager is to help people obtain satisfaction from a job well done. Type x and type y workplaces are sometimes referred to as 'hard' and 'soft'.

2

Building on McGregor's work in the early 1960s, Robert Blake and Jane Mouton devised a managerial chart which defines five leadership styles, as illustrated by the five squares on their chart. Although it's hardly cutting-edge, this model is still considered to be very useful today, and forms the basis of several more recent conflict style inventories. This time the x axis is expressed as 'concern for production', and the y axis as 'concern for people'. Each axis has a scale of nine points, from low to high. The results of a questionnaire on attitudes and opinions are used to plot a manager's position on the grid. For example, a person who scores 'nine, one' – that's to say nine on the x axis and one on the y axis, is defined as having a 'Produce or perish' style. This type of manager is obsessed with achieving goals whatever the human cost, and may seem autocratic and abrasive. Other positions on the grid are the 'country club' style, with a 'one, nine' score, where the manager values the security and comfort of employees at the expense of productivity; and the 'impoverished' style with a 'one, one' score, where managers are interested in neither production nor people, but only in doing the minimum necessary to hang onto their jobs for as long as possible. In the middle of the grid, a score of 'five, five' represents the 'middle-of-the-road' style. This type of manager tries to find a compromise where they can keep people reasonably happy and at the same time achieve reasonable results. Finally, a score of 'nine, nine' is called the 'team' style: by encouraging teamwork and using coaching skills, managers provide high job satisfaction and meet production targets.

3

More recently, Hersey and Blanchard observed that, as an employee gains experience and skills, a manager needs to change styles and adapt to the employee's development stage, hence the arrows on the chart. They redefined 'nine, one' as 'Telling' or 'Directing'. This would be an appropriate style, for example, to manage a new recruit, who needs to be told exactly what to do, and to be carefully directed. 'Nine, nine' becomes 'Selling' or 'Coaching'; 'one, nine' is now 'Participating' or 'Supporting'. Finally, very experienced and autonomous members of staff who can take on complete projects with very little help from their manager, will react best to a 'Delegating' or 'Observing' style of management.

4

All right, let's move on now to models for conflict management. Take a look at this model which was devised by Robert and Dorothy Bolton. Here the x axis measures assertiveness, and the y axis shows responsiveness. Assertive people are considered to be forceful and demanding, whereas responsiveness is a measure of how much awareness of emotions and feelings a person shows. As you can see, the grid is divided into four quadrants: going anticlockwise from 'nine, one' to 'one, one', they are: the Drivers, who are very interested in getting what they want, and not very interested in how anyone else feels about it: the Expressives, who are prepared to be assertive about telling people how they feel: the Amiables, who are prepared to be unassertive in order to keep everyone happy; and finally, the Analyticals, who are quiet, shy and let everyone else get what they want.

5

Now, the last model I want to mention briefly is a conflict management model by Thomas Kilmann. This considers different behaviours in situations of conflict. Starting with the circle at 'nine, one', and going anticlockwise as before, first we have 'Competing', the behaviour of someone who is prepared to do whatever is needed to win. Then we have 'Collaborating', where a person will work hard to try to find a solution which satisfies everyone. Next we come to 'Accommodating'; this is where someone will prefer to sacrifice their own needs or goals in order to satisfy someone else. The circle in the bottom left corner represents 'Avoiding' – as the name suggests, this describes simply avoiding dealing with the problem by procrastinating or sidestepping; and finally, in the middle of the grid, we have 'Compromising' where a person

will look for concessions which will lead to an acceptable deal. OK. I'm sorry if I've covered quite a lot of ground rather quickly today – are there any questions?

4.2 Vocabulary Managing conflict

🔊 1:56–1:63

1

Ed: Things are a bit tense between Lin and Nisha, aren't they?

Jo: Yeah – I heard them having words again this morning.

E: They should never have been put in the same office, they're like chalk and cheese, those two.

J: Hm. They certainly don't seem to have much in common.

2

Dave: D'you hear about Pavel?

Jo: No. What?

D: Apparently he's in trouble again; he lost it with a customer.

J: Really?

D: Yeah, he'd just spent all morning installing a milling machine for Custom Labs and then the Production Manager told him it was in the wrong place – he went ballistic!

J: I'm not surprised – they're a right pain at that company!

3

Lin: I've had it up to here with Mr Jarlberg!

Dave: Why, what's he done?

L: Well, I've been expecting an important call all morning and he wouldn't let me take my mobile into our meeting.

D: Well, you know how obsessive he is about going by the book.

L: I know – he's so blinkered!

4

Ed: Nisha's driving Dave up the wall, you know. She's so fussy.

Jo: Poor Dave – I certainly wouldn't like to be her manager!

E: Me neither – that sort of misplaced perfectionism really gets my goat!

J: Yeah – how long d'you think it'll be before Dave hits the roof?

5

Dave: Oh, for heaven's sake! Jo, look at this!

Jo: What now?

D: Tintex have got our order wrong again, and accounts have already paid the invoice! Those people get away with murder!

J: Right – that's the last straw! Next time we'll take our business elsewhere!

6

Lin: Has Dave told you about that student he's got shadowing him?

Ed: No, why?

L: Well, he's really rubbed Dave up the wrong way already! Keeps interrupting him – and you know how Dave loves the sound of his own voice!

E: Yeah, right, I'm amazed the kid can get a word in!

7

Jo: Hey Ed?

Ed: Yeah?

J: How's the inspection going with that bloke from Head Office?

E: Oh, don't ask! He just doesn't listen, I'm at the end of my tether!

J: Not interested in any of your new ideas then?

E: No. He's got his own agenda and doesn't want to know about anything else.

8

Dave: So, Jo, what did you think of the strategic thinking session with Katrina?

Jo: It was OK, but she wasn't prepared to take on other people's opinions. It was supposed to be a workshop not a lecture.

D: Really?

J: Yeah. She always has to have the last word. People like that really make me sick!

4.4 Management skills
Assertiveness

🔊 1:64–1:67

1

Marc: Linda, I've got a bone to pick with you about my holiday dates. You promised I could have three weeks in June, but now I'm down to cover for Haley ...

Linda: Sorry, Marc, can I get back to you later on? I'm just about to go into a conf call.

M: But you don't understand, I've already booked my flights and everything! It's not good enough!

L: Marc, I understand that you feel upset, but I'd much rather take time to talk this through properly. Can we work something out this afternoon? What time would suit you best?

2

Linda: There was one other thing, Jerry.

Jerry: Yes?

L: Well, I hesitate to ask you this, but I was due for a raise after my last appraisal, and that was nearly six months ago.

J: Oh, well, I don't know ... I'd have to find out – Finance are trying to keep costs down, you know.

L: Well, I realize that this is maybe not the best time, but it was validated in the appraisal report.

J: Yes, but it's not really my decision, you see. Um, I'll look into it, but I can't promise anything. OK?

L: Not really, Jerry. The way I see it is like this: I met my objectives, so it's only fair the bank should respect its commitments.

3

Carmen: Did you switch the TV off again, Linda?

Linda: Yes, Carmen, I did. I'm writing an important proposal here, and I need to concentrate.

C: Why can't you go someplace else?! I'm waiting for the market news.

L: Why can't *you* ...

C: What was that?

L: Carmen, I appreciate that you have your own agenda, but there are eight of us in this office, and I feel strongly that we should respect each others' space. Now, what would be an acceptable compromise? Can we turn the sound off and just leave the picture until the market news comes on?

C: All right, I suppose so.

4

Moritz: Hi Linda!

Linda: Oh, hi.

M: So; what do you think about my idea?

L: Sorry, Moritz, which idea would that be?

M: Spending a weekend on my dad's boat, of course!

L: Oh, right. Well, it's a nice idea, but, erm, I need some time to think it over.

M: Come on, Linda, it'll be great! I know some really nice places to go – just the two of us!

L: Erm, look, Moritz: I appreciate the offer, but no, thanks.

M: But you don't …

L: Moritz: it's really sweet of you, but no.

M: Really?

L: Really.

M: Oh.

4.6 Case study Olvea Brasil

 1:68–1:71

Wilson Holden: OK, at first I thought, fair enough, I won't make trouble, I'll wait and see how things develop. I mean, it's normal when you're new, you expect to be told what to do. So I kept a low profile, and just did what I was asked to do. But, you know, I didn't do five years at engineering school just to stand around and wait for orders from some woman who thinks she's God's gift to engineering!

I know the job, I know a lot about injection moulding, I'm ready to take more responsibility, and I think I can improve the way we do things here. But Carla is completely paranoid! She's a total control freak, and she flatly refuses to allow her people to take even the slightest initiative. Frankly, she's a pain in the neck! There are *good guys* in my team, guys with ideas and potential! But I'll tell you now, they won't stay here long with a boss who won't even contemplate the idea that she might be wrong!

Susan Shipley: I'm glad you set up this meeting – I really need to talk to someone. I can't talk to Vitor, he's never in the office – or if he is, he won't speak to me. I tried to go over his head, to talk to Isabel Correia, but she told me I had to speak to Vitor first. You see, I've been having problems at home; I feel depressed and demotivated, and Vitor just doesn't seem to care. In fact, I'm surprised he even noticed there was a problem. He arrives late, leaves early, and sits in his office with the door closed. When there are problems, he never does anything; he just waits for them to go away. Or he passes the buck and leaves someone like you to pick up the pieces. In our department we call him 'the invisible man'!

Luigi Tarantini: When Isabel was appointed Plant Manager, she was new to the company; we did a lot of stuff together so she could get to know the way we work. That was fine, we got on well, we still do. She's a good manager, demanding, yes, but encouraging and understanding too; always very close to her people. And that's the problem; she's just too close. We have a monthly reporting meeting where I update her on everything that's going on, but no, that's not enough; she wants to be in the lab with me every day. That gets on my nerves! I mean, sure, there are some people that need constant contact with their boss – but I've been here for more than 20 years, and things are going fine – at least they would be if she'd let me get on with my work! I don't need someone constantly looking over my shoulder. If I have a problem, I know where to find her, and I know she values what I'm doing so let's just get on with the job, shall we?

Natasha Gomes: Well, Antony, I mean Mr Middleton, is really nice, you know? I don't want to cause problems, it's just that, well, I don't have very much experience really – it's my first job, and I want to do it well. But when he gives me something to do, he never tells me exactly what he wants. You know, he seems to think I should know what to do. So when I call him and ask him a question, he just says 'What do *you* think?' It's not unkind or anything, it's just like we have to negotiate everything, he can't just say, 'do this' or 'do that'. I just need to know what he wants. When I make mistakes, he doesn't even tell me off – he always looks for something positive first before talking about the problem. Other people in the department are always taking advantage of him – they do whatever they want, because they know he'll always compromise.

5 Marketing and sales

5.1 About business Strategic marketing and partnering

 2:01

Interviewer: Ari, you specialize in business partnering. Am I right in thinking that that's a kind of marriage bureau for companies?

Ari: Well, these days marriage probably implies considerably less sharing and long-term commitment than business partnering! But, no, seriously, we're not in the business of M&A. Perhaps a better analogy would be the cocktail party host who hooks guests up with other people with mutually compatible interests and complementary talents, who can help each other out.

I: I see. Can you give us an example?

A: Sure. Probably the best-known example and certainly one of the most successful, is the partnering strategy between Apple® and Nike. These are two extremely influential corporations with, at first sight, very different product lines. But when you take a closer look at their strategies, you realize that they have something very major in common, because what both organizations offer their customers are lifestyle management solutions. Apple's® core market – no pun intended! – is what could be called the 'creativity culture', and Nike's is clearly the 'sport culture'. Anyway, Nike wanted to provide their customers with performance data from their shoes in real time, and thought that sending data to an iPod™ was the obvious way to do it. Now, the people at Apple®, knowing that around half of their customers use their iPods™ while they work out, were obviously interested. By making the connection with Nike, they created a fantastic opportunity for both companies to promote a whole family of integrated products and accessories for the 'sport-creativity' culture.

I: So they developed shoes which communicate with your iPod™, and can tell you your speed, how far you've run, how long you've been running …

A: … how many calories you've burned …

I: … *and* play music?!

A: Right! But that's only the beginning! Very cleverly, they also exploited the Internet to make maximum use of the data collected from the shoes; so you can now feed your data into Nike's website, and connect with, or even compete against other athletes anywhere in the world! What's more, Apple's® iTunes will sell you music mixes with exactly the right tempos for your personal workout, or your favourite sports stars' recommended playlists!

I: And you can get special Nike running gear with iPod™ pockets, and so on?

A: Absolutely! Shirts, shorts, armbands, jackets … you name it.

I: OK. So are other businesses picking up on this partnering model?

A: Yes, indeed, and in all sorts of sectors, but perhaps most of all in any business which promises lifestyle benefits; fields like travel, entertainment, healthcare, finance, and so on. If businesses believe that you can work with an external partner to develop synergy between your brands, and if you believe that you can deliver added lifestyle benefits to your customers, then partnering is for you. If, in addition, you can enhance your customer experience via the Internet, then you earn yourself a very, very significant bonus.

5.2 Vocabulary Marketing

 2:02–2:07

1

Quizmaster: OK teams, this round is about key marketing terms. Here's your starter; you may confer. All right, fingers on buzzers! What is the fifth P sometimes added to the four Ps in the classic marketing mix?

Student 1: What are the four Ps? Anyone remember?

Student 2: Um, Product, Price, Promotion, um …

Student 3: What about the distribution channel?

S2: Yes, that's Place; so that's four – what's the fifth?

S3: Presentation?

S2: No, that's not it.

S1: OK, I've got it!

Q: Yes, Cambridge?

S1: I think it's Packaging.

Q: Yes, Packaging is the correct answer; you get ten points, and five more questions!

2

Q: The next question is about competitive strategies. Everybody knows the company with the biggest market share is called the market leader. But can you name three more competitive strategy positions?

S1: OK, there's market leader; market follower, that's when you copy the market leader.

S2: Yes, and market nicher, you know, when you just focus on a very specific part of the market, a niche.

S3: Right, so what's the last one? Market climber?

S1: Give it a try.

S3: We think it's market climber.

Q: No, I'm sorry, the correct answer is market challenger.

S3: Oh, yeah!

3

Q: There are generally considered to be four ways in which a market can be divided into segments. One of those is product-related, that's to say based on product benefits like value for money, safety, comfort and so on. But can you name the other three?

S3: Yes, I remember this one! There's demographic, based on things like age, gender and education.

S2: OK, and then there's geographical.

S3: That's right, and the last one is based on opinions, lifestyle and attitudes, um … what's it called?

S1: Is it psychographic?

Q: Yes, indeed!

4

Q: Here's another classic question. This time I want you to name the four stages in the product life cycle.

S1: Oh, that's easy! Introduction, growth, maturity and, um …

Q: Yes?

S1: Um, introduction, growth, maturity and … um …

Q: I'm sorry, Cambridge, I'll have to hurry you!

S3: Death?

S2: No, decline!

S1: Ah, yes, decline!

Q: Just in time!

5

Q: Customers are considered to go through three stages of brand loyalty. The first is brand awareness, or recognition; what are the other two?

S3: Oh, I know there's brand preference, when they choose your brand rather than another if they're offered a choice; but I can't remember the third one!

S2: Isn't it when they refuse to buy any other brand?

S1: Yeah, that's it: brand, um …

S2: Brand insistence!

Q: Yes, well done!

6

Q: Cambridge, you've scored 40 out of a possible 50 so far; here's your last question. There are four main types of promotional activity. Advertising is one, what are the other three?

S3: Oh, I was just going to say advertising!

S2: Yeah, you always know the easy answers!

S3: You cheeky …!

S1: Stop arguing, you two! Advertising, sales promotions …

S3: I knew that too!

S2: Yeah, right!

S1: … and personal selling, you know, face to face or by telephone … but what's the fourth one?

Q: Time's up, Cambridge, I need answers!

S1: Sales promotions, personal selling, and I think … um …

S2: PR. Public relations.

Q: Yes, that's another correct answer!

5.3 Grammar **Prepositions**

 2:08

Right, if we could just focus a bit on our main strategy to grow our North America operation. On balance, what we need more than anything else is a joined-up strategy across our main western centres in California, Washington State and Arizona. In other words, we all need to be focusing on the same strategy, whatever part of the business we're working in. You know, all pulling in the same direction and making sure we all get the three 'Fs' sorted – Focus, Familiarity and Follow-up. Is that clear? So, focus on our core strategy – we've been through all that, build up close familiarity with the local markets, and follow up all leads and opportunities. We can then, as it were, capture the whole market at a stroke. At least that's the plan, if you know what I mean. By the end of this financial year we need to have cracked the West and have our numbers looking good to give us any hope of the Mid-west, and, well, more of that next year.

By the way, have you all managed to have a look through the strategy document, you know, the one I sent round the other day? Did any of you have any particular questions you want to ask about it? Good.

So, our next step is to, well, make the strategy work. I guess that's the hard part. The strategy is, by and large, pretty straightforward – on the one hand focus on the new customer, convince them that they need us, and all that stuff; on the other, well, I'll come on to that in a minute. I should emphasize that we need to be careful with customers at large. They can be a bit demanding so as a rule just fall back on the 'customer is king' thing – you know, just say yes to whatever they want. Within reason anyway – don't leave me with any massive clean-up bills. I don't really foresee anything in particular that can go wrong. In effect it's just like what we've been doing in eastern Europe, though on a bigger scale, of course. I expect it will go like a dream. Oh, one more thing. We must all avoid mentioning that glitch in the software, at all costs. By the same token, make sure you all keep quiet about the temperature thing as well – I still can't believe a bit of heat has such a terrible effect on …

5.4 Management skills **Active listening**

 2:09

Mr Garcia: … and it's not far from the airport, which is handy, of course, but it's not ideal. Then there's the traffic, parking is a nightmare these days, and then the neighbours playing music late at night; they're very friendly, but the walls are really thin, you know!

Agent: I know what you mean! So, if I understand correctly, Mr Garcia, you're saying that basically you'd like to move somewhere quieter?

Mr G: Yes. 22 years I've lived here. I know everybody in the street, and all the shops and restaurants. But I really feel I need more space, and a bit of peace and quiet at night.

A: I see. My guess is that it'll be a wrench for you to leave, am I right?

Mr G: Oh, yes, I'm quite attached to the old place. It'll be tough, but I'll work up the courage to make a move sooner or later.

A: Erm, I'm sorry, Mr Garcia, I'm not too clear about this. What sort of time frame do you have in mind?

Mr G: Well, I don't know really. It depends if I find something I really like. It would be nice to move before the summer, but that's probably too soon.

A: Too soon?

Mr G: Well, there's the financial side to think of as well.

A: Uh-huh?

Mr G: Hm. I suppose I'll need to find out about getting a mortgage if I want something bigger than this place. I expect that'll take several months, you know what banks are like!

A: Yes, they do tend to drag their feet, don't they? But I have a very good friend who works in a bank as a Financial Adviser and sometimes helps me. I can introduce you, if you like? OK, do you mind if I recap? What we've established so far is that you'd like to move somewhere quieter if possible, next spring, if we can find you something really nice to make it worth moving? And you'd like something a bit bigger, but for not too much more than you'll get for the sale of your flat. Is that a fair summary?

Mr G: Yes, you understand my situation perfectly. I can see we're going to get on really well, Miss …?

A: Irina. Yes, I'm sure we will, Mr Garcia! Now then, what I would suggest is that we start by doing a valuation of your flat. Then we'll have an idea of your budget for the new place, and, if necessary, we'll be able to start talking to the bank about how much you'd like to borrow. How does that sound?

5.6 Case study **Presnya Taxi**

 2:10

Ally: Ah, there you are, Volodya. I wanted to ask you something … what's the matter?

Volodya: Oh, it's nothing. How can I help you, Ally?

A: Now come on, I can see there's something wrong; it's written all over your face. Are those the latest accounts?

V: Yes. I just got them today.

A: The drivers are saying we're losing money. Is it true?

V: You know Moscow taxi drivers, Ally. If you believe what they say, the end of the world is only hours away! But things are not too good. Turnover is falling steadily. The taxi business isn't what it was. Too much competition. In the old days, it was a real profession. These days, anyone who can beg, borrow or steal a car is a taxi – and a much cheaper taxi than ours.

A: Hm. And the minivans are a lot cheaper too.

V: Yes. We've lost half of our airport business to minivans. People don't seem to mind sharing if they're all going to the airport.

A: And the buses are getting faster and more comfortable.

V: Not to mention trains, trams, the underground – I've heard they even want to start one of those bicycle services like they have in Paris – you know, you pick up a bicycle in your street, ride where you want to go, and just leave it when you get there.

A: Well, I'm not sure how popular that would be in the winter!

V: I don't know – with all the traffic problems we have, maybe it's not such a stupid idea. That's the other big problem. Even if you drive luxury limousines, nobody wants to spend hours on end stuck in the traffic – and I'm not pretending for a moment that our poor old Ladas are limousines, they're uncomfortable, inefficient and expensive to run. There's still some money in the bank, but we can't afford Mercedes or BMWs. In the old days, it used to take us 20 minutes to drive to Sheremetyevo – now it's usually two hours, or more! How's a taxi supposed to make money when it's not moving?!

A: Exactly. Listen, Volodya, Andrey and I have been doing some thinking about this.

V: Look, I know you went to business school, Ally, but after 40 years in the taxi business, I think I know pretty much everything there is to know. If there was a solution, I'd have found it already. Andrey knows that.

A: Just let us explain our ideas, OK? It won't cost you anything, and it might just help. We think you need to completely rethink your marketing strategy.

V: Ally, this is a taxi company. We don't do marketing, we drive taxis!

A: And that's the root of the problem. Look, just give us a chance to explain our ideas – please?

V: All right, Ally. You know very well a Russian man can never say no to a beautiful woman!

6 Risk management

6.1 About business Crisis management

🔊 2:11

Interviewer: Jack, tell us about Eric Dezenhall.

Jack: Well, Eric is certainly one of the most colourful characters in the PR world. He was once called 'the pit bull of public relations' by a journalist called Kevin McCauley, and the name stuck; I think Eric is probably quite proud of it, actually!

I: Yes. His firm was described by the National Journal as having a 'brass-knuckled, Machiavellian approach' to public relations. Is that an exaggeration?

J: Well, probably, but another journalist, Bill Moyers, went even further in criticizing Dezenhall's firm. This was at the time when Eric was defending the chemicals industry in the debate about the precautionary principle. Anyway, Bill called the firm 'the Mafia of the PR industry'! Of course, he was alluding to the fact that Eric also writes novels that feature the New Jersey Mafia. Well, PR people love calling each other names, but it's true that Eric has made a career out of an aggressively 'anti-spin' approach, and although he's certainly been very successful, he's also made some powerful enemies.

I: Such as?

J: Such as high-profile non-profit organizations like Greenpeace, or the Open Access movement. However Eric argues, and many people would concede that he has a point, that just because these organizations are seen as 'the good guys', that doesn't mean that corporations they attack, like ExxonMobil or the Publishers' Association, shouldn't have the right to defend themselves.

I: OK, so the aggressive approach to crisis management is Dezenhall's USP, basically?

J: Yeah, but although he was probably a bit of a pioneer, he's not alone – other PR firms like Qorvis Communications in Washington and Sitrick & Co. in Los Angeles have successfully exploited the same approach. And they've received plenty of criticism too for representing some very controversial clients.

I: Right. So tell us, Jack, as an experienced observer of crisis management, have these firms got it right? Is it true, as Dezenhall says, that 'whoever attacks wins, whoever defends loses?'

J: Eric has certainly been very successful, but my own feeling is that counterattacking *may* work, but it's always going to be a high-risk strategy. Whether you're totally innocent or guilty as charged, there's always the danger that hitting out at your opponent may backfire and do your image even more damage.

I: Do you have any examples where it hasn't worked?

J: Well, not anything I can talk about on this programme, but I think a measure of the risk involved, is the way that, for example, someone like Eric, who is one of the shrewdest operators I've seen in this business, combines his gloves off aggression with being very extremely low-key and circumspect about who his own clients are and what he does for them: He's extremely discreet and he never gives anything away. He'll tell you he's respecting the attorney-client privilege, but I think he's also very aware that any damage control strategy, however good it is, can sometimes go wrong. It makes sense to give your opponents as little information as possible to work with.

6.2 Vocabulary Risk management and digital risk

🔊 2:12

Interviewer: Steve, your website, Brand Intelligence, claims that digital infringements are costing e-businesses $90 million a day!

Steve: That's right.

I: So, what sort of risks are you open to these days if you're doing your business online?

S: Well, if you have a successful e-business, one problem you're very exposed to is passing off, or ambush marketing. You wake up one day to find someone else has a website which is masquerading as your company, and making money by trading on your company's name – often they will even pirate your own text, images and logo.

I: Nasty!

S: Yeah, and not very easy to deal with. Another classic is cybersquatting – that's when you have an established offline brand and you decide to start an online business to reach more customers. Much to your surprise, you then find out that someone else is freeloading on your reputation by using a domain name featuring your brand name!

I: Hm. And what about hackers?

S: Yes, of course, they're a major problem, and it's still growing as the Internet gets larger and larger – everything from simply defacing web pages to cracking credit card and information databases. Every year nearly half of UK businesses suffer a malicious security incident or breach. But there are also more unexpected risks, what we call protest issues. If your business relies on the Internet to reach an instant worldwide audience, you are vulnerable to protests and rumours of all kinds. It's incredibly easy to incite customers to boycott a company or its products, to try to manipulate your stock price, or simply to bombard a defenceless mailbox with hate mail!

I: Sounds like it's a real jungle out there! But you have solutions, right?

S: Right. We use a combination of unique, highly sophisticated software and specialist analysis to locate and report areas of brand risk, damage and abuse online. For instance, we can scan the Internet to find anyone who is illegally using your logo, even if it has been modified.

I: But what can you do to stop this kind of abuse?

S: Once we've identified the problem, there are lots of solutions; we track perpetrators; we initiate reversal, and then monitor progress.

I: Initiate reversal? Can you be more specific?

S: Each individual case is different, and we adapt to each customer's needs and wishes. At a basic level we issue 'cease and desist' orders to infringing site owners, to get them to remove their sites: we can also get sites removed from ISPs and search engines.

I: So if someone googles my brand, only the real site will come up, not the fakes?

S: Yes. And in more serious cases we get our expert legal trademark partners involved to litigate for damages or pursue criminal and civil action.

6.3 Grammar Perspective and stance

🔊 2:13

Interviewer: So Li, you're an expert in risk management. Could you start by giving us a definition of what risk management is?

Li: Risk management is the attention that organizations must pay in simple terms to things that can and do go wrong. It covers the financial context, technology, human activities, professional and expert activities, and the interface between all of these things.

I: So it's quite wide-ranging then.

L: Oh, absolutely.

I: Do you have a specific example – you mentioned the financial context.

L: Well, in 2007 the United States sub-prime mortgage market crashed. This market was created to help those who either did not have much money or who had a bad credit risk to get onto the mortgage and property ladder. If you put this in simple human terms, if somebody is a bad risk, you would not lend them money. This market turned that idea on its head and the worse the risk effectively the more the banks lent them, not just in terms of the sum of money but also the interest rate that was charged to it.

I: So you mean the banks charged these people higher interest rates? Why did they do that?

L: To make more money out of those who could not pay in the first place. The logical thing would be that, if you haven't got much money, you stand little chance of making a repayment. If you haven't got much money and you are asked to repay a huge sum of money at a higher rate of interest, logically, you are never going to make those repayments and the bank is never going to get its money back.

I: What kind of risk management systems did these banks have in place?

L: They simply assumed that these people would make the repayments, and that is the extent that they went to. From a human point of view, they never studied the likely behavioural response that somebody who is short of money with a large loan will have huge difficulty repaying it. Financially speaking, some of the banks saw the problem coming, and did their best to parcel up the bad debts and sell them on, in some cases to banks in other countries.

I: So in global terms this affected everyone?

L: Yes, it was a global phenomenon and its effects were felt worldwide. The debt parcels had a high asset value because there were high repayments attached to them, but in many cases there was a minimal chance of realizing those assets. So it became a global problem. From the point of view of the banking industry, you can see the logic, but if you look at it from the point of view of the ordinary human being, it was a disaster.

I: I see. Could you just sum up the banks' mistake for us, in one sentence?

L: The mistakes were that they assumed the money would be repaid once it had been contracted, and they also assumed that the asset value could be sold on meaning that if anything did go wrong they would be absolved of all responsibility, and also all comeback.

I: That's very interesting, …

6.4 Management skills
Communicating in a crisis

🔊 2:14–2:21

1

A: Do we really need to keep forking out on risk management?

B: Well, running a business without risk management is like walking a tightrope. It's only a matter of time before you fall off!

2

C: How on earth are we going to find space for another big development project?

D: It's a legitimate question, but I think the bigger issue here is really how we make sure that our competitors don't beat us to market.

3

E: I don't see why we should fix something that's not broken!

F: Quite simply, although the machines we have at the moment aren't broken now, we know they won't go on forever. Even more to the point, the new machines will improve precision, productivity and profitability.

4

G: What sanctions are you planning to take against the strikers?

H: Let's focus on the positives, shall we? The really important thing to remember is that talks are underway, and we hope to be able to release details of an agreement in the next few hours.

5

I: How do you intend to finance rebuilding the homes that were lost in the hurricane?

J: To be honest, I don't really know. We haven't thought about it yet, it's too early to say.

6

K: What sort of compensation will you be offering people who suffer from side effects?

L: Let's not forget that as yet there is no evidence of patients suffering any ill effects: we are simply withdrawing the drug temporarily as a precaution.

7

M: Can you confirm that several company Directors sold large blocks of shares shortly before the profit warning?

N: Let me briefly sum up the current position. An inquiry is currently being conducted with the full cooperation of all staff. The results will be announced in due course, and we are quietly confident that the commission will report that there was no wrongdoing. Thank you.

8

O: Why are you asking us to pump up the advertising budget when the product is hopeless?

P: Well, it's not completely hopeless; of course, we haven't sold as many as we'd like, but the market isn't exactly helping us at the moment.

6.6 Case study Périgord Gourmet

🔊 2:22

Pierre-Yves Gaget: Âllo, oui?

Cindie Hauser: Is this Monsieur Gaget?

PYG: Speaking – how can I help you, Madame?

CH: Cindie Hauser here, from the Washington Police Department.

PYG: Yes?

CH: I'm afraid I have rather bad news for you. Two French citizens living here in DC have been taken to hospital with suspected food poisoning. It seems they'd been celebrating their wedding anniversary with a jar of your foie gras. They're very ill.

PYG: Oh, my God!

CH: We're optimistic they'll recover quickly – fortunately, they went straight to the hospital when they started having muscle spasms. But I'm really calling you for two reasons. The first is to ask whether you are aware of any other similar cases?

PYG: No, no, nothing like this has ever happened before! We have very, very strict quality controls …

CH: Hm. How difficult would it be for someone to get access to your product before it's shipped?

PYG: Well, not very – there are any number of people involved in cooking, packaging, warehousing and shipping – but why do you ask?

CH: We're still waiting for the lab report – but the physician in the ER room said they had all the classic symptoms of strychnine poisoning.

PYG: Strychnine?!

CH: Yeah, it's one of the easiest poisons to acquire – it's found in rat poison.

🔊 2:23

PYG: Hi, this is Pierre-Yves. Sorry to call you in the middle of the night, but it's urgent, and I need you to be working on this first thing in the morning. The good news is, the two people in Washington are making a good recovery. It seems the strychnine dose was too low to be fatal. The bad news is there are three more cases – in Hong Kong. Plus, the animal rights people have hacked into our website and left a message about the poisonings – but they claim they didn't do it. The police are on the case, but no leads yet. The thing is, it's out in the open now, so we can't afford to be seen to be covering up. I want you to call a press conference for tomorrow afternoon. I won't be there – I'm flying out to Hong Kong – so I want you to make a short statement, and then take questions. You know much more about these things than I do, so I'm giving you carte blanche. Good luck.

7 Investment

7.1 About business Investment banks

🔊 2:24

Interviewer: Barry, you're well known as an advocate of the free market, yet you've published several articles calling for greater regulation of investment banks. Isn't that something of a paradox?

Barry: Well, free market theory depends on the idea that a buyer and seller will only agree on a deal if the benefits to each side are greater than the costs.

I: OK.

B: Now, most of the time that works pretty well, because a company's employees and its shareholders share the same interests. If the company does well, it's good for shareholders and it's good for employees, right?

I: Right.

B: The problem comes when the employees' interests conflict with those of the shareholders. For example, in industry, if you pay a salesman solely by commission on the number of sales or the billings he generates, without any thought for margins or value to the company, very quickly you're going to run into difficulties, because you're encouraging the salesman to keep making sales, whatever the cost to the company. And that's precisely what happened in the sub-prime crisis. Because the banks had become corporations, and bankers had become salesmen driven by massive bonuses, they kept on authorizing risky loans and mortgages, knowing that if people defaulted, all the risk would be borne by the shareholders, not by them. The worst that could happen to them was that they could lose their jobs and retire happily on the millions they had already earned.

I: In your industrial example the company goes bust, and the market regulates itself and stops paying salesmen on that basis.

B: That's right. Unfortunately, in banking, we can't afford to let banks go bust because the whole economy would break down, so taxpayers, i.e. you and me, have to bail them out. Which is why we need regulation to make sure that kind of conflict of interest can't happen.

7.2 Vocabulary **Investment choices**

 2:25

Right then ladies and gentlemen, you're going to be thankful that you came along here today. From what I can see, there's a lot of different age groups among you – some more mature ladies and gentlemen if I may say so, rich in experience, quite a few younger ones here, and it looks like one or two teenagers even.

What I want to emphasize to you all today is the importance of investment. The younger ones among you may not want to think about it, but retirement is going to come your way one day, oh, yes, 'the eighth age of man' as they say, it won't go away. And the earlier you start investing for your retirement, the richer you'll be when you retire. It really is something that you can't start doing early enough, the more mature customers amongst you will back me up on that one, won't you?

So, what can you do to make sure you have enough money to see you through your retirement? You may have heard all sorts of investment advice, both good and bad, ranging from topping up your pension pot to buying bottles of vintage wine. And who exactly is going to buy a load of wine years from now? Don't ask me. Well, you may have heard that you should build up a diversified portfolio, all sorts of different investments in different kinds of products, in different currencies even. And I won't disagree with that advice. I know it's going against the herd instinct these days, but investing in different currencies is going to offer you that buffer against market volatility, a bit of protection against the ups and downs of the market.

Ladies and gentlemen, more than anything I would recommend adopting a defensive investment stance to do just that. I reckon if you invest in several currencies you'll actually reduce your overall risk – ever heard of putting all your eggs in one basket? I thought so: all your money in one currency and if it goes down, well, you don't need an expert like me to tell you which way your investment is going to go.

So where was I? Market volatility. Whilst you can't prevent the markets going all over the place what you can do is go for property, ladies and gentlemen, which is why I'm here, as a representative of Properties To Die For Limited. Investing in property means putting your money in bricks and mortar. They're a sure-fire investment, believe me. People are always going to have to live in houses, and the world population is going up and up, so you'll easily find someone to rent your properties out to. The thing is, other property investments you might see here today, charge what you might call a 'premium price'. They're a rip-off in the language of you and me. Now, with Properties To Die For Limited you know where you are. What you see is what you get, fantastic properties that you would actually die for. None of that lack of transparency you'll find if you wander across the floor to one of our lesser rivals. We can offer you prime properties in Spain, in Portugal, in Bulgaria, in Turkey, in the US, you name it. I said 'you name it' – I didn't hear you say anything.

If you don't trust us, all you need to do is ask one of Properties To Die For Limited's valued clients. Do you know I've even seen Felicia Turner here? Well, between you and me she's bought one or two of our plum properties already. That's Ms Turner's retirement sorted. And she's very pleased with what we've sold her so far …

7.3 Grammar **Inversion and emphasis**

 2:26

Well, good morning ladies and gentlemen and thank you for inviting me to talk to you. What I particularly want to talk about today is investment, or to be more specific, ways of finding investment to fund new business ideas. The reason for wanting to focus on this is mainly because what we've found over the years is that the philosophy that's been traditionally taught in business schools, which you could simply say is: write a brilliant business plan, raise $2 million, hire some very expensive executives, doesn't actually work for most of us. Were the business schools to focus on the alternative approach, which I'm going to tell you about, business entrepreneurship would be quite different. I do want to emphasize at this point that I'm speaking from the point of view of the person seeking investment, in other words, the person with the idea for a new business plan. Indeed, the perspective of the investor is quite different.

So, to start off. For most of us aspiring entrepreneurs: you've got a good idea but really no track record so you've really got to do everything yourself. Should you have access to a huge amount of money, you're laughing, but unfortunately most of us don't.

When you're talking about investment there are really two types of investment. There's the financial investment, that you need to, you know, buy a computer, build some code, but more important is what you might call intellectual investment – how do you find a group of partners that you actually work with together and actually build something and bootstrap it into existence? Under no circumstances should you go it alone – you won't succeed. What you need above all, before getting your hands on any investment money, is a core group of people to complement your own skills. For example, if you want to build a social networking site, you might have a brilliant idea, say to build one for the fashion industry.

However, if you can't program then the first thing you need to do is to find a programming wizard so that you can do this. No sooner do you start doing something on the Internet than you need a lawyer. So where can you find an e-commerce lawyer to help you who's prepared to work for equity in the future company? Basically, you haven't got the money to, well, pay anybody, so instead you offer equity. What you're doing is putting together a credible team, Indeed, you're looking for people that can do everything. Not only do you need programmers and lawyers, but also people who can market and sell, people who know about your target market. Only then do you have a credible team and you can actually build something. What investors want to see is what they call traction. They want to see that you've got some customers already. You're on the ground, you've already started and you're ready to go.

7.4 Management skills **Decision-making**

 2:27–2:30

1

Yann: OK, so what conditions would we need to satisfy to find the ideal solution?

Bernard: Climate for one: production start having problems when the temperature hits 30°, so Nice is out of the running for a start, unless we splash out on an air-conditioned production unit.

Claire: Bernard, that's not fair! OK, high temperatures are inconvenient, but they're hardly a make or break factor. We need to draw a distinction between essential requirements and desirable characteristics.

Y: Point taken, Claire, but don't worry, we'll come to weighting in a moment.

B: Communications have to be our number one concern.

Y: OK, but can we quantify that more specifically? In numbers?

B: Sure. Distance from the airport, railway station, motorway; number of international flights per day …

2

Y: All right, some of us have another meeting scheduled at five, so let's get on. What are the options for the new factory?

B: Lyon, period. It has the best communications, and that's our priority. It stands to reason.

Y: Hold on a minute, Bernard; we want to do this scientifically, OK? Let's consider all our options; can we draw up a list?

B: OK – I suppose Lille and Nantes also have to be considered.

Y: Right; so we have Lyon, Lille and Nantes. Does that cover everything, or are there other avenues we should explore?

C: Well, I still feel we shouldn't leave Nice out of the equation. OK, it'll be expensive, but it's a very attractive location for the workforce.

3

Y: Right then, next step: define the relative importance of each of our criteria, give them a weighting. Claire, where would you put cost on a scale of one to five?

C: I'd say, four. It's not the be all and end all of it, but it's pretty important nevertheless.

B: Hang on, Claire, don't you think communications are more relevant than cost? And cost isn't nearly as critical as workforce; I'd only give it a three. What do you say, Yann?

4

Y: So; it would seem that we can rule out Nice. Sorry, Claire, but I think the figures speak for themselves, don't you?

C: Yes, it's pretty black and white, I suppose.

Y: And it appears that the overall winner is Lille: so, do we go for Lille?

B: Like Claire said, it seems an open and shut case.

Y: Lille it is then. Is everybody happy with that?

7.5 Writing Financial reporting

 2:31

Thank you, Sheena. Well, the film buffs amongst you may recognize the name SourceMedia. This is a company that used to be well known for making avant-garde films that won awards at obscure film festivals but never seemed to make any money. Well, they had to tighten their belts when finance for new movies became scarce, but now things are finally looking up for SourceMedia. They reluctantly abandoned the movies, and switched to making TV shows, and they seem to have discovered a recipe for financial success. You may have seen their hit sci-fi TV series *Fax-motor* – today the company announced that it had sold licensing rights for the US, China and South America to 3rd Planet TV. This means we'll be seeing local versions of the series being filmed and aired pretty much all over the world in the next few years. More importantly for SourceMedia, it means regular earnings for at least five years; profits could be as much as £5m next year, and that figure could even double the following year. So after seeing their share price fall steadily for the last five years or so, SourceMedia's shareholders finally have something to shout about! When the market closed a few minutes ago, SourceMedia was up 20 points – the share price hadn't been that high for three years! Look out for a further increase tomorrow; SourceMedia is still considerably undervalued compared to similar companies, so tomorrow should see plenty more investors jumping on the bandwagon!

7.6 Case study Lesage Automobile

 2:32

Mikhail: There you go. No cream anymore, I'm afraid, but there's this skimmed milk powder if you want?

Jack: No, thanks, Mikhail. I'll take it black, like my soul!

M: OK, so how about baring that black old soul of yours, then? Are you intending to back Amelia on this 'no-frills' project?

J: Ah. Amelia wants a Logan. And what the Lesage family want, they generally get.

M: True. But don't you think there's a case for resisting the temptation to go downmarket? Just keep investing in quality, style and service?

J: Maybe. But the Logan is certainly providing growth for Renault, so who am I to say they're wrong?

M: So you think we should produce our own no-frills model? In our French plants?

J: Or maybe go the whole nine yards – build it in eastern Europe. No robots, no electronics, skilled workers on low wages: it's got a lot going for it.

M: Hm. More coffee?

J: Go on then.

M: But listen, Jack; developing a completely new model would take years – why not just take our cheapest existing model, and strip it right down to the essentials?

J: Mm. Worth considering. Another option is a joint venture with the Russians. Basically, we send them the shell, and they put in their own power train. Old-generation technology, but reliable – and cheap.

M: Well, if you want cheap, what about rebadging? Just buy in cars from India, and slap a Lesage badge on them!

J: I wouldn't rule it out.

M: Really? I suppose it all depends whether you're targeting our traditional markets in western Europe: I was thinking more in terms of developing markets in eastern Europe, China, Africa ...

J: Yeah, maybe both.

M: Hm. And perhaps there are other options we haven't even thought of yet. So what's your take on all this?

J: Well, I don't know. I guess the jury's still out. There's a lot riding on this. We're going to have to think it through very, very carefully, look at all the options, weigh up the pros and cons.

M: Yeah. I'm with you on that. You want some more of this?

J: No, I think I've had enough. Amelia's no-frills campaign has gone too far – there's only so much 'affordable' coffee a man can take!

8 Free trade

8.1 About business Free trade

 2:33

Bradley: What annoys me is that these days, saying anything against free trade seems to be politically incorrect.

Rose: Why, don't you think it's a good thing?

B: No, I don't!

R: Why not? I mean, for a start, prices would be much higher if we didn't have free trade.

B: Sure, but most people don't realize how much those low prices really cost. They're only possible because we import stuff from places like China and India, where labour is cheap and largely unregulated, and taxes are low. But that means jobs are lost in the US and in Europe, and we end up having to support millions of jobless people!

R: But the stores make bigger profits, right?

B: Oh, sure. But they're global corporations, not mom and pop stores. The profits they make are not recycled in the local economy, they're moved offshore. Did you know that every year, up to a trillion

dollars of our national wealth gets transferred out of the United States? So the trade deficit explodes, the rich get richer, and the poor get poorer. Free trade is bleeding America dry!

R: But if we manufactured all our electronics, say, in the US, we'd probably have to pay twice as much for them!

B: Possibly, especially if you could eliminate dumping. But we'd make economies of scale – and we wouldn't be encouraging child labour and sweatshops! And we'd be able to regulate exactly what each product could do and what was used to make them – it's very difficult to keep dangerous substances out of the market when stuff's being made on the other side of the world, you know. But the real point is, we'd have full employment, and we'd have control over our own economy and our own politics, instead of being told what to do by the IMF, the World Bank, the World Trade Organization, and so on.

R: Surely you don't subscribe to those crazy, world-domination conspiracy theories, do you?

B: Well, more economic power means more military power, it's a well-known fact.

8.3 Grammar Phrasal and prepositional verbs

 2:34

Dave: First of all, I think we should kick off with a review of the trading laws in South-East Asia …

Jin: Another review? That's the last thing we need. They last forever and it would eat into our valuable time. We've got to crack on with developing our strategy – what the heck is our best way into the new Asian markets?

Sara: Hang on, did you say *Asian* markets? Do you really think this is the right time to try breaking into new markets. What about consolidating our position here in Europe before we start talking about branching out into Asia. That's unknown territory for us.

J: But you know what the CEO said Sara. It's grow or die in our business and we urgently need to come up with a strategy for faster growth. We don't have a choice; Asia is where the action is.

D: Are you really suggesting that we give up our plans for growth in Europe? It might be a competitive market, but it's a high value one and we do have an established presence. I think we need to do more research and weigh up the advantages and disadvantages of such a radical change of strategy before storming ahead with plans for Asia.

J: But David, I never said we should call off the European campaign! I know we need to soldier on with growing our market share in our established market – Europe, but it's a slow business and if we don't try to grab a piece of the action in Asia right now, then someone else will!

S: So you're saying we should stay in Europe but move forward with plans for Asia at the same time.

J: That's exactly what I'm saying.

8.4 Management skills Leading the team

 2:35–2:40

1

Chris, I know you've already done some research on possible distributors in Vietnam. I think you should go ahead and follow up on those contacts, don't you? Just keep me in the loop on what you decide, would you?

2

Paula, do you remember the Japanese market study we did together last year? I wonder if you could get Jack and Ella to do something along the same lines for China? I'm pretty tied up with the partnering discussions at the moment, but I'm sure you can handle it. We'll see how far you've got, say, at the end of the month? Is that OK?

3

You did a great job on the Hong Kong project, Soo-Hyang. I never thought we'd finish it in time, but you really came through! I really appreciate being able to rely on you to get things past the finishing post. This time round, I'd like you to take ownership of the whole logistics side of things – do you feel ready for the challenge?

4

Listen, Henry, you really shouldn't worry about it. I was extremely happy with 99% of your report, and I think you can feel very satisfied with a job well done too. Not picking up on just that one ratio was of no real significance, and it wouldn't have changed our decision in any way. You're a really valuable asset to the team – I don't know where we'd be without you! You've made huge strides in the last six months, so let's just keep up the good work, all right?

5

Just one other thing, Karen; I know you're brilliant at coming up with new ways to improve processes, and I really do appreciate your input – but don't you think that keeping on top of foreign exchange is really Phil's baby? Clearly he doesn't have your creativity, but he does have a lot of experience in his specialist area, so perhaps we should just let him get on with it, what do you think?

6

The thing is Max, until Ling gets back from maternity leave, the team's a bit short on negotiating skills: so if you were able to help us out, I'd really appreciate being able to call on your skills, especially as you've got first-hand experience of working with the Chinese.

8.6 Case study The cartel

 2:41

Toby: Oh, sorry, did you want to use the copier?

Jasmin: It's OK, you go ahead and finish, I'm in no hurry – my boss is off gallivanting in Paris, the lucky devil!

T: Oh, yeah, he's at the meeting with ThreeD-Vision, isn't he?

J: You're not supposed to know about that, young Toby! Don't even think about mentioning it to anyone else, or we can both kiss our careers goodbye!

T: Don't worry, my lips are sealed. But I don't understand why they're meeting our only competitor.

J: A full and frank discussion of mutual interests is the phrase, I believe.

T: You mean fixing prices and production levels, that sort of thing? But that's illegal, isn't it?

J: Now let's not go jumping to conclusions! Yes, cartels are illegal in most countries, but this meeting is to set up an industry trade group, it's completely above board.

T: Hm. So they won't be fixing prices, then?

J: I expect they'll share their ideas on what retail prices should be recommended in different markets: obviously you can't sell at the same price in India or Africa as in the US, so it helps to know what the other side are thinking …

T: Huh! Price-fixing in other words. And I expect they'll be carving up territories between them, sharing out the major markets, or even agreeing to share profits …

J: Toby, I think we're going to have to keep our voices down: it's a very sensitive matter.

T: Sorry. But it just seems very dodgy. Anyway, I don't understand why a company would want to take that kind of risk!

J: Toby, use your loaf! At the moment we can sell everything we can produce, and at a very good price. So can ThreeD. But that won't last: very soon we'll be competing directly for the same customers, and there'll be a price war. Unless there's a, well, let's call it a gentlemen's agreement; it's in everybody's interest – including yours!

T: Hm.

Glossary

The definitions for the words in this glossary are from the *Macmillan Dictionary*. The red words are high-frequency words, that is to say that they are among the 7,500 which native speakers use for 90% of what they speak or write. See http://www.macmillandictionary.com for more information.

Business fundamentals

cyclical /ˈsɪklɪk(ə)l/ adjective referring to a business or stock whose income, value, or earnings fluctuate greatly according to variations in the economy or the cycle of the seasons: *Selling Christmas decorations is a cyclical business.*

EBITDA /iːbɪtdɑː/ noun earnings before interest, tax, depreciation and amortization: *EBITDA is used as a measure of profitability in valuing a company and comparing its financial performance with other firms.*

flawlessly /ˈflɔːləsli/ adverb describes an action done without any mistakes or faults: *He speaks English flawlessly and is a very confident presenter.*

screen /skriːn/ verb [transitive] to get information to decide whether someone is suitable for something, for example a job: *Recruiters are starting to use social media to screen job candidates.*

SG&A /es dʒiː ænd eɪ/ noun selling, general & administrative expenses: *SG&A is found on a corporate income statement as a deduction from revenues in calculating operating income.*

slump /slʌmp/ noun [count] a period when an economy is much less successful than before and people lose their jobs

trough /trɒf/ noun [count] a period when something that rises and falls regularly is at a low level, especially economic activity: *We try to adapt to peaks and troughs in demand.*

1 Personal development

1.1 About business
Developing your career

dress-down Friday /ˌdres daʊn ˈfraɪdeɪ/ noun [count] a day on which employees are allowed to wear informal clothes to work: *I usually wear a suit, but on dress-down Fridays I wear jeans, which makes it easy if I'm going away for the weekend straight from work.*

mind share /ˈmaɪnd ʃeə(r)/ noun [uncount] the amount of awareness an individual or group has about a particular person, product or service: *I pop by each morning to say 'hi' to my boss, and send him regular updates to try to get more of his mind share.*

office politics /ˌɒfɪs ˈpɒlətɪks/ noun [uncount] NEGATIVE the influence of personal relationships and preferences on the day-to-day workings and procedures of an organization: *With many people setting out their own agenda in the workplace, office politics can play a major part in many companies.*

1.2 Vocabulary
Behavioural competencies and setting goals

astute /əˈstjuːt/ adjective good at judging situations and people quickly and able to use this knowledge for personal benefit

SMART /smɑː(r)t/ adjective usually Specific, Measurable, Achievable, Realistic, Time-bound, an acronym used to help formulate objectives, often within corporate performance development: *Make sure your job plan objectives are SMART, or you'll just have to rewrite them.*

time-bound /taɪm baʊnd/ adjective linked to a time frame, must be done by a certain time: *All our projects are time bound and must be completed by the end of the year.*

1.3 Grammar
Tense, aspect and voice

blow your reputation /ˌbləʊ jə(r) repjʊˈteɪʃ(ə)n/ phrase to cause the opinion people have of you to go down: *The Director blew his reputation after being convicted of stealing money from the company.*

Peter Principle /ˈpiːtə(r) ˌprɪnsəp(ə)l/ noun Lawrence Peter's belief that employees tend to be promoted one level too far, to their level of incompetence: *She was a great classroom teacher but made an awful head teacher – a perfect example of the Peter Principle in practice.*

1.4 Management skills
Self-awareness and communication

Arena /əˈriːnə/ noun [count] the quadrant of a Johari window that contains information known to oneself and to others

Blind spot /ˈblaɪnd spɒt/ noun [count] the quadrant of a Johari window that contains information known to others but not to oneself

Façade /fəˈsɑːd/ noun [count] the quadrant of a Johari window that contains information known to oneself but not to others

Johari window /dʒəʊˈhɑːri ˌwɪndəʊ/ noun [count] a tool designed by Joseph Luft and Harry Ingham in 1955 to help people understand how they relate to and communicate with other people

megabucks /ˈmegəˌbʌks/ noun [plural] INFORMAL a very large amount of money: *A $5,000 fine has very little impact on players who are earning megabucks.*

Unknown /ʌnˈnəʊn/ noun [count] the quadrant of a Johari window that contains information unknown to oneself and to others

1.5 Writing
A professional biography

bid /bɪd/ noun [count] an offer to do work or provide a service for a particular amount of money: *They put in a bid for the building contract for the new Olympic stadium.*

broker /ˈbrəʊkə(r)/ noun [count] someone whose job is to organize business deals for other people, especially a stockbroker or an insurance broker: *Independent brokers can bring down your insurance costs by shopping around between suppliers.*

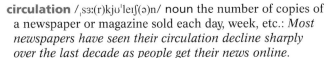

circulation /ˌsɜː(r)kjʊˈleɪʃ(ə)n/ noun the number of copies of a newspaper or magazine sold each day, week, etc.: *Most newspapers have seen their circulation decline sharply over the last decade as people get their news online.*

leverage /ˈliːvərɪdʒ/ verb [transitive] to borrow capital in order to make an investment with the expectation that the profits from it will be greater than the interest payable on the loan: *We are going to leverage private sector investment through loans.*

lobby /ˈlɒbi/ verb [intransitive/transitive] to try to influence politicians or people in authority on a particular subject: *Shopkeepers have been lobbying the city council to try to overturn the ban on vehicles in the city centre.*

1.6 Case study
The glass ceiling

comfort zone /ˈkʌmfə(r)t ˌzəʊn/ noun [count] a situation, place or temperature that you feel comfortable in. In business, it may describe a set of behaviours where risk is avoided, leading to disappointing results: *Genuinely successful people regularly step outside their comfort zone in order to achieve their objectives.*

devil's advocate /ˌdev(ə)lz ˈædvəkət/ noun somebody who pretends to disagree with someone in order to start an argument or interesting discussion: *It can be useful to have a devil's advocate in the team to ensure that decisions are well thought through.*

glass ceiling /ˌɡlɑːs ˈsiːlɪŋ/ noun [count] an unfair system that prevents some people, especially women, from reaching the most senior positions in a company or organization: *Hillary Clinton's candidacy is a reminder that the ultimate glass ceiling remains intact.*

headhunt /ˈhedˌhʌnt/ verb [transitive, usually passive] to try to persuade someone to leave their job and go to work for another company: *He was headhunted by a large electronics company.*

2 Corporate image
2.1 About business
Corporate image

back-to-basics /ˌbæk tə ˈbeɪsɪks/ adjective a return to fundamental principles: *The current approach to climate change is over complex, and isn't working. We need a back-to-basics approach where we can step back and look at the bigger picture.*

fruits of its labours /ˌfruːts əv ɪts ˈleɪbə(r)z/ noun result of work done: *Last week, after weeks of research, the committee presented the fruits of its labours to the forum for consideration and feedback.*

green on the inside /ˌɡriːn ɒn ðiˈɪnsaɪd/ phrase showing concern for the environment as a core principle at the centre of an organization's activities: *Today the question is rarely, why go green on the inside but rather what is the best way to attain a level of sustainability?*

green on the outside /ˌɡriːn ɒn ðiˈaʊtsaɪd/ phrase showing concern for the environment but only superficially: *Although many people claim to be concerned about the environment they are only green on the outside and aren't prepared to give up the conveniences of modern living.*

greenwash /ˈɡriːnˌwɒʃ/ noun [uncount] activities by a business or other organization that are intended to show that the organization is concerned about the environment: *The company is determined to cleanse communications of greenwash because it undermines the validity of genuine green marketing.*

in your face /ˌɪn jə(r) ˈfeɪs/ phrase INFORMAL in a bold aggressive manner: *The film has been described as a modern, in your face World War II epic.*

McLibel /məkˈlaɪb(ə)l/ adjective McLibel Trial, an infamous British court case, which became the longest ever English trial, between McDonald's and two ordinary people who humiliated McDonald's in the biggest corporate PR disaster in history. It was made into a film, released in 2005.

2.2 Vocabulary
Corporate social responsibility

cause-related marketing /ˌkɔːz rɪleɪtɪd ˈmɑː(r)kɪtɪŋ/ noun [uncount] a type of marketing which involves the cooperative efforts of a for-profit business and a non-profit organization for mutual benefit. It differs from corporate giving in that it is a marketing relationship not based on donation: *The survey conducted last year identified the fact that consumers responded extremely positively to cause-related marketing (CRM) partnerships between companies and charities.*

community investment /kəˌmjuːnəti ɪnˈves(t)mənt/ noun [uncount] a type of investment which focuses on how companies manage their activities in the community, and in so doing create a positive impact for both the community and the business: *Many of our employees play a role in our community investment programme through volunteering and fundraising.*

corporate philanthropy /ˈkɔː(r)p(ə)rət fɪˌlænθrəpi/ noun [uncount] activities which demonstrate the promotion of human welfare through business: *Their activities appear to be an example of pure corporate philanthropy. 'We are not doing this for propaganda or visibility. We are doing it for the satisfaction of knowing that we have really achieved and given something to the community in which we are working,' said the CEO.*

eco-efficiency /ˌiːkəʊ ɪˈfɪʃ(ə)nsi/ noun [uncount] the concept of creating more goods and services while using fewer resources, and creating less waste and pollution: *Calculating measures of eco-efficiency alone is not enough to ensure added corporate value. Financial staff must also be involved in the planning of future long-term eco-efficiency improvement.*

2.3 Grammar
The future, tentative and speculative language

carbon footprint /ˈkɑː(r)bən ˌfʊtprɪnt/ noun [count] the amount of carbon dioxide emitted by a person or organization per year: *He drove a car with a six-litre engine and used his private jet all the time, leaving a massive carbon footprint.*

signage /ˈsaɪnɪdʒ/ noun [uncount] signs and how they are presented: *There's hardly any signage in that building, so you can't find where anything is.*

2.4 Management skills
Time management

brainstorm /ˈbreɪnˌstɔː(r)m/ verb [intransitive/transitive] to develop new ideas by exploring all possible solutions before choosing the best ones: *Effective brainstorming involves four basic rules: 1 suspend judgement during the discussion; 2 record all ideas, however unrealistic they seem at first; 3 encourage participants to build on others' ideas; 4 think 'outside the box' by disregarding traditional assumptions and conventions.*

delegate /ˈdeləgeɪt/ verb [intransitive/transitive] to give part of your work, duties or responsibilities to someone who is junior to you: *Effective delegating involves the OMMDC formula: giving a specific Objective, specifying the Method and the Means that should be used, agreeing a realistic Deadline, and Checking that the task has been successfully completed.*

Paired Comparison Analysis /peə(r)d kəmˈpærɪs(ə)n əˌnæləsɪs/ noun [count] a decision-making technique where different options are compared: each possibility is compared with each of the other options, and given a score. Adding up the total scores for each option provides an indication of their relative importance: *Paired Comparison Analysis is particularly useful for making comparisons where no objective data is available.*

2.5 Writing
Newsletter articles

gasp /ɡɑːsp/ verb [intransitive] to breathe in suddenly, for example because you are surprised, shocked or in pain: *Some members of the Board gasped with amazement when they saw the huge jump in the sales figures.*

thinly disguised /ˈθɪnli dɪsˈɡaɪzd/ phrase pretending to be something else, but it is easy to see what it really is: *The CEO's end-of-year review speech was a thinly disguised attack on his predecessor's policies.*

2.6 Case study
Pixkel Inc.

endorsement /ɪnˈdɔː(r)smənt/ noun [count] an occasion when someone famous says in an advertisement that they like a product: *We've got endorsements from top athletes for the running shoe's new design.*

firefighting /ˈfaɪə(r)ˌfaɪtɪŋ/ noun [uncount] the activity of trying to stop a serious problem that suddenly happens by reacting quickly and effectively. In business, it frequently refers to wasting time and energy dealing with problems that would not happen if managers were more proactive: *According to a survey, IT managers spend too much time firefighting, and not enough time developing new ways to improve their business.*

flavour of the month /ˈfleɪvə(r) əv ðə ˌmʌnθ/ phrase something or someone that is very popular for only a short time: *She is very much flavour of the month in Hollywood.*

hit the ground running /ˈhɪt ðə ˌɡraʊnd rʌnɪŋ/ phrase to be successful from the start of an activity: *The squad will have to hit the ground running from the very first game.*

Intel Inside /ˌɪntel ɪnˈsaɪd/ TRADEMARK a classic 1990s brand campaign: *By persuading computer manufacturers to place an 'Intel Inside' sticker on machines containing its processors, Intel transformed itself from an anonymous manufacturer of computer components into a household name.*

real McCoy /ˌrɪəl məˈkɔɪ/ noun INFORMAL something that is real and not a copy: *There are lots of sparkling wines that you could drink instead of champagne, but this is the real McCoy.*

swoosh /swuːʃ/ noun [uncount] something which moves through air or water with a smooth gentle sound. Nike's sportswear logo, created in 1971 and now one of the most recognized brand logos in the world.

3 Supply chain
3.1 About business
Outsourcing

data crunching /ˈdeɪtə ˌkrʌntʃɪŋ/ noun [uncount] dealing with large amounts of information or calculations very quickly: *There are times when data crunching doesn't give you the whole picture: however much market data you have gathered, sometimes you still have to rely on your instincts.*

in silico /ɪn ˈsɪlɪkəʊ/ phrase an expression used to describe research or models developed on a computer or in virtual reality, as opposed to 'in vivo' or 'in vitro': *Reports state that extensive use of in silico technologies could reduce the overall cost of drug development by as much as 50%.*

knowledge drain /ˈnɒlɪdʒ ˌdreɪn/ noun [count] when a company loses specialist skills and know-how because experienced staff leave the organization for reasons such as redundancy, retirement or lift-out: *Companies are failing to consider the knowledge-management implications of offshoring manufacturing and other processes; the resulting knowledge drain has an immediate impact on productivity and thus directly affects the bottom line.*

lift-out /ˈlɪft aʊt/ noun [count] when an external provider hires staff who used to do the same job for the customer. They may continue to work on their former employer's site, or be moved to the provider's own premises: *A major advantage of the lift-out model lies in acquiring a team with intimate knowledge of the client's business, thus making the new provider fully operational from day one.*

roll out /rəʊl ˈaʊt/ phrasal verb [transitive] to introduce a new product or service: *Australia will roll out the prototype of its new jet fighter in January.*

3.2 Vocabulary
Logistics

JIT /ˈdʒeɪ aɪ tiː/ adjective BUSINESS Just-In-Time, bought sent or produced at the last possible time: *JIT is a management philosophy that aims to eliminate sources of manufacturing waste and cost by producing the right part in the right place at the right time.*

reverse logistics /rɪˌvɜː(r)s ləˈʤɪstɪks/ noun [uncount] the activity of product management that goes beyond a manufacturer's normal distribution and delivery system: in particular, the reverse flow of products and materials for returns, repair, remanufacture and/or recycling: *The complement to the traditional supply chain, reverse logistics treats used products or materials as valuable industrial nutrients instead of disposing of them as trash.*

3.3 Grammar
Noun phrases

vertically integrated /ˈvɜː(r)tɪkli ˌɪntɪɡreɪtɪd/ adjective companies which own operations at different levels of a production process, such as farms, processing plants and distribution facilities, in order to increase economies of scale: *MyCoffee is a vertically integrated company which runs its own coffee plantations as well as a shipping company.*

3.4 Management skills
Managing change

CPFR /siː piː ef ˈɑː(r)/ noun [uncount] Collaborative Planning, Forecasting and Replenishment, the activity of sharing forecasts and business information with business partners in order to optimize the supply chain: *The businesses which have benefited most from CPFR are those that have to live with significant variations in demand.*

force field analysis /ˈfɔː(r)s fiːld əˌnæləsɪs/ noun [count] a method used in change management for displaying and evaluating factors that may drive or obstruct change: *Performing a force field analysis helps build consensus by allowing people to express, discuss and resolve their objections.*

think outside the box /θɪŋk ˌaʊtˈsaɪd ðə bɒks/ phrase to find new ways of doing things, especially of solving problems: *Employees are encouraged to think outside the box and develop creative solutions.*

3.5 Writing
Emails

batch /bætʃ/ noun [count] a quantity of a substance needed or produced at one time: *We liked two of the designs from the first batch of samples and one from the second batch.*

coating /ˈkəʊtɪŋ/ noun [count] a thin layer that covers something: *The metal parts of the machine have acquired a thin coating of rust and will need to be replaced.*

fastening /ˈfɑːsnɪŋ/ noun [count] a screw, bolt or hinge used to assemble parts of a structure, machine or vehicle: *They use stainless or brass steel fastenings for the outside of the submarine because both metals are resistant to corrosion.*

galvanized /ˈɡælvənaɪzd/ adjective galvanized metal is covered with a layer of zinc to protect it from damage, especially rust: *It wouldn't have got so rusty if they had used galvanized steel.*

micron /ˈmaɪkrɒn/ noun [count] a unit for measuring very small lengths in the metric system. There are one million microns in a metre: *The machine will print a new line of data each time the paper moves 44.5 microns.*

3.6 Case study
WEF Audio

scorecard /ˈskɔː(r)ˌkɑː(r)d/ noun [count] BUSINESS a table of the most important information needed to achieve an objective, consolidated and laid out so that the information can be monitored at a glance: *The balanced scorecard is a strategic planning and management system which adds strategic non-financial performance measures to traditional financial metrics in order to provide a more 'balanced' view of organizational performance.*

the writing's on the wall /ðə ˈraɪtɪŋz ɒn ðə ˌwɔːl/ phrase INFORMAL used for saying that it seems likely that something will soon go wrong or stop existing: *Is the writing on the wall for tobacco advertising?*

USP /juː es ˈpiː/ noun [count] BUSINESS Unique Selling Proposition, or Unique Selling Point. The thing that makes a product or service special or different from others: *Your USP is your competitive advantage, the benefit you offer that your competitors can't provide. It's the reason why customers buy from you and not from anyone else.*

4 Managing conflict
4.1 About business
Management style

gunslinger /ˈɡʌnˌslɪŋə(r)/ noun [count] a gunman in the American Wild West in the past can also mean someone who is forceful and adventurous in their particular sphere of activity: *He's a gastronomic gunslinger who has revolutionized modern French cooking.*

hell for leather /ˈhel fə(r) leðə(r)/ phrase INFORMAL as fast as possible: *He came rushing out of his office and tore up the stairs, hell for leather.*

meat and drink /miːt ənd ˈdrɪŋk/ phrase INFORMAL something that someone enjoys doing or can do very easily, usually because they do it often: *This kind of shot is meat and drink to a player like him.*

4.2 Vocabulary
Managing conflict

get somebody's goat /get ˈsʌmbədiz ˌgəʊt/ phrase INFORMAL to annoy someone: *It really gets my goat – the way she keeps interrupting all the time.*

harassment /həˈræsmənt/ noun [count] annoying or unpleasant behaviour towards someone that takes place regularly, for example threats, offensive remarks or physical attacks: *We encourage anyone who has been the subject of racial harassment to report it.*

4.3 Grammar
Conjunctions

hearts and minds strategy /ˌhɑː(r)ts ən ˈmaɪndz ˌstrætəʤi/ phrase a plan to win over the feelings and opinions of people: *The Kidz Konfection Kompany used a hearts and minds strategy to get parents on their side by presenting evidence that their chocolate was actually healthy.*

turn the tables on somebody /ˌtɜː(r)n ðə ˈteɪb(ə)lz ɒn sʌmbədi/ phrase to change a situation from being bad for you and good for someone else to the opposite: *First, they were losing market share, but they managed to turn the tables on the market leader by presenting the rival product as environmentally unfriendly.*

4.4 Management skills
Assertiveness

have a bone to pick with somebody /hæv ə ˈbəʊn tə pɪk wɪð ˌsʌmbədi/ phrase INFORMAL to want to talk to someone about something they have done that has annoyed you: *I've got a bone to pick with you.*

hearing /ˈhɪərɪŋ/ noun [count] LEGAL a meeting of a court of law or official organization to find out the facts about something: *A court hearing has been scheduled for 31 August.*

4.5 Writing
Letters

grievance /ˈɡriːv(ə)ns/ noun [count] a complaint about being treated in an unfair way: *The managers were presented with a long list of grievances from their unhappy employees.*

infringe /ɪnˈfrɪndʒ/ verb [intransitive/transitive] to limit or reduce someone's legal rights of freedom

remonstrate /ˈremənˌstreɪt/ verb [intransitive] FORMAL to argue with, complain to or criticise someone about something: *He remonstrated with for her disastrous decision to close down the department.*

statutory /ˈstætʃʊt(ə)ri/ adjective controlled by a law or statute: *a statutory minimum wage*

wilful /ˈwɪlf(ə)l/ adjective done deliberately in order to cause damage or harm: *The enforced closure of the factory is the result of the firm's wilful neglect of health and safety regulations.*

4.6 Case study
Olvea Brasil

concern /kənˈsɜː(r)n/ noun [count] something that worries you. In Human Resources, a person whose performance is in some way inadequate, disappointing or worrying: *The team have consistently underperformed this season: in particular, coach Jack Harris has labelled outfielders Darren Hollins and Marty Schneck as concerns.*

to go over somebody's head /tə ɡəʊ ˌəʊvə(r) ˈsʌmbədiz hed/ phrase to go to a more important or powerful person in order to get what you want: *I was furious that he went over my head and complained to my manager.*

5 Marketing and sales

5.1 About business
Strategic marketing and partnering

air time /ˈeə(r) taɪm/ noun [uncount] the amount of time given to someone or something in a radio or television broadcast: *We need more air time for the new advertising campaign.*

be up to something /bi ʌp tu ˈsʌmθɪŋ/ phrase doing or planning something secretly: *We knew they were up to something because they had been shut up in the conference room all day in a special meeting.*

M&A /em ən ˈeɪ/ noun [plural] BUSINESS Mergers and Acquisitions, the activities of companies that combine with or take control of other companies: *Visit our web page for the latest M&A news, including recent consolidations, hostile takeovers and other corporate deals.*

sign on the dotted line /saɪn ɒn ðə dɒtɪd laɪn/ phrase to sign a contract or other legal agreement: *They have agreed to the contract, but they haven't signed on the dotted line yet.*

testimonial /ˌtestɪˈməʊniəl/ noun [count] a formal statement about someone's qualities and character, usually provided by an employer. A more usual word is 'reference'.

workhorse /ˈwɜː(r)kˌhɔː(r)s/ noun [count] a very useful piece of equipment that you use a lot: *My old laptop is a real workhorse - I've had it for ages and it's never broken down - but I need something lighter and faster.*

5.2 Vocabulary
Marketing

Generation Y /ˌdʒenəˈreɪʃ(ə)n ˌwaɪ/ noun people born between 1979 and 1994: *The baby boomers were followed by Generation X, the children of the sixties and seventies, who were themselves succeeded by Generation Y.*

5.3 Grammar
Prepositions

joined-up strategy /ˌdʒɔɪnd ʌp ˈstrætədʒi/ noun a plan which carefully links all parts of the company so that they all follow the same strategy: *Your job is to ensure we have a joined-up strategy by liaising with every department involved in the operation.*

5.5 Writing
Business proposals

concessive clause /kənˌsesɪv ˈklɔːz/ noun [count] a concessive clause is a subordinate clause referring to a situation that contrasts with the main clause: *Although the company is expanding rapidly, we haven't yet recruited any additional personnel to help manage the workload.*

credentials /krɪˈdenʃ(ə)lz/ noun [plural] personal qualities, achievements or experiences that make someone suitable for something: *The company is looking to enhance its environmental credentials.*

metrics /ˈmetrɪks/ noun [plural] standards of measurement used to measure, compare and track the performance of a process or product: *Market analysts use metrics to compare the performance of different companies.*

prowess /ˈpraʊes/ noun [uncount] great skill or ability: *Our technical prowess has enabled us to develop products of ourtstanding quality unmatched by our competitors.*

6 Risk management

6.1 About business
Crisis management

canard /ˈkænɑː(r)d/ noun [count] a false story or piece of information, especially one that is intended as a joke or to make someone stop respecting someone: *If this type of canard is repeated often enough people start believing it's true.*

feel-good guru /ˈfiːl gʊd ˌgʊruː/ noun [count] an expert or teacher who makes people feel better by telling them want they want to hear: *Talking to her was like talking to a feel-good guru. She made it sound as though nothing was impossible.*

pit bull /ˈpɪt ˌbʊl/ noun [count] a type of small very strong dog originally trained to fight other dogs, can also mean a person who is very determined and aggressive: *He came in like a pit bull and literally forced them to offer us better terms.*

whistle-blower /ˈwɪs(ə)l bləʊwə(r)/ noun [count] someone who reports dishonest or illegal activities within an organization to someone in authority: *Fearing retaliation, the whistle-blower in the case changed his name and moved to another city.*

6.2 Vocabulary
Risk management and digital risk

cease and desist order /ˌsiːs ən dɪˈzɪst ɔː(r)də(r)/ phrase an order from a lawyer, court or government agency prohibiting a person or company from continuing specific behaviour: *They received a cease and desist order, advising them that if the unlawful practice of downloading copyright material from the website continued, the company would seek all appropriate legal remedies without prior notification.*

ERM /iː ɑː em/ noun [uncount] Enterprise Risk Management, an approach to optimizing the way a company manages risks by taking an integrated view of the various uncertainties involved across the organization: *Following a series of high-profile corporate finance scandals, enterprise risk management has become one of the most important aspects of corporate governance.*

6.3 Grammar
Perspective and stance

property ladder /ˈprɒpə(r)ti ˌlædə(r)/ noun houses, with the expectation that as a person gets richer they can buy more expensive houses: *With house prices sky-high I can't get a foot on the property ladder in my hometown.*

6.5 Writing
Reports: making recommendations

libellous /ˈlaɪbələs/ adjective LEGAL containing written statements about someone that are not true: *We sued the magazine for their libellous comments about our environmental policy in this article.*

opportunity cost /ˌɒpə(r)ˈtjuːnəti kɒst/ noun [count] BUSINESS the amount of money that a company or organization loses by deciding to do one thing rather than another: *The time and cost involved in writing the proposal to get the construction contract will be considered an opportunity cost.*

posit /ˈpɒzɪt/ verb [transitive] FORMAL to say that something is true or that something should be accepted as true: *He posited the basic universal laws of the free market as the basis for the company's policy.*

7 Investment
7.1 About business
Investment banks

bail out /beɪl aʊt/ phrasal verb to help a person or organization that is having problems, especially financial problems: *During the financial crisis, the government was obliged to bail out several of the high street banks.*

call the shots /kɔːl ðə ʃɒts/ phrase to be in a position of control or authority: *He has it made it clear to the team that he will be the one calling the shots on this project.*

fat cat /fæt kæt/ noun [count] SHOWING DISAPPROVAL a very rich and powerful person, usually in business or politics: *Fat cat investment bankers earn salaries that most people can only dream about.*

going rate /ˈgəʊɪŋ reɪt/ noun the usual amount of money that people are paying for something: *I was disappointed by the salary offered, but was told that this is the going rate for inexperienced web designers.*

grind to a halt /graɪnd tʊ ə hɔːlt/ phrase if a process or a country grinds to a halt, things gradually get slower until they stop: *If the fuel deliveries don't arrive soon, production will grind to a halt.*

market volatility /ˌmɑː(r)kɪt vɒləˈtɪləti/ phrase an unpredictable and fluctuating investment market: *Given recent market volatility, today's investors need either a strong stomach or deep pockets, or both.*

weigh in /weɪ ɪn/ phrasal verb [intransitive] to become involved in something

7.2 Vocabulary
Investment choices

buy-to-let /ˌbaɪ tə ˈlet/ phrase to buy a property in order to rent it out and make money: *Following years of easy credit the buy-to-let market is finally cooling as sources of finance dry up.*

downshift /ˈdaʊnˌʃɪft/ verb to change from a higher-pressure well-paid job to a potentially more satisfying lower-paid job and possibly new area of the country: *After years of commuting to the City my brother's decided to downshift and go and open a tearoom in Wales.*

eighth age of man /ˈeɪtθ ˌeɪdʒ əv mæn/ phrase the final stage of an old person's life, following Shakespeare's seven ages: *With medical advances and greater longevity, more and more people are reaching the eighth age of man than ever before.*

quids in /kwɪdz ˈɪn/ phrase to make good money out of a deal: *I'll sell you ten T-shirts for 100 quid, you can easily double that on your market stall and you'll be quids in.*

7.3 Grammar
Inversion and emphasis

bootstrap /ˈbuːtˌstræp/ verb to pull yourself up from a poor position by working very hard: *First, get a great business idea then bootstrap yourself up without borrowing too much money.*

intellectual investment /ɪntəˌlektʃuəl ɪnˈves(t)mənt/ noun investment in good ideas and people with particular skills rather than financial investment: *What we need now is a top team – we need intellectual investment not money right now.*

strategic defence /strə'tiːʤɪk dɪˌfens/ noun protecting a country's important industries such as defence from foreign takeovers: *You may call it protectionism, but we call it strategic defence.*

7.5 Writing
Financial reporting

ballpark figure /'bɔːlˌpɑː(r)k 'fɪɡə(r)/ noun [count] a rough estimate: *We know this isn't going to be cheap, but we've got very little idea of the going rates. Can you give us a ballpark figure?*

bite the bullet /baɪt ðə 'bʊlɪt/ phrase INFORMAL to force yourself to do something difficult or unpleasant that you have been avoiding doing: *We've tried very hard to avoid laying off staff up to now, but this time we're just going to have to bite the bullet.*

credit crunch /'kredɪt ˌkrʌntʃ/ noun a period of economic depression in which lenders stop lending, credit is difficult to obtain and interest rates are very high: *The global credit crunch deepened on Monday as ANZ Bank of Australia warned its annual profit could fall by as much as 25% and hiked its bad loan provisions, triggering a massive share sell-off in the country's financial services sector.*

punt /pʌnt/ noun [count] a bet: *He was always top of the class in our MBA course and we've got a punt on him being headhunted into a top job.*

sit tight /sɪt taɪt/ phrase INFORMAL to stay where you are, or to not take action until the right time: *We've done all we can to improve sales and now we've just got to sit tight and wait for the end of year results to come in.*

tuck away /tʌk əˈweɪ/ phrasal verb [transitive] to put money or securities in a safe place so that you can use them later: *Every time I've earned some extra money, I've always tried to tuck some of it away for my retirement.*

7.6 Case study
Lesage Automobile

clamour /'klæmə(r)/ verb [intransitive] to say that you want something and must have it

no-frills /'nəʊ frɪlz/ adjective used for referring to something that is good enough but has no unnecessary extra features: *No-frills airlines have achieved spectacular growth in the European market since the scheduled airline market was fully liberalized in 1997.*

oversell /'əʊvə(r)ˌsel/ verb [transitive, usually passive] BUSINESS to sell a customer features they do not need: *Read our buyer's guide and never be oversold on a car again.*

8 Free trade

8.1 About business
Free trade

archipelago /ˌɑː(r)kɪ'peləɡəʊ/ noun [count] a large group of small islands: *The territory of the Republic of the Philippines consists of an archipelago of 17-18 islands in the Western Pacific Ocean.*

commensurately /kə'menʃərətli/ adverb FORMAL in a directly proportional way: *If we could halve the amount of money we spend on consultants, other costs would fall commensurately, and our profitability would increase.*

DRM /diː ɑː(r) em/ noun Digital Rights Management – access control technologies limiting the use of digital content and devices after sale: *Opponents of DRM believe that it limits the possibilities enabled by digital technologies by placing them under the control of a few.*

dub /dʌb/ verb [transitive] MAINLY JOURNALISM to give someone or something a particular name or description: *His colleagues dubbed him 'Mr Speedy' 'because he always finished his projects first.*

funky /'fʌŋki/ adjective unusual and showing a lot of imagination: *Our products were successful because of their funky new features which no-one else had and which appealed to our teenage audience.*

hothouse /'hɒtˌhaʊs/ noun [count] a building made of glass that is used for growing plants that need a warm temperature: *Microsoft's summer camps were a hothouse of innovative ideas and creativity where young programmers developed their talents.*

hurdle /'hɜː(r)d(ə)l/ noun [count] one of several problems that you must solve before you can do something successfully: *Our small size and modest amount of available investment capital are hurdles we will have to overcome if we want to grow the business.*

lint /lɪnt/ noun [uncount] MAINLY AMERICAN very small pieces of hair, dust or cloth that stick together or to the surface of something else: *Clean your keyboard regularly with a soft cotton cloth free of lint.*

8.4 Management skills
Leading the team

in/out of the loop /'ɪn/'aʊt əv ðə ˌluːp/ phrase INFORMAL belonging or not belonging to a group that has information and makes decisions about something: *When changes are being made in the organization, keep your team in the loop so they know what to expect.*

8.5 Writing
Style

alliteration /əˌlɪtə'reɪʃ(ə)n/ noun [uncount] LITERATURE the use of the same letter or sound at the beginning of words in a sentence, especially in poetry: *The slogan for Fila sportswear - 'functional, fashionable and formidable' is an example of alliteration used in an advertising slogan.*

all-nighter /ˌɔːl 'naɪtə(r)/ noun [count] something that continues for the whole night: *The end of the project was an all-nighter: we worked through until the next morning to finish it.*

booth /buːð/ noun [count] a small enclosed space where you can buy things, look at things or use a service: *Members of the public can use the computer terminals in the booths at the back of the store to search for products and check availability.*

woo /wuː/ verb [transitive] to try to persuade people to support you or to buy something from you, especially by saying and doing nice things: *The company wooed him with offers of a excellent salary and exceptional career development opportunities until he finally agreed to take the job.*

8.6 Case study
The cartel

duopoly /djuːˈɒpəli/ noun [count] BUSINESS a situation in which two companies, people or groups control something such as a business activity or industry: *Intel and AMD's long-standing duopoly in the PC processor market could be challenged by the arrival of new players like VIA Technologies.*

oligopoly /ɒlɪˈɡɒpəli/ noun [count] BUSINESS a situation in which only a few companies, people or groups control something such as a business activity or industry: *In an oligopoly such as the domestic gas market there are so few sellers that a change decided by any one of them will have a measurable impact on all competitors.*

Macmillan Education
Between Towns Road, Oxford OX4 3PP
A division of Macmillan Publishers Limited
Companies and representatives throughout the world

ISBN 978-0-230-43804-0

Text © John Allison, Rachel Appleby and Edward de Chazal 2013
Design and illustration © Macmillan Publishers Limited 2013
The authors have asserted their rights to be identified as the authors of
this work in accordance with the Copyright, Design and Patents Act 1988.

This edition published 2013
First edition published 2009

Original design by Keith Shaw, Threefold Design Ltd
Designed by Keith Shaw, Threefold Design Ltd
Illustrated by Coburn, Mark Duffin, Peter Ellis and Peter Harper
Cover design by Keith Shaw, Threefold Design Ltd
Cover image: Getty Images/Altrendo Images
Picture research by Susannah Jayes

Authors' acknowledgements
John Allison
I would like to thank everybody at Macmillan; Lidia Zielinska and the
English teachers at Cracow University of Economics; my colleagues at
Infolangues; and last but not least, Brigitte and my family.

Rachel Appleby
I would also like to thank family and friends, and colleagues and students
in Hungary and the UK for their many ideas and considerable patience.

Edward de Chazal
I would like to thank my family for their continuing support during the
writing process.

The publishers would like to thank the following people for piloting and
commenting on material for this coursebook:
Paul Bellchambers, Business and Technical Languages, Paris, France;
Bunmi Rolland, Pôle Universitaire Léonard de Vinci, Paris, France;
Prof. Vanessa Leonardi, Faculty of Economics, University of Ferrara,
Italy; Prof. Paola De La Pierre, Faculty of Economics, University of Turin,
Italy; Elżbieta Typek, Cracow University of Economics, Poland; Marlena
Nowak, Cracow University of Economics, Poland; Lucyna Wilinkiewicz-
Górniak, Cracow University of Economics, Poland; Jolanta Regucka-
Pawlina, Cracow University of Economics, Poland; Sebastian Florek-
Paszkowski, Cracow University of Economics, Poland; Bożena Bielak,
Cracow University of Economics, Poland; Małgorzata Held, Cracow
University of Economics, Poland; Anna Wróblewska-Marzec, Cracow
University of Economics, Poland; Lidia Zielińska, Cracow University of
Economics, Poland; Olga Druszkiewicz, Cracow University of Economics,
Poland; Maciej Krzanowski, Cracow University of Economics, Poland;
Lubov Kulik, Moscow Lomonosov State University, Russia; Irina
Ekareva, The Russian Plekhanov University of Economics, Russia; Larisa
Tarkhova, The Russian Plekhanov University of Economics, Russia;
Irina Schemeleva, Higher School of Economics, Russia; Irina Matveeva,
The Academy of Social and Labour Relations, Russia; Galina Makarova,
Denis' School, Russia, Liam James Tyler, IPT, Russia; Tatiana Efremtseva,
The Russian International Academy of Tourism, Russia; Tatiana Sedova,
The University of Finance, Russia; Tony Watson and Kim Draper,
MLS Bournemouth, Bournemouth, UK; Louise Raven, Marcus Evans
Linguarama, Stratford-upon-Avon, UK.

The publishers would like to thank the following people for piloting and
commenting on material for the original edition of this coursebook:
Jacqueline Cruz, Target Inglês Instrumental, Brazil; Terry Bland,
Università Carlo Cattaneo, Castellanza, Italy; Stephan Cooper, Economics
University, Turin, Italy; Nicole Ioakimidis, Commercial School, Geneva,
Switzerland; Dr Soe Than, Assumption University, Bangkok, Thailand.

The author and publishers would like to thank the following for
permission to reproduce their photographs: **Alamy**/AA World Travel
Library p88, Alamy/Bernhard Classen p103, Alamy/Corbis Super
RF p91, Alamy/Fancy p46(cr), Alamy/PE Forsberg p72(t), Alamy/
Imagebroker p8, Alamy/Losevsky Pavel pp38(bcl), 73(cl), Alamy/
Photocuisine p84(cr), Alamy/Ulrich Schade p94(tcl), Alamy/Peter
Scholey p94(bcl), Alamy/Sergey Shcherbakov p73(tcl), Alamy/Karen
Spencer p59(tr), Alamy/Mikael Utterström p95, Alamy/Wavebreak
Media Ltd p9, Alamy/Westend61 GmbH p46(bcr); **Cartoonstock**/
www.cartoonstock.com/S.Harris p96; **Corbis**/Bettmann p65, Corbis/
Creasource p106, Corbis/Oswald Eckstein p30, Corbis/Holger Hill/
fstop p32(bl), Corbis/Juice Images p110, Corbis/Beau Lark p29, Corbis/

Hans Neleman p20, Corbis/Ocean p67, Corbis/Chuck Savage p10,
Corbis/Zhang Jun/Xinhua Press p63(tr); **Getty Images** p45(tr), Getty
Images/AFP p24, Getty Images/Thomas Coex/AFP p81, Getty Images/
Philippe Huguen/AFP p82, Getty Images/Assembly p78, Getty Images/
Eric Audras p18, Getty Images/PhotoAlto/Eric Audras p33(bcr), Getty
Images/Barcroft Media p76, Getty Images/Christopher Bissell p55, Getty
Images/Bloomberg via Getty Images p22, Getty Images/Bongarts p71,
Getty Images/Flavia Celidonio p58, Getty Images/Elisa Cicinelli p59(tcr),
Getty Images/Clerkenwell p33(br), Getty Images/Comstock Images
pp14, 21, 46(tcr), Getty Images/Tony Cordoza p46(cmr), Getty Images/
Digital Vision p64, Getty Images/Fabaziou Collection p16, Getty Images/
Fuse pp50, 94(cl), Getty Images/Tom Grill p31, Getty Images/Bartosz
Hadyniak p40, Getty Images/Gabriela Hasbun p90, Getty Images/Noel
Hendrickson p33(cr), Getty Images/Jason Hetherington p98(tr), Getty
Images/IMAGEMORE Co., Ltd p85, Getty Images/Image Source pp36,
89, Getty Images/Zigy Kaluzny p92, Getty Images/Don Klumpp p26,
Getty Images/Carol Kohen p12, Getty Images/Rob Lewine p33(tr), Getty
Images/Steve McAlister p79, Getty Images/Jose Luis Pelaez Inc pp45(tl),
49, Getty Images/Perkus p102, Getty Images/Adrian Pope p32(tr), Getty
Images/PT Images p59(bcr), Getty Images/Radius Images p59(br), Getty
Images/Chris Ryan p56, Getty Images/Stefanie Senholt p84(t), Getty
Images/Simone Spada p47(br), Getty Images/Thinkstock p19, Getty
Images/Mike Timo p75, Getty Images/Susanne Walstrom p42, Getty
Images/Art Wolfe p37; **Glow Images**/Stock Connection/Gary Bistram
p72(bl), Glow Images/Henkelmann/F1online p100, Glow Images/
Imagebroker/GTW p104, Glow Images/PictureIndia/Alex Mares-
Manton p107, Glow Images/Blend RF/John Lund/Nevada Wier p53,
Glow Images/Ojo Images/Adam Gault p97, Glow Images/Superstock
p68; **Hindustan Times** p63(b); **Imagebroker** p62; **Image Source** p33(tcr);
Photoshot pp73(tl),101; **Press Association**/VADIM GHIRDA p98(bl); **Rex
Features**/AGF s.r.l p108; **Stockbyte** p38 (cl).

The authors and publishers are grateful for permission to reprint the
following copyright material:
Business Week for extract from "Got 5,000 euros? Need a new car?" by
Gail Edmondson & Constance Faivre d'Arcier 4 July 2005 copyright
© Business Week www.businessweek.com; Extract from 'Steer well
clear of meetings…. Guy Browning offers 20 top tips for surviving life
in the workplace' copyright © Smokehouse Ltd 2006, first published
in The Guardian 18.10.06, reprinted by permission of the publisher;
Guardian News & Media Ltd for extracts adapted from 'Judgement
Days' by Liz Hollis published in *The Guardian* 14 July 2007; and "The Big
McMakeover" by Patrick Barkham published in *The Guardian* 28 January
2008 © Guardian 2007, 2008; Extracted material from 'Damage Control'
by Eric Dezenhall and John Weber copyright © 2007 by Eric Dezenhall.
Reprinted with permission of ICM Partners; The Outsourcing Institute for
an extract adapted from "Preparing for lift out" by John Conley published
on www.outsourcing.com; Material from articles 'The Price of Being a
Fortress' by David H. Holtzman, copyright David H. Holtzman 2007 and
'The Indian Machine' by Chris Anderson, copyright Chris Anderson 2004,
both printed with permission of the publisher; Material from article 'The
Three Faces of Risk Management' by Joanne Sammer, first published in
Business Finance Magazine December 2000, reprinted by permission of
the publisher; Phrasal verb index/definitions from Macmillan English
Dictionary, reprinted by permission of the publisher.

These materials may contain links for third party websites. We have no
control over, and are not responsible for, the contents of such third party
websites. Please use care when accessing them.

Although we have tried to trace and contact copyright holders before
publication, in some cases this has not been possible. If contacted we will
be pleased to rectify any errors or omissions at the earliest opportunity.

Printed and bound in Thailand

2017 2016 2015 2014 2013
10 9 8 7 6 5 4 3 2 1